W9-DHF-655

UNITED STATES TRADE
AND INVESTMENT
IN LATIN AMERICA

UNITED STATES TRADE AND INVESTMENT IN LATIN AMERICA

Opportunities for Business in the 1990s

Chris C. Carvounis
Brinda Z. Carvounis

Q

Quorum Books
Westport, Connecticut • London

HF
1456.5
L3
C37
1992

Library of Congress Cataloging-in-Publication Data

Carvounis, Chris C.
    United States trade and investment in Latin America : opportunities for
business in the 1990s / Chris C. Carvounis and Brinda Z. Carvounis.
        p. cm.
    Includes bibliographical references and index.
    ISBN 0–89930–786–8 (alk. paper)
    1. United States—Foreign economic relations—Latin America.   2. Latin
America—Foreign economic relations—United States.   3. Investments,
American—Latin America.   4. Structural adjustment (Economic policy)—
Latin America.   I. Carvounis, Brinda Z.   II. Title.
HF1456.5.L3C37   1992
337.7308—dc20   92-12719

British Library Cataloguing in Publication Data is available.

Copyright © 1992 by Chris C. Carvounis and Brinda Z. Carvounis

All rights reserved. No portion of this book may be
reproduced, by any process or technique, without the
express written consent of the publisher.

Library of Congress Catalog Card Number: 92-12719
ISBN: 0–89930–786–8

First published in 1992

Quorum Books, 88 Post Road West, Westport, CT 06881
An imprint of Greenwood Publishing Group, Inc.

Printed in the United States of America

The paper used in this book complies with the
Permanent Paper Standard issued by the National
Information Standards Organization (Z39.48—1984).

10 9 8 7 6 5 4 3 2 1

FLORIDA STATE
UNIVERSITY LBRARIES

AUG 30 1993

TALLAHAS   IDA

To Professor Robert J. Alexander

Contents

Acknowledgments   ix

1 The United States and Latin America in an Era of
Global Economic Regionalism   1
The Enterprise for the Americas Initiative   **1**
Outlines of a New World Order   **2**
The Consequences of Regionalism for the Western Hemisphere   **6**
EAI and the Economic Future of the Western Hemisphere   **11**

2 Latin American Debt and Adjustment   17
Causes of Debt   **19**
The Debt Overhang Debate   **23**
Capital Flight   **25**
The International Debt Strategy   **29**
Secondary Market for Latin Debt Paper   **37**
Adjustment   **41**

3 United States Policy toward Latin America   47
The Reagan Administration   **47**
First Two Years of the Bush Administration   **48**
The Enterprise for the Americas Initiative   **48**
The Environing Factors   **50**
Roots of the EAI   **52**
The Lack of an Integrative Mechanism in Latin America   **63**

4 The United States–Mexico Free Trade Agreement and the
Mexican Economy   69
Historical Evolution   **69**
Contents   **75**
Direct Commercial Gains   **77**
Adjustment Gains   **87**

Political Gains   **100**
Advocates and Opponents   **105**
The Current Outlook   **110**

5   First-Tier EAI Candidates:
        Chile, Venezuela, Colombia, and Bolivia   **113**
        Chile   **114**
        Recent Economic Performance   **121**
        Venezuela   **125**
        Political Factors   **133**
        Boliva   **134**
        Adjustment   **134**
        Economic Performance   **139**
        Political Factors   **139**
        Colombia   **140**
        Adjustment   **140**
        Economic Performance   **142**

6   Second-Tier EAI Economies: Brazil, Argentina, and Peru   **143**
        Brazil   **144**
        Adjustment   **144**
        Economic Performance   **156**
        Political Factors   **157**
        Argentina   **160**
        Economic Performance   **168**
        Political Factors   **168**
        Peru   **170**
        Adjustment   **170**
        Economic Performance   **175**

        Bibliography   **177**

        Notes   **187**

        Index   **195**

        About the Authors   **201**

Acknowledgments

I wish to extend my gratitude to my colleagues at St. John's University: Anthony Angelini, Maximo Eng, Francis Lees, Chaman Jain, Stanley Lawson, John Dobbins, Larry Boone, Valerie Englander, Arlene Furfero, Robert Goch, Sara Gordon, Lee Lattimer, Michael Liechenstein, Charles Little, Robert Lucy, Lawrence Mauer, Ronald Moy, LeRoy Pagano, Anthony Pappas, Gregory Pizzigno, Christine Rider, Ralph Terregrossa, Frederick Schmidt, and Athanasios Vasilopoulos. Appreciation is also due to the staff of St. John's Loretto Memorial Library, particularly to Eugene Hunt and Rose Leonardi.

UNITED STATES TRADE AND INVESTMENT IN LATIN AMERICA

CHAPTER 1

The United States and Latin America in an Era of Global Economic Regionalism

THE ENTERPRISE FOR THE AMERICAS INITIATIVE

On June 27, 1990, President George Bush announced a long-range proposal to remove trade barriers with the nations of Latin America, to stimulate private investment there, and to provide the economies of the region with official foreign debt relief. Termed the *Enterprise for the Americas Initiative* (EAI), the Bush plan was unveiled with little fanfare and received scant coverage in the North American press. Given the vagueness of its objectives, its lack of a definite timetable, and the offhand manner in which it was presented, the EAI appeared to be more of a rhetorical intimation than an authentic blueprint for hemispheric economic integration.

Government leaders in Latin America paid much closer attention to Bush's statement than did the American media in their coverage of that summer's first presidential press conference. They had far more at stake, since the EAI spoke of removing protectionist barriers to their chief export market, of providing fresh infusions of sorely needed capital to facilitate privatization, and of alleviating the crippling debt burdens that had disfigured Latin American economies during the "lost decade" of the 1980s. Beyond this natural interest, the officials in the region had also been following the chain of events that led up to the EAI announcement.

To begin, the Bush administration had already taken a series of constructive steps in recasting American policy toward Latin America. These included preliminary background work on a free trade agreement with Mexico, successful implementation of the Brady Plan for debt reduction in that country, as well as Venezuela and Costa Rica, and the replenishment of the Inter-American Development Bank as a lending resource.

Latin American leaders also knew, as many in the United States had not yet recognized, that their region itself had undergone a fundamental transformation in the recent past. The entire continent was now governed by democratically elected leaders; and these same heads of state had either held fast to economic adjustment programs inherited from their predecessors, intensified those programs, or initiated new ones. In the course of adjusting both to their own debt burdens and to adverse events outside their borders, many of these same leaders had endeavored to restructure their economies along free-market lines, liberalizing their trade and direct investment regimes and their domestic sectors. In fact, some Latin countries were already prepared to play a full role in economic partnership with the United States. Seen in this context, the EAI proposal suggested that America was close to acknowledging the "sea change" that had taken place in Latin America.

But the momentum behind the Bush proposal was more powerful and far reaching. It could be interpreted as a basic change in American policy, not only toward Latin America but, in response to cardinal shifts in power occurring around the globe, to such diverse regions as the European Community, the Pacific Basin, and the newly liberated nations of the erstwhile Eastern Bloc. Only in this broader framework can the challenges and the opportunities underpinning the EAI be grasped in full.

OUTLINES OF A NEW WORLD ORDER

The Broad Shape of Things to Come

Entering the final decade of this century, the outlines of a new world order began to emerge with an astounding speed as historical events of systemic magnitude followed each other in rapid succession. While the exact shape of this order remains unclear, through a process of elimination coupled with a good deal of speculation, we can project what the future may hold for the global economy at large and America's fortunes in particular.

Just a few years ago, the assumption that the world economy would move toward an irreversible globalization seemed to be an unshakable axiom of modernization theory. While that plank is still sound, its utility as a predictive foundation for thinking about the future has been undermined by the emergence of economic regionalism. Today, a loose but broad consensus in both business and scholarly circles has come together around the notion that three major regional trade and financial groupings will come to dominate international commercial flows and that their individual efforts to achieve relative advantages will bring them into intensified competition and conflict. Meanwhile, continental sections outside these three centers will not achieve anything like the clout and dynamism.

On the Sidelines: Eastern Europe, Africa, and the Middle East

By a straightforward process of elimination, the first cut in the construction of a future global economic model can be rendered. For the time being, a number of potential players in the coming order have been relegated to the sidelines as a result of their deeply rooted structural problems. Although it is always hazardous to engage in sweeping generalizations, Eastern Europe, sub-Saharan Africa, and the Middle East (led by the Organization of Petroleum Exporting Countries) [OPEC]) all fall in this category.

Despite the worldwide euphoria that arose in the immediate aftermath of the abortive coup in the Soviet Union in August 1991, prospects for Eastern Europe becoming a major force in the global economy are at present more remote than ever. It is by now apparent that the transition from central planning to a market-based economy in what was the Council for Mutual Economic Assistance (CMEA) Bloc, and especially in the Soviet Union, will be a prolonged and arduous undertaking, with both near-term and long-range outcomes remaining uncertain.

In a joint study conducted by the International Monetary Fund (IMF), the World Bank (IBRD), the Organization for Economic Cooperation and Development (OECD), and the European Bank for Reconstruction and Development, entitled *The Economy of the USSR,* one of its working premises is summarized in the statement that "there is no example of a successful modern centrally planned economy."[1] This assertion implies that *perestroika*-type reforms will occur simply because the Soviets have no alternative but to embrace some form of capitalism. By the same token, it must be observed that recent history provides us with no cases of a command economy of the USSR's complexity and size undergoing a successful capitalist transformation. Indeed, despite marginal progress in some Eastern European economies, we have no evidence that such a metamorphosis can be accomplished. While the possibility is rarely mentioned, communism may be not merely a macroeconomic malady that requires strong and distasteful medicine but in fact a terminal condition. After generations of living under a centrally planned economy, the citizens of Eastern Europe may lack the motivation, the requisite know-how, and the productive resources to join the world capitalist system as full-fledged "players." It is by now plain that, with the exception of East Germany, all the economies of this region, particularly those of the nations that comprised the Soviet Union, will remain on the periphery of the international economy for some time to come.

The outlook for sub-Saharan Africa varies from nation to nation, but it must generally be characterized as fairly dismal. Virtually all the forty-odd countries in this part of the world continue to suffer from a lack of domestic and foreign investment, a secular decline in terms of trade on the raw and semiprocessed commodities they export, and an overhang of external debt that rules out all save concessional resource transfers from bilateral and multilateral official sources.

There are, to be sure, some bright spots. Despite declining export prices, export receipts, and terms of trade since 1980, many of these countries have adopted strong reform programs aimed at placing their macroeconomic policies on a sound footing and restructuring their economies for eventual entrance into the global mainstream. In this, the nation's of Africa have enjoyed substantial help from the West. The share of net official development assistance (ODA) disbursements earmarked for sub-Saharan Africa almost doubled between 1970 and 1987 to about 30 percent. As important, their debt-service burdens have been lightened of late as official creditors have formally acknowledged that the loans of the 1970s and 1980s will not be repaid in full, if at all. Nevertheless, the promise of a vibrant Africa is unlikely to be kept any time soon.

For decidedly different reasons, the energy-rich Middle East is also likely to be a spectator to the new economic order. During the 1990–1991 Persian Gulf crisis, the specter of world economic conditions being determined through the policies of OPEC loomed large. Having experienced two oil "shocks" in the 1970s, the energy-importing countries, industrialized and developing alike, had ample reason to fear OPEC's capacity to control global economic and financial flows.

But it was not OPEC's strength that came to the fore in the wake of Iraq's invasion of Kuwait; instead, it was the acknowledgment by its membership of the need to maintain price stability and, tacitly, of the region's continued dependence upon the West. When the Bush administration announced that it would release only a tiny fraction of America's Strategic Petroleum Reserve, prices for Persian crude plummeted considerably faster than they had increased in the weeks following Saddam Hussein's invasion. At bottom, the Middle East suffers from an inordinately narrow export base; a lack of import-substitution; and thin, inefficient financial markets. In the new world order, OPEC is likely to assume a supporting, if not a cameo, role. While the cartel may be able to influence the world economy briefly from time to time, it will remain constrained in the scope and durability of its power.

Two of the "Big Three" Players:
The European Community and the Pacific Basin

With these three regions ruled out as prospective epicenters of economic power, the more obvious side of our perspective on the new world order is in place, and we must turn to more affirmative yet more problematic statements. Fortunately, while there are those who depart from what has become the orthodox reading of the future, the majority of government experts, private business analysts, and university academicians subscribe to remarkably uniform understanding.

The opening assumption of this interpretation is that with the passage of the Cold War, economic power has increased in importance relative to military might. From this, it follows that economic events occurring almost anywhere will take on a greater ability to influence domestic economic, political, and social conditions within each of the world's nation-states. The political boundaries between nation-states have been subsumed by a far more fluid and amorphous economic structure. Concurrently, while forces encouraging worldwide economic integration have gathered momentum as a consequence of the events of the late 1980s and early 1990s, powerful regionalizing tendencies are also operative. In this context, *regionalism* denotes intensifying pattern of trade and factor flows within a given geographical region. The share of cross-border flows of products and services — of capital, labor, and technology — within the region becomes progressively greater, at the expense of flows from the region to other parts of the global economy. This, in turn, will tend to create regional blocs within multilateral institutions (such as the General Agreement on Tariffs and Trade [GATT]), as nations within specific regions develop stronger and more united stands on the issues addressed through international organizations. As this takes place, the viability and the power of these global institutions will come under mounting pressure. Some of these bodies will find their power diminished; others will move into new areas, and most important, regional bodies will assume some of the tasks previously performed by organizations with worldwide memberships.

To be more specific, the world seems to be heading toward a tripolar distribution of economic clout, consisting of the European Community, a Pacific Basin bloc led by Japan and the newly industrialized countries (NICs) of the Pacific Rim, and some Western Hemispheric counterpart as yet to be organized by the United States. These three blocs will be the principal forces in the sense that each will be able to initiate changes with global repercussions. Thus, contrary to the optimistic assumptions that have guided integration theory, the limbo state of regional economic divisions is likely to be with us for some time and to be characterized by a high degree of contention among regions.

Although the sudden unification of Germany has tended to overshadow the unification of the European Community (EC) to be achieved through the EC-92 program, it has also underscored the fact that Europe's integration under EC-92 will be far more than an administrative change or a marginal transfer of power from individual European capitals to Brussels. Although both German unification and the larger process of resurrecting Eastern Europe have made the EC-92 program more complicated and may even slow it down, a greater Germany and a redeemed Eastern Europe will enlarge the significance of this program within and outside Europe. Thus, while the process formally initiated with Lord Cockfield's 1985 white paper may be delayed by events in the East, the sacrifices the EC will be compelled to make in response to them will tend to deepen its commitment to that program. There is no sign whatsoever that Eastern Europe's liberation will derail the EC-92 drive.

The European Community is unique in having longstanding organizational and institutional arrangements that favor (indeed, that mandate) regional economic integration. The same cannot be said of what was once termed the Far East and has since been conceptually expanded under the label *Pacific Basin*. A decade ago, it was customary to describe the Far East as a set of isolated production, trading, and financial centers, notably Japan and its clones — the "four tigers" of South Korea, Taiwan, Hong Kong, and Singapore. Rendered in such broad strokes, two incipient but important dimensions of the Far East picture were obscured. The first was internal to the region — the growth of intraregional trade and factor flows that have integrated the Far East (including Malaysia, Thailand, and Indonesia, along with Australia) to a level that approximates the integration of Western Europe. In fact, albeit without the fanfare that has heralded EC-92, longstanding regional associations like ASEAN (Association of South East Asian Nations) have been joined by "new" confederations like Asian-Pacific Economic Cooperation (APEC) effort.

The second factor was external to the original concept of the Far East — that the region's geographical sphere would be confined to the Orient. Based in part on a Western cultural bias, this view expected that some regional enlargement (to the Philippines, for example) might occur. This artificial limit on the frame of the Far East has now been broken by an incipient Pacific Basin bloc that encompasses most of the economies of both North and South America.

THE CONSEQUENCES OF REGIONALISM FOR
THE WESTERN HEMISPHERE

Impact on the United States

For the United States, as for all other nations of the world, the trend toward regionalism will have both positive and negative consequences. The emergence of three blocs or regional groupings does not necessarily imply that the world will enter a new era of protectionism. Ideally, the formation of these blocs would encourage member countries to open their markets globally as well, so that any trade diversion would tend to be offset by trade creation. Since the Pacific Basin and the European Community represent America's largest and second-largest regional export markets, the boost to growth that regional associations will bring to them should fuel some absolute export growth if the implicit protectionism of regionalization is not overwhelming. At the same time, the emergence of a Big Three of the industrialized world — Europe, Japan, and the United States — will place a higher premium on coordination, especially in the realms of monetary and fiscal policy.

On the other hand, the different strategies chosen by the Big Three in the quest for the market shares and wealth may become incompatible if they lead to permanent imbalances. A prime example of this is the perennial trade and current-account surpluses of Japanese exporting and the acrimony they have generated among that country's trading partners. As Japan and the EC use their own resources to finance regional integration and as their competitive edge is honed by intraregional production, conflicts over trade and trade-related issues may well escalate.

From a short-term perspective, the principal economic reason to believe that the formation of regional groupings will create more intense conflict is the likely advent of a world capital shortage and its attendant pressures on international financial markets. Reacting to the projected costs of German reunification and the financial needs of Eastern Europe, the governor of the Bank of England, Robin Leigh-Pemberton stated that "the industrial world is in for an era of high interest rates."[2] With the EC issuing more debt paper to underwrite both the EC-92 program and development assistance for Eastern Europe, its currencies will appreciate as international investors trade non-EC currencies for Deutschemarks, pounds, and francs to take advantage of increasingly attractive yields. This, in turn, will reduce the competitiveness of EC products in external markets in the short-run, transforming the current account surpluses registered by the Europeans in the 1980s into deficits during the first half of the 1990s. Presumably, these disequilibriums will prompt Europe to take an even more aggressive stance on trade and boost incentives to investment. Meanwhile, the Japanese are planning vast infrastructural improvement programs over the next quarter-century. Although domestic savings may be sufficient to furnish the wherewithal, Japan's role as a net exporter of autonomous capital will probably diminish.

Should an international credit crunch occur, higher global interest rates are likely to have a stronger drag on the U.S. economy than on those of Europe or Japan. At the end of the 1980s, the U.S. Federal Reserve (the Fed) faced a seemingly intractable dilemma. In order to stimulate growth, the Fed has been pressured to loosen the monetary screws and thereby facilitate lower interest rates. While concern for domestic price inflation limits the Fed's capacity to perform this stimulative function, a second constraint is that less attractive rates will inhibit the flow of capital into the United States and prompt a wholesale extraction of credit. This quandary effectively undercuts America as it tries to exercise leverage against the EC and the Japanese on crucial trade issues.

In the long-term, the competitive advantages of regional integration in the EC and the Pacific Basin will also be felt by the United States as exports are reduced relative to intraregional exchanges there, as stronger platforms for EC and Pacific Basin blocs permit penetration of American markets, and as share of third-country markets decline when U.S. firms square off against European and Asian firms supported by regional resource power, scale, and major public-sector investment stimuli. Having dug itself into a current-account and foreign-debt hole, the United States will be stymied in trying to garner the trade and investment receipts needed to remit payments on past borrowings from Europe and Asia.

Impact on Latin America

But the United States is *not* the area where economic regionalization of the world may exercise its strongest negative effect. Latin America is bound to suffer even more as a region trying to cast off the strictures of foreign debt and the misguided development strategies of the past. As is detailed in the next chapter, Latin America is currently on the sidelines of both the global economy and the trend toward economic regionalism. Not only have its trade and factor exchanges with the rest of the world failed to keep abreast, its intraregional flows have also been stagnant. In the area of trade, the emergence of European and Pacific economic groupings is likely to create a strong bias against positive net trade revenues and resource flows between these quarters of the developed world and Latin America. Concurrently, the enhanced competitiveness of European and Asian firms in the world economy will create a barrier to the growth of nontraditional exports from Latin America to markets outside the EC and the Pacific Basin.

The accompanying tendency for capital to coalesce within geographic groupings gives economic regionalism its most debilitating impact for most Latin countries, which generally need foreign investment to meet their current account needs, solidify adjustment, and extricate their economies from developmental stagnation.

Latin America was a major recipient of net investment flows during the 1960s and 1970s; but in the 1980s, foreign debt repayment, coupled with a widespread decline in traditional funding sources, left the region transferring huge sums to the developed world with no compensatory inflow of fresh money. Since 1982, Latin America has sent net resources of around $200 billion back to the United States, Western Europe, and Japan, an amount equivalent to nearly half its total foreign debt. Even under optimistic assumptions about Latin American output and trade growth (now clouded by the likely impact of regionalism), the nations of the region will be able to repay their borrowings on a sustainable basis only if they obtain an additional $15 billion a year in capital from the outside world during the 1990s. As for the amount of funding Latin America could absorb into productive capital, a study prepared by the Inter-American Development Bank sets Latin America's investment gap in 1989 at about 8 percent of GDP, that is, about $70 billion.³ Even after substantial debt reductions under the Brady Plan, if renewed net positive flow of resources to major Latin America countries fails to materialize, powerful economic and political constraints will impede the continued stabilization and liberalization of these economies; and the adjustment registered to date in several Latin American nations may slow down or halt altogether.

For Latin America to satisfy its current account requirements and a portion of its investment needs, there are four sources from which it can draw: (1) commercial bank, bilateral official, and multilateral official loans; (2) direct investment, either straight or as part of debt conversions or formal privatization programs; (3) international capital markets for issues of bonds and stocks by private Latin American enterprises and government bonds, along with equity offerings in conjunction with privatizations; and (4) repatriation of capital flight money.

Of these sources, fresh voluntary loans are unlikely to come anywhere near meeting Latin America's capital needs; indeed, they are not likely to counterbalance debt-service flows on the repayment of existing loans. As for American banks, all small banks and most regional institutions have left the Latin market and closed their Third World loan windows. For their part, the big U.S. banks—the nine money-center institutions that now hold the bulk of existing Latin American private loans—have made it clear that they will either stand pat or try to reduce their exposure to Latin America even further. Japanese banks have stronger balance sheets than American institutions, which are reeling from rising delinquencies and defaults on domestic debt paper; but the Japanese Ministry of Finance is now steering banks away from new lending to Third World borrowers except in rescheduling packages that include debt-equity conversions.

During the last half of the 1980s, official government-to-government loan flows from the developed world to Latin America increased by around 20 percent. However, trends in bilateral official development assistance (ODA) suggest that it will not fulfill a major part of funding needs for this part of the world. Many bilateral official lenders, especially export credit agencies, have reduced their net flows to these countries; and, indeed, one factor behind the demise of the Baker Third World debt plan was the failure of these governments to reach the aggregate lending targets set by the U.S. Treasury secretary in 1985. Two of the major European lender nations, Germany and France, have already written off official Latin American loans and became disinclined to take on another wave of bad sovereign debt. In Japan, since early in 1991, the administration of Toshiki Kaifu has been adopting a hard line on official debt reduction for Third World countries, vocally criticizing the Brady Plan.

Multilateral official loan sources (the World Bank, the International Monetary Fund, and regional banking institutions) have picked up much of the external financing burden of developing countries dropped by banks and individual Western governments. Today, the International Bank for Reconstruction and Development (IBRD) or World Bank is the single largest source of new financing for the heavily indebted countries of Latin America, but there are problems here as well. The capital resources of the World Bank are not unlimited, and many Latin American nations are reaching ceilings set by the IBRD for resource transfers to them. Moreover, as a bank, the IBRD expects to be repaid on the credit that it extends to sovereign borrowers. As new loans dwindle and grace periods on old loans lapse, Latin American debtor nations will start making net outward transfers to the IBRD. Indeed, this situation has already occurred with regard to loans extended to Latin American governments by the International Monetary Fund. The chances that Latin America can meet its foreign investment needs from composite loans source are zero; and on balance, commercial debt repayment will demand greater outward capital resource transfers than official lending will provide.

Although there is some potential for direct investment to fulfill Latin America's external financing needs during the decade ahead, it is necessary to distinguish between direct investment made in conjunction with official debt-equity swap programs and conventional foreign direct investment (FDI). Here the prospects are substantially brighter, but pitfalls remain. Many multinational corporations are eager to purchase Latin American real assets at a deep discount through debt-equity swaps, but most Latin American governments are trying to limit the amount of direct investment taking place through these channels. Not only can such swaps undermine stabilization efforts, since capital inflows are diverted to extinguishing existing debt, but very little new money actually reaches the affected economies through this route. To date, direct investment in Latin America outside debt-equity conversions has been spotty and shallow. A broad increase in FDI will take place when these economies are stable, and "deep" investment will occur with the liberalization of their external and domestic sectors. Some Latin American governments are close to meeting such conditions if they can bolster their current accounts; others are not. For direct investment to play its part in the commercial revitalization of Latin America, host economies must display strong growth trajectories, but this will not take place until the region's external accounts are stabilized by an increase in foreign capital flows.

Reflecting the extent to which some Latin American countries have progressed in improving their investment environments, a new source of capital has emerged, one that could eventually become the workhorse of the region's foreign capital inflows. Several private corporations in Latin America have begun to issue bonds and stocks on international capital markets. This source of foreign financing could potentially lift Latin growth rates and thereby induce an even greater flow of money from both this source and others. Officials at Salomon Brothers estimate the market for new Latin American bonds could grow to $80 billion in two or three years and eventually reach *$250* *billion.*[4] Indicative of this growth potential is the fact that in 1991 private Latin American bonds were bid down to yields slightly higher than those on debt offerings from their counterparts in the United States. Even some Latin American governments have been able to access this source of capital, albeit for very limited amounts.

This new source of funding could reach a magnitude commensurate with Latin American capital needs. Several caveats are nevertheless in order. As yields rise on public and private debt issued by the Europeans and Japanese, ever higher rates of return will be required to keep Latin paper attractive to international investors. More important, capital from this source can be withdrawn as rapidly as it is mobilized. Hence, there is a significant danger of speculative inflows undercutting Latin America should its progress toward the resumption of growth hit a snag. For the sake of investors and recipients alike, extensive use of this source demands stable conditions in the recipient economy. As Latin American economies move in that direction, capital markets could furnish the wherewithal for further adjustments and growth advances. But for the time being, the latter depend on substantial increases in external financing.

From any perspective, Latin American investment needs would be best met by a reflux of capital flight. Some signs that such a reverse flow could be in the offing were seen in Mexico after its Brady Plan debt workout, and modest reflows have been experienced by Venezuela and Chile as well. Capital flight reflux has taken place through international capital markets as well as direct repatriation. Nevertheless, the permanent return of flight capital in substantial magnitude is likely to be a medium-term phenomenon, coming after macroeconomic stability has been reestablished. The prerequisite for harnessing flight capital in the service of Latin American renewal is achieving economic stability in the economies of origin.

This preliminary survey of possible capital sources for Latin America shows that many sources of funds may become available if the necessary investment conditions are met. The propensity of capital to circulate within geographical areas that is inherent in economic regionalization tends to raise the level of underlying stability that Latin economies must attain if they are to attract and retain the funds they need to resume growth.

EAI AND THE ECONOMIC FUTURE OF
THE WESTERN HEMISPHERE

Against this backdrop of changes and shifts, the central argument of this book assumes its full meaning. In the chapters that follow, it is argued that the United States must take an active and leading role in the construction of a hemispheric economic entity in order to compete against the regional blocs now forming in Europe and the Far East. In a period when nations are joining to gain greater regional economic and political leverage, America must look to Latin America and seek to restore not just buoyancy to its previously thriving export markets but developmental momentum so that the nations of this region can become genuine partners in common resource usage.

Plainly, the attainment of such aims will require a transformation in U.S. policy. From the announcement of the Mexican amortization moratorium in August 1982 until the end of the decade, the United States placed the debtor nations of Latin America on hold. The Reagan administration prosecuted an anachronistic Cold War struggle against the Sandinistas, but otherwise the U.S. government effectively ceded control over its Latin American policy to the International Monetary Fund, the World Bank, the Paris Club and, least appropriately of all, a shifting assemblage of bank steering committees at pains to extract debt repayments. Meanwhile, American protectionism against Latin American exports and chronic American inability to put the nation's financial house in order both handicapped Latin America's ability to adjust and raised the cost of servicing its debts. During the second half of the 1980s, heavily indebted Latin American nations made net resource transfers to North American, Western European, and Far Eastern creditors, both official and private, laboring under the combined weight of repayment obligations and adjustment programs aimed at bringing their external accounts into balance. It has become increasingly apparent that Latin America cannot become a genuine partner in a hemispheric economic grouping under these circumstances.

Under President Bush, there are signs that the atrophication of U.S. Latin American policy is at last coming to an end. Although the Brady debt-relief plan for developing countries is a broad initiative intended to help less developed countries (LDCs) around the world, its principal beneficiaries are the middle-income economies of Latin America. By itself, the Brady Plan has proved laudable but insufficient to the task at hand. What is required at this juncture is precisely what the EAI calls for, supplemental debt relief on official loans, incentives for domestic and overseas investment, and the liberalization of trade in both directions. Under the Enterprise for the Americas Initiative, prospects for improvement in the investment climate of Latin American economies would be significantly raised. Official debt reduction under the EAI would reduce pressures on Latin American current-account balances. EAI funds to augment ongoing privatization programs would reduce public outlays to cover the losses of state-owned enterprises (SOEs) and force privatized production entities to operate according to the dictates of market forces. More important, opening U.S. markets to Latin American goods would provide the region with additional export receipts. Liberalized trade with the United States would both put pressure on Latin American producers of rival goods to become more efficient and enhance the competitiveness of Latin exporters using American-made capital and intermediate goods. Of itself, EAI will not give Latin America the ability to compete against powerful regional blocs for export sales and investment capital. Further restructuring of Latin economies will be needed if they are to withstand greater competition for trade and factor flows that will occur as regional groupings take shape. Acknowledging this, EAI includes an explicit conditional adjustment dimension.

Since the EAI proposal calls for substantial transfers to Latin America, most of the immediate gains would accrue to economies there. Nevertheless, the prospective benefits from an EAI would be mutual, and the United States can expect to receive important gains. By implementing a program of economic partnership with the nations of Latin America, the United States can achieve at least four types of advantages.

The first benefits are general economic advances that have the most direct consequences for U.S. firms. Consistent with classical economic theory, the liberalization of trade and factor flows between the United States and Latin America offers the promise of enhanced efficiency in resource allocation at the regional, national, and enterprise levels for all parties to the plan. EAI would help to resurrect a major U.S. export market and to maintain or increase the U.S. share of world goods and services delivered to that market. It would also have a salutary influence on a direct investment outlet that has languished for nearly ten years, offering the prospect of boosting regional competitiveness through production-sharing arrangements. EAI would both bolster Latin America's capacity to repay existing loans to the U.S. government and American banks and stimulate new interest-bearing commercial credit flows from the latter. Last, it would assist Latin nations in tapping international financial markets, expanding opportunities for American investors to realize comparatively high rates of return on Latin American private and public bond issues and stocks offerings.

A second cluster of benefits are political in nature, with indirect but powerful implications for American commercial interests. The EAI proposal would generally enhance U.S. relations with a region it has neglected and thus permit America to build upon the far more positive attitude toward the United States that has emerged there during the last part of the 1980s. Demonstrating support for these nations would enable the United States to support fledgling democratic regimes that are strongly committed to open societies and free markets. Plainly, this improvement in relations would bode well for American companies looking to Latin America for new trade and investment outlets.

At the same time, EAI affords the United States the chance to take advantage of significant changes that are occurring in the policies of international organizations and to increase its leverage within these global bodies at a time when the power configuration among them is itself shifting. Joining Latin nations in an economic alliance would furnish the United States with additional leverage in future GATT negotiating sessions. The Bush proposal is congruent with the revision of IMF and World Bank approaches toward Latin America, notably the recognition that external debt reduction is required if these economies are to resume growth. EAI would feature a linkage to the Inter-American Development Bank (IDB) at a time when the IDB is moving toward lending policies consistent with the conditional dimension of the Bush package. It would also fill a void in the institutional landscape of Latin American integration that has opened as the import-substituting strategy of the old Latin cooperation organizations became more and more irrelevant, just as it would preempt any return to that discredited strategy at a regional or subregional level. Thus, at multiple levels the EAI would further American commercial interests by increasing the leverage of the United States chief international trade and financial institutions of the world and by establishing a leading role for America in those regional bodies that are likely to become increasingly significant.

A final set of benefits pivots on the conditional nature of the proposed program. EAI eligibility is contingent on continued adjustment to and extension of processes already under way in most Latin American nations as a consequence of their grappling with debt burdens. During the 1980s, external debt burdens compelled adjustment by Latin American nations, often under the supervision of the IMF as part of a conditional loan program. As time elapsed, the ingredients of the IMF adjustment recipe became fairly standardized. Derived chiefly from neoclassical economic theory, what will be called the *orthodox approach* is based on the assumption that lasting adjustment must encompass both domestic and foreign sectors of an economy and that in each of these spheres the attainment of balance and discipline in the near term must be supported by structural reforms leading to full reliance on the free operation of market forces.

The extent to which individual Latin American countries have pursued adjustment and the degree to which they have been successful vary substantially from country to country. Some economies, those of Mexico, Chile, and Bolivia, have undergone substantial change; others, such as Venezuela and Peru, are committed to deep reforms that have not yet been realized; still others, like Argentina, have encountered serious roadblocks along the way; and some, the most important being Brazil, have adjusted half-heartedly and haphazardly. Consequently, because EAI imposes conditions, it offers additional potential gains for the United States, both economic and political. Participation in EAI would provide individual Latin American nations with recognition of adjustment made to date and create both incentives for and conditions favorable to further changes. Such acknowledgments and incentives would plainly raise the attractiveness of Latin America as a trading partner, a direct investment outlet, and a source of equity and debt paper.

The fact that EAI imposes conditions is central to the analysis and working methods of this study. The degree of adjustment undertaken to date by individual countries furnishes us with a yardstick of their readiness to act as economic partners with the United States. It is assumed that the capacity of an economy to take part in a mutually beneficial program of economic integration with one or more other economies can be directly measured by the extent to which its external accounts are in balance and its trade and foreign direct investment regimes are open. Anticipating the sort of deep commitment a free-trade pact would require, a given economy's long-term attractiveness as a trade or investment partner requires that its domestic affairs be in order and underpinned by market mechanisms. In brief, a demonstrated capacity for adjustment toward a stable, open economy is a useful rule-of-thumb index to the probability that union with a prospective trade or investment partner will work out and pay off. A comparative appraisal of adjustment thus far points out which nations are now prepared for EAI talks.

CHAPTER 2

Latin American Debt and Adjustment

An examination of the aggregate accounts of Latin American nations during the 1980s reveals little cause for enthusiasm about a future hemispheric economic grouping. For Latin America, the 1980s were an era of both relative and absolute immiseration during which real growth rates were either negative or well below those of the 1960s and 1970s – all accompanied by fiscal crises, outbursts of hyperinflation, and grinding poverty. As John Williamson reports, Latin America as a whole has not yet rebounded from the deep decline it suffered at the start of the 1980s.

As the decade [1980s] ended, the region remained mired in stagflation, burdened by foreign debt, disfigured by the world's most inegalitarian income distribution, and crippled by a continuing lack of confidence on the part not only of its foreign creditors but also of its own entrepreneurs, manifested in low domestic investment and massive holdings of flight capital.[1]

A brief survey of Latin America's recent macroeconomic performance indicators confirms Williamson's evaluation. For 1990, composite Latin America GDP growth came in at only 1 percent, with only a slight improvement (to 2 percent output growth) projected for 1991. During the 1980s as a whole, the aggregate Latin American GNP growth rate dropped to 1.1 percent a year, compared to 5.9 percent in the 1970s. Having achieved some recovery in the mid-1980s, Latin American growth rates declined considerably in the late 1980s as a result of insufficient domestic savings and a continuing erosion in terms of trade. In many instances, this second drop in growth was accompanied by rapid price inflation that led to the worst-case-scenario phenomenon of stagflation. Lack of investment, which as a share of GDP has fallen by one-third, from nearly 24 percent between 1974 and 1980 to 16 percent be-

tween 1983 and 1989. Worse, any evaluation of the region's economic performance must be adjusted for its rapid growth of population, which is on
the order of 2.5 percent to 3 percent a year. In this context, marginal output
expansion has not kept abreast of population growth. During the 1980s, the
region's average per-capita product declined at a rate of nearly 1 percent a
year, so that by the end of the decade, GDP per capita for the region as a
whole was 8.1 percent lower than it had been in 1980. At the end of the
decade, only two of the major debtor countries—Brazil and Colombia—had
achieved levels of per-capita income higher than those prevailing at its start.
The collapse of the unsustainable Brazilian debt-led expansion during 1990
leaves Colombia the only large nation in the region to have attained any real
progress on this front.

The brunt of this prolonged recession was borne by the region's working
class. Throughout Latin America, real wages were lower in 1989 than they
were in 1982; in Mexican industry, for example, workers now receive pay-
checks some 40 percent smaller in real purchasing power than they were prior
to the onset of the debt. Long before the current growth contraction hit Latin
America, disparities in wealth and income were sharper than in any other
LDC region. During the lost decade of the 1980s, both the absolute number
and the percentage of people living in extreme poverty rose substantially.

In Latin American external accounts, some positive developments in trade
have continued through the 1980s. For instance, acknowledging the secular
deterioration of terms of trade on primary commodities, nations have both
increased the proportion of manufactured goods in their aggregate export
bundles from 12 percent in 1960 to 31 percent in 1986 and expanded the
range of agricultural products destined for markets overseas. Indeed, Chile,
Brazil, Mexico, Colombia, and Costa Rica have all experienced impressive
growth in nontraditional exports (NTEGs) during the 1980s. For Latin
America as a whole, however, aggregate exports since 1982 have essentially
been stagnant. Despite the growing component of nontraditional goods in
the export bundles, total Latin American exports have declined as a percentage of global shipments. Imports, notably purchases of American goods
and services, have dropped in both relative and absolute terms (leaving aside
Mexico's 1989–1900 import surge). Victor Urquidi has succinctly summarized
the general trajectory of the continent's international stature during the
1980s: "In other words, Latin America's participation in the world economy
has declined."[2]

The president of the Inter-American Development Bank, Enrique Iglesias,
ascribed the decline of Latin America's fortunes to two basic and interrelated
causes: (1) the mismanagement of Latin economies over the last thirty years
and (2) the accumulation of a massive external debt burden.[3] Gross external
debt rose from a low and manageable U.S. $26 billion in 1973 to more than
$360 billion in 1984, while the region's debt coefficient (debt-service ratio of
annual export receipts to scheduled foreign debt repayment) rose from 13

percent to 36 percent during the same period. Some progress has been made in reducing short-term debt and rescheduling repayments on lengthier maturities, but little has been accomplished to date in the reduction of medium- and long-term debt. At the end of 1990, external debt stood at $426 billion, three-quarters of it owed by Argentina, Brazil, Chile, Mexico, and Venezuela. Although this sum is less than half the estimated $1.3 trillion in outstanding external debt of all developing countries, the bulk of Latin America's debt is owed to commercial banks rather than official bilateral or multilateral lenders and was originally contracted on hard terms — at market interest rates plus a margin. Moreover, this outstanding debt is heavily concentrated in the portfolios of nine American money-market-center banks.

Given the frequency with which commercial banks reschedule debt among Latin American borrowers, it is possible to cast the course of Latin debt repayment in the 1980s in a positive, if not glowing, light. William Cline has observed that today it is not the debt-service-ratio (DSR) of total annual debt repayment to export receipts but the ratio of external interest payments (exclusive of payments on principal) to export revenues that provides the true working measure of the region's debt burden. Cline points out that: "the region as a whole has reduced its interest/export ratio from 41 percent to 30 percent since 1982; Brazil from 57 percent to 34 percent; and Mexico from 41 percent to 29 percent."[4] Nonetheless, all the pertinent debt ratios are well beyond the pale, and any attempt to explain how Latin America became entrapped in its current bind must necessarily examine the accumulation of foreign debt.

CAUSES OF DEBT

The causes of the Latin American debt problem have been extensively analyzed elsewhere,[5] and require only the most cursory survey at this time. Until the late 1980s, analyses of the debt crisis often displayed a polemical character, taking the form of a debate over who was to blame. Of late, scholars both from the industrialized nations and from Latin America have come to agree that errors were made on all sides, that no party is exclusively responsible for the situation as it now stands.

Borrowers

The most straightforward explanation of the debt crisis is that Latin debtors simply borrowed too much money from international lenders to begin with. According to a Federal Reserve Board study written by Steven Kamin, Robert Kahn, and Ross Levine, overborrowing was the heart of the problem.[6] This version is something of an oversimplification. Kamin and his colleagues concluded that Argentina, Brazil, Chile, and Mexico actually benefited from external borrowing in the 1970s. At its precrisis peak, real GDP per capita in these nations was 4 percent to 16 percent beyond the level it would have reached if the rate of real external borrowing had remained unchanged from 1975 to 1987. More pointedly, official wisdom maintains that this same group of major borrowers would have been better off, "if their external borrowing . . . had been used as efficiently as their borrowing has been before the buildup of external debt in the 1970s."[7]

This is the crux of the problem, and it provides both a lesson about the past and a glimmer of hope for the future. Many of these nations used borrowed funds to finance import-substituting industrialization strategies. These misguided programs were yoked to protectionist measures for infant industry. By shielding these state-financed and managed entities from foreign competition, these countries created vast networks of loss-making SOEs that could not generate the foreign exchange earnings necessary to service external debt and in fact siphoned resources from productive sectors. Hence, among the causes of the debt crisis on the debit side of the ledger S. Shahid Husain places the rapid expansion of the governments into functional areas better handled by the private sector alongside overregulation and the politicization of economic decisions at the top of his list.[8] Amplifying the general problem, prior to the quiet revolutions that ushered civilian governments into power in Latin America during the 1980s, many major debtor nations were controlled by the military. Thus, a significant portion of the external public debt accumulated by 1982 was the result of expanded arms imports in the 1970s and early 1980s.[9]

As Latin governments extended their reach into the traditional province of the private sector, inefficient state-run enterprises contributed to poorly conceived and badly implemented domestic macroeconomic policies. Losses generated at the level of the SOE were absorbed by the public sector through deficit financing, the accumulation of domestic debt, and lax monetary policies aimed in part at monetizing the latter. The burden of import-substituting industrialization was thus shifted to the private sector, causing the bankruptcy of many Latin American business entities, often preceded by spurts of private-sector foreign borrowing. To be sure, smart money in Latin America circumvented absorption by the state through capital flight.

When the external shocks of the early 1980s rippled through Latin America, there was an immediate need to achieve domestic balance through fiscal and monetary discipline and external balance through devaluation and other import-compressing measures. Many governments elected to treat these adverse external developments as temporary aberrations and to postpone adjustment. Wise investors realized that a day of reckoning was approaching that would include drastic devaluations, hyperinflation, and direct confiscation of wealth. Faced with this prospect, they exported still more capital. When halfhearted adjustment policies that combined delay with reliance on heterodox emergency measures were adopted by Latin American governments, cautious citizens took whatever steps they could to circumvent their impact.

Lenders

While Latin governments and private agents may have borrowed too heavily, their creditors erred by lending too much. The money-center banks extended too much credit to Latin governments during the 1970s, using the device of variable-interest loans to transfer the burden of risk onto the shoulders of the borrowers and the form of the syndicated loan to divide the remaining risk among themselves. During the 1970s, stagflation in the industrialized nations and a superabundance of petrodollars generated by windfall oil profits led to negative interest rates in real (inflation-adjusted) terms. At the same time, Latin America remained one of the world's most dynamic regions, and its traditional export commodities enjoyed a brief price increase. These factors contributed to a virtual explosion of commercial bank lending to Latin America.

Temporary conditions during the 1970s led bankers to overestimate the amount of credit that could be extended to sovereign Latin American borrowers. However, even if we factor out the probable distortions seeping into bank lending decisions from short-term extrapolation, as Bahram Nowzad stated, "It should have been clear that lending at negative interest rates could not continue indefinitely."[10] With demand for credit weak elsewhere and bankers eager to cultivate new clients, the international lending community simply chose to overlook the inevitable.

Of course, the inevitable did occur. Tight monetary policies in OECD nations caused interest rates to rise sharply. Simultaneously, the brief respite from long-term deterioration in Latin terms of trade came to a halt. Early in the 1980s, as commodity prices plummeted and real interest rates soared, syndicated bank loans to Latin nations that were already heavily indebted vanished overnight. Sere credit markets exerted a powerful negative influence on Third World growth everywhere; but while the average nonindustrialized country experienced a decline of about 40 percent in external financing between 1981 and 1983, the average Latin American country experienced a drop of approximately 90 percent in net capital inflows. As Edwards and Larrain underscore the point, total net capital inflows to Latin America, which reached an all-time high of $37.5 billion in 1981, declined to $20 billion in 1982 and $3.2 billion in 1983, "a drop of 90 percent in two years!"[11] Having enjoyed a cumulative net capital influx of over $70 billion between 1976 and 1981, Latin America suffered a net outflow in excess of $130 billion during the next five years. As the debt crisis deepened and several major borrowers suspended amortization payments, the banks closed ranks and formed steering committees to confront their borrowers. This cartelization enabled them to impose stringent rescheduling terms on debtors and to maintain an almost complete shutdown of new loans.

While the loan shutoff of the 1980s can be justified as a market correction (or even an overcorrection), bank steering committees engaged in a practice far less conscionable. A large portion of their outstanding debt portfolios consisted of loans made to private-sector businesses and individuals, originally devoid of any government guarantee of repayment. As these loans went sour, rather than turning to bankruptcy courts to effect debt-equity swaps with delinquent private debtors, the banks insisted that the debtor governments assume responsibility for servicing the private debt. The steering committees were able to extort the assumption of private debt from Latin American governments by threatening to refuse to reschedule publicly guaranteed debt. Between 1982 and 1986, the publicly guaranteed share of Latin America's total debt rose from 53.7 percent to 79.5 percent. Figures for some nations display an even greater proportion of what Felix and Caskey call "socialized" debt, the percentage of publicly guaranteed Argentinean debt growing from 36.4 percent to 93.5 percent and Chilean from 30.5 percent to 80.0 percent.[12] The aftershock from this activity played havoc with Latin American budgets as many countries issued costly domestic debt to garner scarce foreign exchange from private citizens.

External Shocks

As mentioned earlier, the Latin American financial situation was adversely affected in the early 1980s by external shocks. While these were not completely unpredictable, their magnitude was greater than virtually anyone could have anticipated. During the 1980s, Latin American terms of trade dropped by some 21 percent, with an especially sharp decline taking place at the start of the decade. Simultaneously, after being negative during most of the 1970s (with an average of − 3.4 percent for the decade), real interest rates on international loans climbed to 19.9 percent in 1981, 17.5 percent in 1982, and 17.4 percent in 1983. In fact, when Bianchi et al. estimated the combined impact of these tandem shocks in 1987, they found that the deterioration of nonoil export prices and the surge in world interest rates account for almost 50 percent of the increase in Latin America's current-account deficit during 1981 and 1982.[13] Although some downturn in volatile and secularly declining terms of trade might have been expected, this magnitude of erosion in relative prices was extremely difficult to forecast.

On their part, the governments of the industrialized countries are directly culpable in the sense that they strenuously encouraged financial institutions to recycle petrodollars during the 1970s but subsequently exhorted these same commercial lenders to refinance during the first years of debt crisis. Moreover, given not only this support but also the existence of a safety net provided by the Federal Deposit Insurance Corporation (FDIC), it is likely that the banks had good reason to hope for a government bailout in the event of trouble. Last of all, loose bank regulatory policies and oversight practices by OECD governments may have had a part in allowing excessive lending to occur.

Policies in the Developed Countries

Many observers believe that the governments of developed countries have a significantly deeper responsibility for the Latin American debt crisis (and, indeed, for the debt problems of all developing nations), a perception widespread among adherents of the structural or *dependencía* school. Keith Griffin has assembled statistics that support a causal analysis of Third World debt ascribing its rise to skyrocketing real interest rates in early 1980s, coupled with a slowdown in the pace of growth in world trade, and linking both these "shocks" to policies pursued by OECD governments.[14] At the time of the first oil price hike, monetary authorities in the developed world tried to restrain import demand and thereby dampen inflation by adopting a tight policy that translated into a high real interest repayment burden. Thereafter, lack of fiscal discipline in some industrialized nations, notably the United States, extended tight credit and, at the same time, drew in world capital to finance perennial budget deficits. As Nowzad observes, these profligate domestic policies had a devastating impact on indebted LDCs from the start of the crisis to the present.[15]

Equally important, while the industrialized nations are all subscribers to the GATT and impose comparatively low tariff rates on LDC imports, many have erected or extended nontariff barriers to trade, the most glaring example being the Multi-Fiber Arrangement (MFA). Retaining quotas to prevent "market disruptions," these same governments have periodically threatened to apply trade sanctions to developing countries that use tariffs or nontariff barriers (NTBs) to compress imports from OECD producers. It is hard to imagine how indebted LDCs could be expected to garner the foreign exchange earnings they need to service their external debts when they find their exports to the developed world constrained by nontariff barriers and face the threat of even higher protectionist measures should they attempt to conserve foreign currency holdings by limiting imports.

THE DEBT OVERHANG DEBATE

At this point, any analysis of the roots of Latin American debt appears to be a dead issue. However, the way the causes of the debt problem are regarded powerfully influences discussion of its effects and remedies. It pervades not only the ongoing debate concerning the influence of debt overhang on growth within heavily borrowed developing countries but also any discussion of capital flight.

On the surface, it is intuitively easy to grasp a relationship between a large burden of publicly guaranteed external debt and low growth within the debtor economy. It stands to reason that when resources are transferred abroad they cannot be used to underwrite public investment. But at the heart of the debt-overhang concept as it is applied to indebted developing nations is the observation that external debt exercises a pernicious influence on private sector behavior.

The poor investment and growth performance of the highly indebted Latin American countries during the 1980s is often attributed to the burden of their foreign debt (a high ratio of external debt to GDP), a phenomenon known as *debt overhang*. According to the debt-overhang hypothesis, foreign debt functions like a tax on future output by inhibiting the productive investment plans of the private sector. Private-sector investors anticipate that any increases in production or in exports of the indebted country must generate revenues that will be used to repay current debt obligations. That being so, onerous taxes on such revenue streams will be imposed by the government. Investors therefore decline to move into or expand productive activities that might be subject to levies of this sort. High debt-service payments that mandate high tax rates thus discourage capital formation and the repatriation of flight capital.

If large amounts of accumulated external debt do indeed repress private sector activity, two conclusions directly relevant to the handling of foreign debt can be made. On the one hand, since external debt functions like a tax, indebted countries should be better off buying back a portion of it at a discount on the secondary market, even if it means expending scarce foreign exchange resources to do so. Most analysts agree that the advisability of this approach depends on specific circumstances, especially the source of the foreign exchange used to buy debt back. On the other hand, and more paradoxically, reducing the overhang via debt relief may actually be to the lender's advantage. "In the extreme, there may even be a debt Laffer curve, in which case creditors can actually gain by forgiving part of the debt, since the prospects for repaying the remainder would increase so dramatically."[16] Such a debt reduction might lead to an increase in economic efficiency in the debtor country that in turn increases the value of outstanding claims on that economy. In the end, creditors who retain their existing claims rather than sell or exchange them can benefit from good economic performance in the debtor economies following debt reduction. Ironically, if the debt overhang thesis is valid, lenders have an immediate and concrete motive to participate in debt-reduction exercises. Sums lost via debt forgiveness will be outweighed by the increased value of the outstanding debt as the economy in question is freed of its debt overhang.

The central controversy about the debt-overhang concept is the extent to which the debt problem is responsible for low growth in some major debtor countries. Despite its common-sense plausibility, many analysts differ in their appraisals of its impact. The main reason for this is the possibility that the direct effect of the debt overhang on investment may not be reflected in the empirical analysis because it is, in large measure, associated with expectations about future events. In particular, while some scholars maintain that slow growth in heavily indebted LDC economies is in part a result of external debt, others have argued that it stems from some other sources, such as structural deficiencies combined with macropolicy mismanagement, which also cause excessive debt.

Jeffrey Sachs has stated unequivocally that debt overhang does retard growth.[17] His·position has received some support from a recent empirical study. Investigating the relationship between outstanding foreign debt and GDP growth in the Philippines, Eduardo Borenzstein found empirical evidence of a debt overhang effect, concluding that "all results show a significant negative relationship between foreign debt and investment."[18] His findings indicate that the median effect of a $1.3-billion debt reduction operation in the Philippines would be to increase investment demand by about one percentage point of GDP. Borenzstein's study indicates that it is neither the existence nor the amount of debt per se that is exclusively responsible for debt overhang but the source of the debt and, with it, the terms on which it is contracted. "When the significance of the effects on investment of debt from private and from official sources is statistically tested," he concludes, "the results support only the existence of an effect from private bank debt. There is no evidence that debt with official creditors (both international and bilateral) has any adverse effects on private investment."[19]

By contrast, Jeremy Bulow and Kenneth Rogoff have argued that slow growth hit Latin economies before they were required to make significant repayments to commercial creditors. Hence, they see debt overhang as a symptom rather than a cause of weak growth, the latter stemming from economic mismanagement and external shocks.[20] In support of this stance, they comment that "it is often overlooked that a large fraction of the growth shortfall in the Highly Indebted Countries occurred from 1980 to 1983, *before* the countries were required to make any significant debt repayments."[21] Gross macroeconomic statistics lend credence to this view in application to Latin America. Private investment in Latin America during the late 1980s stood at 18 percent of GDP. This was only two percentage points lower than the average for the period from 1960 to 1973, and it represented a smaller decline than the one experienced in industrial countries over the same period of time.

Finally, even among those who subscribe to debt-overhang hypothesis there is still disagreement about how much debt relief is required to activate growth and overcome the debt-overhang effect. Some have asserted that the growth-retarding effects of external debt have exercised a remedial influence on LDC economies by compelling them to undertake stabilization and liberalization programs. In this interpretation, debt overhang can serve as a catalyst for change, an external lever that international financial institutions, like the IMF and the World Bank can manipulate to force overdue reforms.

CAPITAL FLIGHT

There is a similar division of opinion about Latin American capital flight, a subject also plagued by myriad theoretical and empirical problems. As in the case of debt overhang, the central issue—whether external debt causes capital flight or capital flight arises from the same general conditions as the excessive accumulation of foreign debt—is still unresolved.

The difficulty of determining whether an international transfer of funds actually constitutes *capital flight* becomes evident when we consider that Japanese or Kuwaiti transfers of capital to the United States are generally labeled *foreign investment* while similar transfers from Latin America are disparaged as capital flight. As a working definition, the term might be glossed as *the transfer of funds abroad by private investors in an attempt to escape the control of domestic authorities and flee abnormal market risks at home.*

No matter how it is conceived, the definitional problems embedded in the phenomenon of Latin American capital flight spill over into methodology when the substantive question of how much capital has fled Latin America is broached. Nevertheless, although precise measures remain slippery, the significance of private Latin American capital migrating toward safer havens than those provided by domestic economies becomes apparent in light of the observation that many estimates of total capital flight—including money diverted to foreign direct investment such as corporate stock and Florida real estate—actually exceed the book value of government and government-guaranteed debts of the countries involved. Bulow and Rogoff have stated that by the end of 1988 Latin American *bank deposits alone* held in the North come to more than $100 billion and approximated the value of this debt.[22] Novak has calculated that some $326 billion in Latin American capital was transferred to the United States in the late 1970s and 1980s.[23] *If* these figures are close to the truth, some highly indebted Latin American countries may even be net creditors, and the possibility must be considered that Latin economies have been suffering more from a crisis of confidence among domestic investors than from the fallout of foreign debt.

In their survey of studies dealing with capital flight, Lessard and Williamson assert that the causal factors behind it can be grouped under two headings, with different analysts tending to stress one set or the other.[24] The first of these revolves around overall investment climate in an affected economy, including government adjustment programs such as the correction of an overvalued currency through stiff official devaluation. John Cuddington, for one, has concluded that Mexican capital flight is correlated with overvaluation of the peso, disbursements of public debt, and past capital flight—fear of devaluation being the major stimulus.[25] The second set of causal variables comes as discriminatory treatment of resident capital "in the form of differential taxation, financial repression, different currency denomination, or investment guarantees and their subordination to nonresident claims in the event of financial crisis."[26] Dooley has delineated the ways source countries explicitly or implicitly use to impose discriminatory taxes on domestic asset holders—not only outright taxes but also takings through inflation, interest ceilings, or multiple exchange rates—and finds them to be strongly correlated with capital flight movements.[27] There is a unifying thread in both models — in one sense or another (broad or narrow), these constructions of the causes of capital flight point to macroeconomic mismanagement in the source country as chief force behind it.

No matter how we construe capital flight, it is bound to have negative effects on the economy from which it flows. Virtually by definition, capital flight entails a loss of both investment capital and the stream of tax revenue from those funds. According to Felix and Caskey, were deeply indebted Latin countries able to use the foreign assets of their nationals to collateralize the foreign debt or the income from those assets to service it, 46 percent of Latin America's overall debt and 51 percent of its privately held debt could be retired.[28] Moreover, capital flight may exercise indirect negative effects as investors follow their capital abroad. Domestic capitalists who find themselves with a large part of their wealth abroad for a lengthy period are tempted to start looking for investment opportunities more challenging than passive ownership of financial assets and real estate. In time, they begin to purchase corporations in the developed countries; and eventually not just their wealth but their entrepreneurial energies and their economic stake in national policies as well are lost to their home countries.

The critical issue at this time is this: given that an indefinite (but large) amount of capital has been shipped from Latin America to tax havens in the industrialized world, how can a reflux of this money be induced? A 1986 evaluation of capital flight from the Morgan Guaranty states that handling capital flight is crucial to the resolution of the Third World debt crisis:

LDC capital outflows have to be tackled as part of the solution to the debt problem, not as something that need be addressed only later. If capital flight is given a free ride in the caboose of the LDC debt train, the train has little hope of making the station.[29]

In attempting to fashion policies that will attract a return of flight capital, developing nations find themselves on the horns of a dilemma. No matter how strenuous their adjustment efforts may be, changes in macroeconomic policy are unlikely to permit the restoration of growth until the foreign-exchange constraint is broken. However, flight capital is unlikely to return and help break the foreign-exchange constraint until growth resumes. Consequently, flight capital "is both a cause and an effect of financial instability, creating a vicious circle that is extremely hard to break."[30]

Capital flight can be handled in three ways. The first is the imposition of exchange controls. For example, during the late 1970s and early 1980s, Argentina, Mexico, Uruguay, and Venezuela all experienced massive capital outflows; but those from Brazil, Chile, Colombia, and Peru were relatively modest. The latter group of countries all maintained restrictions on capital outflows that made the accumulation of unregistered foreign assets illegal. At this stage, however, simply imposing capital controls is akin to closing the stable door after the horse has gone.

Under a second approach, Latin American governments could alter their policies regarding the taxation of capital sent abroad by their residents and enforce these policies in cooperation with haven countries. This measure would entail both legislation within Latin American nations to make such income legally liable to tax and information-exchange arrangements to permit tax obligations to be enforced. Hence, this method would require not only appropriate policies in both source and haven countries but also the conclusion of an international tax convention among them.[31]

Although both exchange and capital controls and an announced change in the tax status of overseas investment might deter future capital flight episodes, it would also tend to inhibit a reflux of existing flight capital. Stiffening the rules regarding capital flight is bound to engender the fear that repatriation will expose the investor to penalties for taxes that were unpaid or exchange-control regulations that were violated. Experience shows that imposition of exchange controls actually deters a reflux of flight capital and that their removal encourages its return.

Of late, there have been some positive developments on this front insofar as Latin American economies are concerned. They have found that a repatriation of flight capital sometimes occurs spontaneously, often linked to an event that raises investor expectations for an improvement in the home country's economic conditions or dispels apprehension about Draconian penalties. When Mexico rescheduled its commercial debt under the Brady Plan in 1989, for example, an estimated $10 billion in flight capital returned in the following eighteen months. While no empirically verifiable relationship can be shown, there appears to have been some connection between this massive debt workout and the return. Similarly, when it became apparent that Venezuela would undergo Brady Plan treatment, Venezuelans repatriated about $2 billion in 1989 and 1990. On the other hand, capital flight reflux has sometimes taken place without such a triggering event. In the summer of 1991, Peru experienced the unexpected repatriation of an estimated $600 million to $700 million in flight capital. Peruvian investors seem to have been influenced by the perception that the Peruvian chief executive, Alberto Fujimori, was committed to an adjustment program of stabilization and liberalization.

Repatriation can also occur indirectly when Latin American owners of flight capital purchase the public or private bonds and stocks of their nations in international markets. During 1989 and 1990, there was tremendous growth in Euromarket trading in bonds and equities issued by Latin American firms and entities, much of it stimulated by Latin American investors, primarily Mexicans and Argentineans wanting to repatriate flight capital. In the final analysis, flight capital repatriation requires exactly the conditions in its country of origin that massive foreign debt and the debt overhang work against. Today, the chief instrument for creating those conditions is the international debt strategy.

THE INTERNATIONAL DEBT STRATEGY

The Latin American debt crisis created a need both to ease the strain of debt repayment (and the underlying impediments to debt repayment) and to manage foreign debt in cooperation with creditors through rescheduling and voluntary debt reduction. Since 1982, an international debt strategy has taken form and evolved in fairly distinct phases, the current stage beginning in 1989 and revolving around the provisions of the Brady Plan. At this juncture, it seems useful to briefly chronicle the evolution of this strategy.

It is essential to note from the outset that the chief objective of international debt management changed during the 1980s. Early in the debt crisis, there was considerable concern that widespread repudiation of sovereign debts by LDC governments would bankrupt a number of thinly capitalized banks. After years of steady decline in the exposure ratios of the most heavily exposed banks, the risk of a banking crash resulting from the debt crisis is now virtually nonexistent. L. William Seidman has calculated that each of the nine American money-center banks with substantial exposure to Latin America could write off all its claims upon that region's six largest debtors and still remain solvent.[32]

As time has passed and the banks have strengthened their balance sheets, the main focus has shifted to the stagnating economies of the highly indebted countries. Initially, the chief goal of debt strategy was taken to be the return of a debtor country to normal and voluntary access to international capital markets. Since the inception of the Baker Plan, the goal has become the restoration not just of creditworthiness but also of economic growth and development. Even after the Brady Plan went into operation, debtor-nation growth was to be achieved primarily through infusions of fresh loan money. Unfortunately, any optimistic assumptions about the willingness of international banks and Western governments to supply the requisite funds underpinning the Baker approach vanished during the late 1980s. Most analysts now believe that the debt burden should be reduced, not only for the sake of the debtors but also for the sake of the creditors, who have an important long-run stake in allowing developing countries to surmount the crisis. At bottom, the Brady Plan is grounded in the recognized need for a reduction of the debt burden. However, whether the debt relief offered by the Brady Plan will be sufficient in itself remains debatable.

From the Mexican Moratorium to the Baker Plan

When the Latin American debt crisis began in 1982, the guiding assumption of debtors and creditors alike was that it was a temporary liquidity problem that could be managed through restructured payment schedules. LDCs would have to do their part through adjustment to external shocks such as declining terms of trade and very high real interest rates on both current loans and outstanding balances due on floating terms. Creditor governments and private financial institutions would hold up their end by simply permitting revisions in payment schedules.

Problems with this approach appeared early on, for while the banks were initially prepared to defer repayment of principal, they were unwilling to do the same for interest payments. This meant that additional resources of new money had to be assembled to refinance interest obligations falling due. Under these circumstances, a difficult issue arose: how to compel commercial lenders in the aggregate (and even more significant, individual banks) to supply more capital to nations whose creditworthiness had already deteriorated? The heart of this quandary hinged upon the existence of a "free rider" problem. While the banks shared a collective stake in supplying debt-strapped LDCs with new money, individually each bank had an even more compelling interest in limiting its role as a supplier of new credits and in seeing others handle the refinancing. Hence, a mechanism was needed to keep individual creditors in the fold, to compel their participation in debt refinancing.

The mechanism that emerged was "forced," "involuntary" or "concerted" lending, and its institutional setting was the International Monetary Fund. From the start of the debt crisis, lender banks relied heavily on the IMF to furnish indebted LDCs with modest financial assistance and, more important, to design and monitor the balance-of-payments adjustment programs required to return them to timely debt service. This gave the IMF leverage against lenders reluctant to extend new loans to debtor nations as part of rescheduling workouts. Early in the process, the Fund moved to forced lending. It insisted on the need to obtain an agreement on the provision of additional bank and official resources *before* the approval of a Fund-supported arrangement. Absent such an agreement, the Fund would simply refuse to play its part. Because of this stand, the role of the IMF in relation to commercial banks in the management of the debt crisis changed from that of certifier to that of mobilizer of capital. Directing manager of the IMF, Jacques de Larosière, asserted that "one key feature of the approach was that no party provided medium-term financing until all parties were ready to do so. This was the policy requiring a 'critical mass' of financial support from the commercial banks and creditor governments."[33] The Fund decided that developing-country debt would be dealt with on a case-by-case basis, with the IMF selecting the "cases" and then orchestrating them by linking debtor-country adjustment programs and involuntary loan packages.

This approach and its descriptive terminology proved faulty. The banks closed ranks and formed steering committees to represent their side in debt rescheduling. They imposed onerous terms on the new money they supplied, with higher margins above prevailing international interest rates. As previously mentioned, they also required that debtor country governments guarantee private loans on a post hoc basis. It is not simply that the banks worked as cartels or that they drove hard bargains with the debtors that undermined the "case-by-case" approach. It was that they often failed to distinguish among LDC borrowers. Thus, a nation like Chile, which was making a strong adjustment effort and realizing some positive results, was treated in the same manner as Brazil or Argentina, where genuine adjustment was essentially absent. Moreover, with an individual country, even after a substantial change in policy and performance (for better or worse), no change took place in rescheduling terms. In the end, "there was no true case-by-case approach."[34]

Given the rosy assumptions underpinning this initial strategy, the form that debt rescheduling first took was not as critical for the actual outcome as was the persistence of external shocks upon Latin economies. Although interest rates began to decline after 1982, most LDC debtors, including those of Latin America, experienced a further deterioration in terms of trade. Consequently, when this occurrence was compounded with the inherent defects of the opening debt strategy, within a few years it became evident that the case-by-case approach was foundering. Debtor-country export earnings were not growing as had been expected. Worse, indebted Latin American governments became increasingly reluctant to deal with the IMF, which was asking for more austerity but providing less emergency credit. In 1985, the principal debtor countries in Latin America came to the conclusion that a unified suspension or repudiation of foreign debt was not in their best interest. Still, the mere phantom of a debtor's cartel arising in Latin America to coordinate a moratorium on debt payments was a reflection of how far relations between the debtors and their creditors had deteriorated under the case-by-case approach.

From the Baker Plan to the Brady Plan

Against this backdrop, the Baker Plan was proposed in October 1985 at the annual IMF-IBRD meeting in Seoul, where U.S. Treasury Secretary James Baker put forth a three-part program for sustained growth to deal with the debt problem. The Baker Plan had three elements. The first called upon the debtor nations to adopt comprehensive macroeconomic and structural policies, supervised by the IMF and the World Bank. The second created a role for the IMF as a continued lender in conjunction with increased and more effective structural-adjustment lending by multilateral development banks like the World Bank to provide financing for major changes in debtor economies beyond near term stabilization. Finally the Baker Plan required increased lending by the private banks to support comprehensive economic adjustment programs. After outlining his program, Secretary Baker asked the multilateral institutions and banks to adopt specific new targets for lending to fifteen highly indebted countries, all of which were engaged in adjustment programs supervised by the IMF. Ten of the nations were Latin

American: Argentina, Bolivia, Brazil, Chile, Columbia, Ecuador, Mexico, Peru, Uruguay, and Venezuela.

The Baker Plan failed simply because the players in the scenario refused to perform their own assigned roles but pointed to each other's shortcomings to rationalize their own counterproductive behavior. With the benefit of hindsight, it is easy to identify the commercial banks as the main culprits in the Baker Plan's demise. Secretary Baker called for about $20 billion in net new lending by commercial banks to the fifteen countries on his roster during the 1986–1988 period. The banks fell far short of those targets, actually reducing their claims on some developing-country borrowers. Only a few months after the adoption of the Baker Plan, IMF director de Larosière indicated that a shortfall was at hand on this front, stating that banks' new loan commitments (in 1986) to major debtors "appear to be well short of the amounts implied in the U.S. debt initiative."[35] There is some disagreement about precisely how much the banks did advance to the Baker fifteen since they were compelled to recapitalize LDC interest arrears amounting to some $6 billion. But this aside, the banks themselves advanced only $6.6 billion to LDCs in 1986–1988. Truman has calculated the proportion of new money disbursements to total scheduled interest payments and concluded that the "banks disbursed about two bits for every buck they received in interest."[36]

But if the banks fell short of the mark set for them under the Baker Plan, the indebted LDCs failed to live up to their end of the bargain by relaxing their adjustment efforts. The aims of the Baker Plan were undercut by a dramatic change in the international economic environment shortly after it was announced — the collapse of international oil prices in 1986. Many oil-importing developing countries enjoyed a current-account windfall as the cost of oil declined. Unfortunately, this positive development weakened perceptions of the need to adopt economic policy reforms, and adjustment programs were pursued with less vigor or jettisoned altogether in favor of reflation.

The multilateral development banks (MDBs) also fell short of the lending goals set under the Baker Plan. Secretary Baker had anticipated MDB disbursements over the 1986–1988 period would total $27 billion. As it turned out, they were about $22 billion, 20 percent less than expected. Even the IMF failed to reach its goal, albeit because of the departures from adjustment programs by the indebted LDCs. As one consequence of the shortfall in economic reform efforts, many countries fell out of compliance with IMF-supported programs or declined to accept new ones. Thus, IMF conditional loan disbursements declined, and net transfers from the Fund to the major debtors turned negative. Over the 1986–1988 period, the IMF received net repayments of principal from the Baker-fifteen countries of about $3 billion.

The growing perception that the Baker Plan was not working was reinforced by two major developments during 1987 that in turn paradoxically set the stage for the Brady Plan. First, there was a substantial increase in the number of countries in the region that partially or wholly suspended service on their foreign debt. This group included Bolivia, Brazil, Costa Rica, Ecuador, Honduras, Nicaragua, Peru, and later, Argentina. Most important, on 20 February 1987, the Brazilian government decided to suspend interest payments to foreign banks.

Partly in reaction to this unilateral move, on 19 May 1987 Citicorp (Brazil's largest commercial creditor) added some $3 billion to its reserve for possible losses on its Third World, specifically Brazilian, loan portfolio. This move triggered a chain reaction—other money-center banks and about twenty regional banking companies proceeded to "follow the leader."[37] Between mid-1987 and the third quarter of 1988, U.S. banks reduced their claims on all developing countries by more than $20 billion. More than half of this represented a reduction in claims on highly indebted countries, that is, the Baker fifteen. Under these circumstances, a war of nerves began as the LDCs feigned lack of interest in resolving the debt crisis and continued to suspend payments while the banks demonstrated that they were preparing for the worst and threatened a permanent shutdown of their developing-country loan window. These two trends led to a vibrant secondary market for discounted Latin debt paper (discussed in the next section), as small regional banks increased the supply of secondary loans by selling off their Latin debt holdings. The brief respite afforded by debt repayment moratoriums allowed some Latin debtors to accumulate the foreign exchange reserves needed to buy this debt back. Their perception that the crisis would ultimately demand resolution also prompted them to use these funds to repurchase discounted debt on the secondary market. It is evident from price movement of Latin debt paper on the secondary market, however, that the confrontational tactics of banks and debtor nations initially led to an erosion of confidence in a lasting solution to the problem. Between July 1985 and August 1987, the average price across eight major debtors fell by 31 percent. The decline in the value for some individual countries over this period was Brazil (32 percent), Argentina (26 percent), Mexico (36 percent), Peru (82 percent), and Venezuela (20 percent).[38]

By early 1989, the likelihood that Latin American debtors could work their way out of the "lost decade" had diminished. Commercial banks had already indicated this by building up reserves against LDC loan losses and by selling loans in the secondary market at deep discounts. Each year saw both a further buildup of debt and the absence of any conviction among foreign and domestic savers that there had been a decisive improvement in the prospects for sustained growth. The likelihood of a return to normal access to credit markets for indebted countries was receding into the horizon. During this time, the case for debt reduction was strengthened by the virtual absence of voluntary new loans by commercial banks to Latin American countries. Thus by 1989, the international debt strategy was amended to include debt reduction, backed by the IMF, the World Bank, and other resources.

The Brady Plan

Although the current Brady Plan was a U.S. policy initiative, it was antic-ipated at the 1988 IMF-IBRD meeting in Berlin where the IMF Interim Committee proposed that the Baker-style approach be broadened to include "voluntary market-based techniques which . . . reduce the stock of debt without transferring risk from private lenders to official creditors."[39] The aim of the international strategy was thus shifted from raising outstanding debt through new loans to reducing debt, signaling a fundamental change in the official interpretation of the debt problem.

On 10 March 1989, U.S. Treasury Secretary Nicholas F. Brady prefaced the introduction of the Brady Plan by observing that, "serious problems and impediments to a successful resolution of the debt crisis remain, [and there-fore declared that] the path toward greater creditworthiness and a return to the markets for many debtor countries needs to involve debt reduction."[40] Like the ill-fated Baker Plan, Brady's initiative had three main provisions. First, Brady called on commercial lenders to allow debtor nations to buy back debt at a discount, the price to be determined by secondary-market valuation. He specifically called for a three-year waiver of clauses in existing loan agreements that stood in the way of debt reduction to accelerate sharply the pace of this process and pass the benefits directly to the debtor nations. Creditor banks not agreeing to take a loss on capital could elect to exchange old debt for new forms carrying concessional rates of interest. The value of these exchange instruments (generically, "Brady bonds") would be enhanced by credit guarantees with international organizations (the Fund and the Bank) furnishing the bulk of funds to purchase the enhancements. Alternatively, those electing to stay the course could fulfill their obligations by extending new loan money in proportion to their exposure. Second, in return, the debtor nations would agree to continue under new adjustment programs supervised by the IMF and IBRD, and these multilateral bodies would supply some financing for the debt buybacks and debt conversions. Under the original Brady proposal, the Fund and the Bank were expected to provide up to $20 or $25 billion, divided roughly equally for use in the reduction of principal and the reduction of interest payments. With supplemental funding coming mainly from Japan, this figure was later increased to $30 billion to $40 billion. Last, the entire program would remain conditional, and LDCs undergoing Brady treatment would need to adopt and maintain adjustment programs under IMF-IBRD supervision to become eligible.

The precise terms of the debt-reduction packages would be worked out in rescheduling exercises at which the proportion and amount of outstanding debt to be bought back or converted would be decided in negotiation. Indi-vidual banks would be able to choose one of the three main menu options. Hence, case-by-case negotiations were required between sovereign debtors and bank steering committees to reduce debt principal and/or interest rates and to supply new loans on more favorable terms. Despite the format of individual agreements and the complexity of the coming workouts, Brady originally estimated a 20 percent reduction in existing debt for thirty-nine countries conditionally eligible for such assistance.

Assistant U.S. Treasury Secretary David Mulford presented the details of the Brady Plan at a meeting of the IMF-World Bank Interim & Development Committee in April 1989. Although the initiative met with distinctly tepid support, the committee eventually agreed that the Fund should provide appropriate financing to help debt-reduction operations in countries undertaking sound economic reforms. On May 23, 1989, the IMF executive board adopted broad guidelines for the Fund's role in the Brady Plan. Meanwhile, the World Bank moved in parallel to establish guidelines to provide support over three years for the reduction of countries' debt and debt-service payments. Events moved rapidly thereafter, as the IMF extended new credits to Mexico, Costa Rica, and the Philippines within days of the executive board meeting.

It seems self-evident that indebted Latin American nations should welcome the Brady Plan and eagerly accept help in reducing their foreign debts. When the Brady Initiative was announced, more than a dozen countries were in long-standing open arrears to commercial bank creditors, to official lenders, to the IMF-IBRD, or to some combination of these three. For many of them, however, a key question was whether they should try to achieve debt settlements through the medium of the Brady Plan, through either unilateral (or joint) moratoriums or repudiations, or through demands for a new debt strategy. Some academics argued against LDC acceptance of the Brady proposal and for a unilateral suspension as well.[41] Even after the Brady Plan was unveiled, international scholar Rudiger Dornbusch left open the question of whether indebted Latin nations should seize this opportunity, asserting that "A good debt strategy is essential for the return to growth [and] one such strategy is to postpone all debt service until reconstruction is accomplished."[42]

Within eighteen months, however, two major Latin American debtors, Mexico and Venezuela, joined the Philippines and Costa Rica as successful Brady Plan patients. As it became evident that progress toward debt reduction could be achieved through the Brady Plan mechanism, Latin American sovereign debtors put aside talk of unilateral action. By the end of 1990, virtually every eligible debtor country was requesting Brady Plan treatment.

A substantially different response to the Brady Plan came from creditor banks. Soon after the initiative was laid out, Brady met personally with bankers, but he failed to persuade them that the plan had merit. Rather than readying new loan issues to the thirty-nine countries on the treasury secretary's list, the banks put even more of their cash into reserves against Third World loan losses. By sharply boosting these reserves, U.S. money-center banks seemed intent upon scuttling the Brady initiative. A year after the plan was announced, the top banking lobby, the Institute for International Finance, released a report criticizing Brady for imposing the pain of debt forgiveness on the commercial banks without giving them the financial support they wanted from the IMF and World Bank.[43]

The banks also scored the plan for its lack of any complementary provision to reduce official debts of Third World borrowers to agencies of developed country governments through the Paris Club. Consistent with the practices of the Paris Club, bilateral lenders had never offered to reduce outstanding principal in debt restructurings conducted through that forum. Thus, the banks complained (with some justification) that they were being asked to reduce the face value of their claims on LDCs by governments that were themselves unwilling to do the same.

Although Baker had counted upon and failed to receive the good will of commercial lenders, the Brady Plan uses more coercive methods to secure participation from lenders. The Treasury Department exerted mounting pressure on reluctant banks to secure their cooperation. Indirectly, other U.S. authorities turned up the heat on the banks as well. In 1990, for example, federal bank regulators noted that Brazilian loans had not been paying interest for more than a year and forced commercial banks to acknowledge a loss on Brazilian accounts equivalent to 20 percent of their exposure to Brazil.

The IMF has also applied pressure to the banks through a technical change accompanying its revised role under the Brady Plan. Until 1989, the IMF required nations that sought conditional adjustment loans to settle outstanding arrearages on commercial bank debts. Because banks dragged their feet in sealing deals with debtor countries and sought to circumvent Brady Plan workouts, the IMF changed tack in the spring of 1989 and began to agree to adjustment programs with countries in arrears on their payments to commercial banks. As total interest arrearages rose from $14 billion at the end of 1989 to more than $18 billion at the end of March 1990, bankers complained to the Fund about the change in stance and about the Brady Plan as a whole. The IMF, however, ignored the bankers' concerns and continued to praise the Brady Plan.

The Brady Plan has been criticized from a number of other quarters and on a variety of grounds. The most frequently raised objection is that it is too little, too late. "The Brady Plan has proved to be little more than a stop-gap measure, and not a very effective one at that," Wayne Smith stated in 1991.[44] The plan goal of a 20 percent reduction for major LDC debtors has been characterized as marginal and vulnerable to "washing out" should another external shock take place. Observing that the 20 percent average debt reduction that the treasury estimates the thirty-nine debtor countries may receive under the Brady initiative is roughly equivalent to a reduction in their cost of borrowing of 2 percentage points, Islam observes, "that a 2 percentage point increase in the interest rate the banks charge the countries can wipe out all of the debt relief of the Brady initiative."[45] Moreover, along with the banks, many independent observers remarked that the Brady plan was flawed insofar as it did nothing to reduce official debt. Others, like Bulow and

Rogoff, contend that buybacks at market discount at the heart of the Brady Plan reduction mechanism may result in an enormous leakage of public aid to creditor banks.

Under the Brady blueprint, governments of the industrialized countries are planning to devote at least $30 billion to $40 billion over the next three years to help buy back Third World debt at discount. Recent academic research on buybacks suggests that a very substantial fraction of these funds will end up in the hands of private banks, without benefiting the debtors.[46]

Finally, the U.S. credit agency, Moody's, has criticized the plan because it exacts more than the banks can handle at this time but offers too little help to indebted LDCs.[47]

Despite this litany, several analysts have suggested that Brady is about right. In June 1990, Fischer and Husain noted that "it is safe to say that over the past year an important corner has been turned."[48] Recently proposals have been made to offer a comprehensive approach to official debt relief through the Paris Club that would parallel the reduction of bank debt of the Brady Plan. In subsequent chapters of this study, generally positive results are described in the Brady Plan treatments extended to Mexico and Venezuela. The clearest indication that the plan has raised chances for a successful resolution of the Latin debt crisis, however, comes from the movement of prices on the secondary market. In the year after announcement of the plan, Salomon Brothers' developing-country debt index rose from 30 cents to 37 cents on the dollar. This suggests that international investors interpret the plan as a major step in the right direction although they do not yet see a clear-cut resolution to the Third World (and Latin American) debt problems.

SECONDARY MARKET FOR LATIN DEBT PAPER

Since its inception in 1982, the secondary market for developing-country loans has grown quickly. Between 1985 and 1989, the total volume of loans traded increased from around $6 billion to over $60 billion. Now that "Brady bonds" have been added to the mix, according to initial estimates, the turnover has reached $100 billion. Latin American debt paper has dominated trading on the secondary market from the outset. Although the growing number of participants has added to market liquidity and strengthened its cohesiveness, most transactions have still been concentrated in the debts of a few countries. In 1988 and 1989, for example, transactions in the liabilities of Argentina, Brazil, Chile, and Mexico accounted for roughly 85 percent of debt conversions.

The factors behind the growth of the secondary market in LDC debt are manifold and accompany watersheds in the evolution of the international debt strategy, the expansion of the market into new functions, the emergence of new forms of debt conversion, and (as cause and consequence of the latter) the entrance of new buyers and sellers into the market.

Initial growth of the secondary market in Latin debt paper was fueled by the introduction of formal debt-conversion and debt-reduction programs in several Latin American economies. After 1984, formal debt conversion programs were launched in several major debtor countries (Chile, Argentina, Brazil, Mexico, and the Philippines). These programs stimulated the growth in cash transactions which were triggered by conversions of debt into equity and included discounted purchases by some countries of their own debt.

The secondary market was given a major boost in 1987 with the Brazilian payment suspension and the subsequent spurt in bank loan loss provisioning. These developments significantly activated the secondary markets for Latin American debt and increased the discounts at which the debt was traded. Ironically, Brazil was one of the nations to make the greatest use of the secondary market. In 1988 Brazilian agents retired some $12 billion in external debt in this way, nearly five times the amount transacted the previous year. But the most prolific growth of the secondary market in Latin American loans came about as an adjunct to the Brady initiative, for it explicitly endorsed the concept of securitizing debt into bonds.

Ultimately, the secondary market has grown because it performs useful functions for both lenders and debtors. For the debtor nations, it offers a tool with which they can pare down their level of existing debt. Several countries, including Brazil, Chile, and Mexico, have substantially reduced their commercial bank debt by using the secondary market for various debt conversion schemes. While the largest reduction in absolute terms has been for Brazil, the most comprehensive reductions have been undertaken by Chile, Costa Rica, and Bolivia, each of which has cut commercial debt by half or more via secondary market deals. The market also creates channels through which lenders can reduce exposure, alter the composition of portfolios, and exit from individual countries or Third World lending as a whole, albeit at a cost.

For all parties, the secondary market provides a useful index of how the market values outstanding debt and thus an informal appraisal of economic adjustment. Indeed, by providing a market-based valuation of developing-country loans, the market has strengthened the Brady initiative. After the precipitous decline in the prices of Latin American debt paper between 1985 and 1987 came the subsequent rise in the value of those same assets after the initial successful implementation of Brady Plan treatment for Mexico and Venezuela. This same positive appraisal continued in 1991 – virtually all countries' debt rose in value on the secondary market during the first months of that year. The most dramatic improvement occurred in Latin American debt – the average for the region as a whole moved from around 36 percent at the start of the year to nearly 45 percent in May 1991. This seems to confirm the remedial course implicit in the debt overhang hypothesis. While it is possible that markets may associate the granting of debt reduction with a less firm commitment to service obligations in the future, as shown in the upward movement of Latin debt on the secondary market, the favorable effects of debt reduction seem to outweigh that consideration.

As the secondary market has grown, new players have entered it. At first, the original holders of debt — commercial banks — were the principal participants. During its first few years, most secondary market transactions took the form of interbank debt swaps aimed at rearranging bank portfolios to reduce risk or enhance tax benefits. Then, as remains the case today, most direct sales of debt paper came from smaller regional European and American banks. The money-market-center banks with larger exposure remained reluctant to sell their loan paper at a discount because of uncertainty about the extent to which accounting standards would require that other loans to the relevant countries be similarly discounted. During the second half of the decade, however, new players entered the arena, notably multinational corporations purchasing Latin American debt at a discount for eventual use in debt-equity swaps and Latin American investors indirectly repatriating capital flight money.

Secondary market exchanges may be classified under five rubrics. The simplest transactions are *loan-to-loan swaps* in which one bank simply trades loans with a second bank. Nearly as straightforward are *cash sales* in which either a bank or an investor pays cash in exchange for a loan. This conversion method has been used by many small regional banks to exit, albeit at a loss, from involvement in a particular country.

In a *debt buyback,* a debtor country retires a debt at a discount by paying cash to a creditor. Until quite recently, straight buybacks with cash have been comparatively rare because of the lack of foreign exchange in indebted LDCs. Outside a Brady Plan framework, the chief example of a debt buyback took place in March 1988 when Bolivia purchased roughly half its $670-million dollar debt for 6 cents on the dollar.

Debt-equity swaps are among the most commonplace forms of Latin debt conversion. These exchanges involve the purchase of a debt instrument in the secondary market (usually at a discount) in exchange for an equity investment in the borrowing country. While there are several variations, a typical debt-equity swap is a three-step process. The first step begins when a bank sells at a discount an outstanding loan made to a public-sector agency (or sometimes to a private-sector enterprise) in an indebted country. Second, an investor, often a multinational corporation, purchases the loan at a discounted price and presents it to the central bank of the indebted country, which redeems it at face value or at a modest discount in domestic currency at the prevailing exchange rate. Finally, the investor acquires equity in the indebted country with this domestic currency, which it has purchased on more favorable terms than the investor could have obtained through the regular foreign exchange market transactions.

Although they discourage direct sales for cash, commercial banks have strongly encouraged countries to introduce debt-equity programs, especially in the context of new money negotiations. This has occurred notably in Chile and Mexico. For reasons detailed later in the book, few Latin American debtors are enthusiastic about this form of debt conversion. Today, most debtor nations see swaps as a concession to the banks worthwhile within the overall framework of a comprehensive debt settlement. Indeed, one of the few advantages of the Brady Plan, as seen from the perspective of the lender banks, is that these workouts have often included clauses calling for formal debt-equity swap programs within debtor nations. Thus, after falling from favor in the late 1980s, debt-equity trading prompted by the Brady Plan has enjoyed a resurgence.

Receiving considerable attention in the press is a special form of debt-equity swap known colloquially as a *debt-for-nature swap*. These transactions can be divided into two major categories: (1) conversion of debt into local currency or local debt instruments to be donated to local environmental organizations to fund specific projects and (2) official debt relief tied to environmental policies and investments. During the 1980s, the impact of debt-for-nature swaps was limited—only a small fraction of debt was converted under these schemes. However, under initiatives launched by the United States, including foreign aid outgrowths of EAI, debt-for-nature swaps may become a primary debt-reduction mechanism.

In the fifth generic type of secondary-market transaction, debt exchanges transform bank loans into other types of external debt obligations, usually bonds, often called *debt-exit bonds,* of which Brady bonds are now the premier example. These instruments frequently include credit enhancements, as was the case when Mexico purchased U.S. Treasury zero-coupon bonds to guarantee the repayment of principal on its Brady bonds.

The growth of debt conversions on the secondary market has fueled a lively debate about their merits and disadvantages to indebted countries. On the positive side, the low price of debt on the secondary market encourages the view that a debtor country can take advantage of bargains. Buybacks or debt-equity swap programs seem to afford the opportunity for banks to get out and for debtors to pay off their debt on terms far less onerous than the face values of contracts. Some types of conversions offer advantages beyond the simple reduction of debt overhang. For example, although debt-equity conversions only partly reduce external liabilities of a given country (as the discounted debt-type liability is converted into a foreign investment liability), they can also shift the risk of not meeting future foreign exchange obligations from borrower to foreign investor.

The question then arises: Why not simply rely upon exchanges in the secondary market to resolve Latin America's debt crisis? The answer is that debt conversions in themselves furnish Latin American borrowers with little or no new money to underwrite domestic investment and they carry substantial drawbacks to debtor economies, especially in terms of the attainment of monetary stabilization objectives. Indeed, debt conversion has many drawbacks. It uses scarce current resources, unleashes inflationary pressures, increases domestic debt, raises interest rates, reduces private investment, and encourages inequitable transactions in which domestic elites or foreign investors receive fire-sale bargains.

ADJUSTMENT

In essence, Latin debtor nations have three ways of coping with their debt problems: (1) reschedule debt payments, (2) reduce outstanding debt through conversion or debt relief, and (3) modify economic policies to enhance debt-service capacity. We have already covered first two of these channels in this chapter. Modifying economic policies to improve debt-service capacity is customarily referred to as *adjustment*—these reform programs are most often constructed and carried out as balance-of-payments adjustment programs orchestrated by the International Monetary Fund, with disbursements of IMF concessional loan resources conditional upon their adoption and successful implementation. As the pressures of foreign debt repayment have led to recurrent payment crises in many LDCs, IMF has expanded its traditional objectives to include policy changes aimed at putting these economies on permanently sound footings. Thus, adjustment now encompasses two elements: stabilization and structural reform or liberalization. The former refers to the attainment of balanced, stable internal and external accounts. Structural reform was originally more closely associated with the World Bank than with the IMF; but as the policies and functions of the Bretton Woods institutions have converged, structural reform has become a prominent dimension of IMF adjustment packages as well. According to John Williamson, what the IBRD (and the IMF) really mean by "structural adjustment" is "liberalization," that is, "the replacement of a traditional statist system by a market system."[49]

A Descriptive Model of Adjustment

For our purposes, we can grasp "adjustment" through a "2 × 2" paradigm that consists of four cells: (1) stabilization and (2) liberalization measures aimed at the adjusting economy's external sector along with (3) stabilization and (4) liberalization policies aimed principally at the adjusting economy's domestic sector. Of these four adjustment "domains," external stabilization is attained when the current account (including external debt payments) is either in equilibrium or displays a deficit that can be met through sustainable foreign capital inflows. Thus, this objective entails servicing existing foreign debt on original contract terms or on revised terms agreed to by lenders in the course of debt rescheduling exercises. Ideally, of course, the adjusting economy would have avoided the buildup of foreign debts; and in this light, high levels of external debt may be seen as the consequence of failure or delay in meeting the adjustment demands of the past. To adjust in the present means that the growth of debt must be slowed or reversed, that existing liabilities be serviced by means other than simply paying off old loans with new ones, for example, by attracting non-debt–creating capital inflows, including the repatriation of flight capital.

External restructuring or liberalization can be facilitated through measures that liberalize trade, encourage (or at least do not deter) foreign direct investment, and yield a competitive exchange rate. Trade liberalization requires that protectionist barriers to imports be lowered. This, of course, exposes domestic producers of import substitutes to intensified competition from abroad. It is generally believed that lowering tariff and nontariff barriers to imported goods and services ultimately forces domestic firms to operate more efficiently or fall by the wayside. At the same time, import liberalization that increases access to imports of intermediate production inputs and capital goods at competitive prices is thought to be essential for export growth. Recognizing that protected economies may undergo radical dislocations if imports are completely liberalized, the conventional wisdom maintains that tariff rates should be lowered gradually while import licenses and quotas are replaced by tariffs, so that at least some revenue stream is generated to the public sector.

Liberalization of an adjusting economy's external sector also includes the reduction of barriers to foreign direct investment, either "at the border" or through discriminatory treatment vis-à-vis purely domestic investments. Direct investment, the bulk of which occurs through multinational corporations, is often opposed by LDC governments or by political factions within them as foreign exploitation of factor endowments – of inexpensive wage labor, land, or natural resources – and has been viewed as an infringement upon sovereignty. Nonetheless, liberalization of foreign direct investment rules is now seen as a crucial means through which adjusting LDCs can garner capital (including foreign exchange), technology, and technical and managerial know-how.

Attaining and maintaining a realistic foreign exchange rate may be considered an element of external stabilization; but because institutional arrangements in many adjusting economies have led to permanently overvalued exchange rates, it can also be seen as a liberalization reform. At one time, orthodox adjustment theory showed a strong preference for exchange rates that are unified and set by market forces. While the preference for unified rates remains strong, that for rates determined purely by market forces has diminished somewhat. Today, the dominant view is that achieving a competitive exchange rate is more important than deciding how the rate is to be determined. Hence, a realistic exchange rate can be achieved through market mechanisms, through currency auctions, or by administrative means as flexibly "fixed" rates. The achievement of competitive exchange rates remains among the most controversial of orthodox IMF conditions since this normally means currency devaluation with both inflationary and recessionary side effects.

Internal stabilization encompasses the attainment of a balanced public-sector budget, a public-sector expenditure profile that emphasizes capital and human investment, and a tax regime that is both fair and capable of supporting government outlays. The demand for fiscal discipline has always been a core requirement of IMF adjustment programs, the sine qua non of adjustment efforts under its aegis. IMF-sponsored adjustment programs normally call for the elimination of deficit spending by the central government in fairly short order and the prompt, steady reduction of the deficit in relation to GDP prior to fiscal convergence.

In order to achieve balanced budgets, adjusting LDCs have often leveled their budget axes on politically inexpensive items—their capital accounts and their spending on welfare. Their purpose in doing so is to avoid the backlash that would occur if broad consumption subsidies or the state payroll were slashed instead. The result has been the neglect of long-term development, especially the accumulation of human capital through adequate educational and health provisions. Lasting adjustment requires that such public expenditure priorities be reversed. The primary target for government spending reduction should be indiscriminate consumption subsidies, which drain public coffers and impair price setting by free market forces. In addition, the size of the state apparatus must be cut. Here the principal candidates for this in Latin America are the parastatal entities that often account for as much as 50 percent of GDP. To rectify the neglect of the past, however, spending on both physical and human infrastructure may need to be increased.

Tax reform to increase central government revenues and distribute the burden of taxation more broadly is, of course, a key feature of domestic stabilization. Tax rates may need to be raised high enough to support fiscal balance but not so high as to choke off growth or induce capital flight. More important, the tax base should be expanded to include all productive sectors (including agriculture and finance), loopholes must be closed, and tax collection and enforcement of tax laws bolstered.

If progress toward fiscal balance is achieved through reductions in spending, rearrangements of budget priorities, and expansion of the tax base, then the internal conditions for a disciplined monetary policy will fall into place. The two guiding principles of monetary policy in adjusting economies are first that it should not be used to finance or monetize debt and second that a central bank should be able to ensure noninflationary growth, with stronger emphasis upon noninflation than upon growth. In many cases this may require that the central bank be insulated from political pressures through laws that give them autonomy.

The final dimension of orthodox adjustment is internal liberalization. Among the policy steps recommended to free the domestic economy, financial liberalization (epitomized by interest rates that are determined by market demand) is seen as crucial to the long-term well-being of adjusting economies. In order to temporarily stimulate growth, Latin American governments have frequently fixed interest rates by fiat at artificially low levels. Given high rates of price inflation, administratively set rates are often negative in real terms. Such practices not only deter private savings and impel capital flight, they also contribute to even higher levels of inflation. Thus, programmatic liberalization of the domestic sector requires that interest rates be market-determined and that real interest rates be positive.

Privatization of production entities that have been established or assumed by the government is a cardinal tenet of orthodox adjustment. The purpose of putting state-owned enterprises into private hands is basically twofold. First, sale of such entities assists in fiscal closure, not only by generating much-needed revenue but also (if these units have been operating at a loss, as is often the case) by eliminating a perennial source of expenditure in the form of direct or indirect subsidies. The IMF specifically endorses privatization as a means of short-run public expenditure reduction. Equally important, divestiture of SOEs is widely perceived as a measure that leads to efficiency gains of three kinds. First, gains in allocative efficiency result if relative output prices in the economy more closely reflect scarcity values, because of the reforms. Second, gains in productive efficiency arise from a more optimal use of resources within the enterprise after divestiture. Third, "x" inefficiencies at level of firm are likely to be eliminated as the workers begin to toe the line and exert more effort under private ownership. Like many facets of orthodox adjustment, privatization has been heavily criticized, and it remains a controversial topic in the developing world. As in the case of debt-equity swaps, there is a widespread perception that privatization programs frequently offer inordinate bargains to privileged domestic or (worse) foreign investors. This aside, privatization may lead to a concentration of ownership and oligopolistic structure, a point made by Glade who noted that "not much is gained . . . if a public monopoly is simply converted, other things remaining equal, into a private monopoly."[50]

For privatization to have an efficiency-boosting impact, substantial deregulation of the adjusting economy is often necessary. Simply divesting production entities and expecting them to perform well although the government continues to restrict private-sector activities is not sufficient. Thus, beyond simply selling their SOEs, Latin American governments must reduce their intervention within their economies. Given the extent to which Latin American governments are entwined with private-sector activities through extensive regulation, this is a massive undertaking in itself that bears substantial political liabilities.

A Critique of Adjustment

On the surface, it appears that the orthodox adjustment model, an attendant policy prescription, provides a blueprint. Not only are there drawbacks to each of these recommended measures, however, as questions arise regarding the proper sequence of adjustment reforms, the timing of temporary departures, and the use of heterodox policy instruments, but also the crucial issue remains whether adjustment will be rewarded by a return to satisfactory output growth. On the first count, Marcelo Selowsky has argued that adjustment should unfold in a fairly set sequence consisting of stabilization first, structural reform second, and finally, growth-promoting measures.[51] In his conceptualization, adjusting LDCs must first combat debt accumulation and inflation with fiscal and monetary discipline. Only after stabilization has been achieved may the focus shift to structural reform. Once the economy has been liberalized, the government can concentrate upon devising noninflationary measures to reactivate output expansion. While Selowsky's three-stage model seems sound and sensible, several Latin American economies have either undertaken stabilization and liberalization in one fell swoop (e.g., Bolivia) or sought to liberalize economic structures before stabilization objectives have been fully attained (e.g., Mexico).

In some developing countries, orthodox adjustment may not result in lasting stabilization, and this observation is especially true of antiinflationary policy steps. Public expectations of price increases may persist in spite of proclamations. Under such circumstances, it may be advisable to deviate from the orthodox course and impose heterodox solutions such as wage-price freezes to break inertial inflation. Some analysts believe that LDC governments can use heterodox policy shocks as supplements to (but not substitutes for) orthodox adjustment, while others eschew any departure from free-market principles.

The criticism of adjustment on the lines sketched above voiced most often is that it neglects the third stage in Selowsky's sequential model—the restoration of growth. Because adjustment implies a short-term sacrifice in growth, orthodox adjustment programs are frequently characterized as austerity or belt-tightening measures. A constant complaint leveled at IMF conditional adjustment is that it imposes recession. For its part, the IMF insists that its approach is intended to place the adjusting economy in a position where long-term growth can take place. Former managing director of the IMF, Jacques de Larosière, makes the point that "adjustment as perceived by the International Monetary Fund is not synonymous with lower growth or economic retrogression."[52]

As is detailed in subsequent chapters, orthodox adjustment has been pursued during the 1980s in several Latin American countries without return to the high-growth pattern that prevailed before debt crisis. Of the countries where adjustment has been diligently implemented, only Chile has returned to a strong growth trajectory. This disappointing result is exacerbated by the need for high levels of growth simply to repay existing debt. The World Bank has stated that heavily indebted nations must achieve growth rates in the range of 4 to 5 percent per year over the next five to seven years to work their way out of indebtedness.[53] To date, the results suggest that in itself — even with allowance for a time lag — unaided orthodox adjustment will not yield output growth at this level.

At the same time, it has been observed that the impact of adjustment normally falls most heavily upon the working class and the poor. Economic sacrifices to adjust to the foreign debt have not been shared equally by different segments of Latin American society. Instead, the brunt of austerity has been felt by wage earners and the unemployed poor. This situation, in turn, creates latent grassroots pressures to abandon adjustment altogether. Accordingly, although orthodox adjustment may bring the accounts of debtor nations into equilibrium, its capacity to stimulate renewed growth is suspect, its ability to counter erosions in investor and consumer confidence is problematical, and its treatment of economic policy is divorced from the political imperatives that confront Latin America today.

CHAPTER 3

United States Policy toward Latin America

THE REAGAN ADMINISTRATION

During the administration of President Reagan, U.S. policy toward Latin America was dominated by two preoccupations. The first of these was the battle between the Sandinistas and the Contra "freedom fighters" treated by the Reagan administration as a natural outgrowth of the Cold War struggle between the free world and communist dictatorship. Since Castro's Cuba had voluntarily relinquished the role of exporter of revolution to mainland Latin America in the late 1960s, Daniel Ortega's Nicaraguan regime was cast into this role. The Cold War conceptions and rhetoric that enveloped the invasion of Grenada were accompanied by President Reagan holding a televised press conference and pointing to a map of South America with heavy lines connecting Managua with insurgent communist movements throughout that continent, and others linking the Nicaraguan capital to Havana and the Kremlin. Immediately after that press conference, Reagan received a phone call from Brazilian President José Sarney informing him that his nation had no insurgent communist movement within its borders. This fact apparently did not register, for Reagan was determined to seek and destroy the red menace in his own backyard. That this crusade created enmity toward the United States within the bulk of Latin America also did not seem to matter.

What might be called a "radical laissez faire" toward the issue of external debt dominated the other aspect of Reagan's stance toward Latin America. As Jeffrey Sachs summarizes it: "For the past several years, the U.S. government has managed the debt crisis with the preeminent goal of sustaining the flow of debt servicing payments from the debtor countries to the commercial banks."[1] Even with the Baker "growth" Plan, the aim was not so much to assist Latin America as to stimulate growth so that debt could be repaid. Indeed, the most obvious exception to perceived harmony of interests between the United States and Latin America was (and is) continued receipt of debt service. "Some (but not all) believe this consideration to have been important in motivating Washington's support for policies of austerity in Latin America during the 1980s."[2] The Reagan administration viewed the debt crisis as an opportunity to force something like the Chilean free market model on the other debtors.

FIRST TWO YEARS OF THE BUSH ADMINISTRATION

To critics of U.S. Latin American policy, the first year of the Bush administration proved a considerable disappointment. True, the president seemed ready to jettison the narrow and obsolete Cold War assumptions that had guided America's relations with this region under his predecessor; and he periodically praised the "quite revolution" unfolding there. But his expressions of support for the renewal of popular government were not matched by specific steps to provide resources to alleviate the extraordinary economic and social pressures that confronted fledgling democracies in Latin America. By early 1990, many specialists on Latin America from both parties were becoming increasingly critical of the administration's equivocal record in the hemisphere.[3] Indeed, although Bush had taken steps to resurrect the Organization of American States (OAS), his hot pursuit of General Noriega that culminated in the invasion of Panama was a high-handed unilateral action in clear violation of Article 18 of the OAS Charter. This appeared to confirm the view that although fighting communism was no longer the beacon of U.S. policy in this quarter of the world, America's basic patronage orientation toward Latin America had not changed.

In fact, by the start of 1990, considerable changes in U.S. policy toward Latin America could already be seen both in the Brady debt-reduction plan and off-stage maneuvers in response to Mexican overtures for a free-trade agreement. The prospect of a major shift in policy was heightened dramatically on 27 June 1990 when President Bush announced the Enterprise for the Americas Initiative. The proposal, in fact, "could signal a fundamental U.S. policy decision of great potential significance: to build strong Western Hemisphere partnerships for the 1990s."[4]

THE ENTERPRISE FOR THE AMERICAS INITIATIVE

The EAI has three broad planks: a program of trade preferences toward the creation of a regional free-trade zone, U.S. incentives for private sector investment in Latin America, and debt relief.

Trade Liberalization

The Bush program calls for long-term discussions on the creation of a hemispheric free-trade zone that would extend from Point Barrow, Alaska, to Tierra del Fuego at the southernmost tip of Argentina. Quite obviously, an undertaking of this magnitude would require several years to complete. In the interim, the EAI will be moved forward through a series of bilateral negotiations aimed at the establishment of free-trade-agreement "frameworks" with individual nations. Even before this preliminary work begins, the EAI speaks of both unilateral tariff reductions on Latin American goods bound for U.S. markets and close cooperation between the United States and its Latin American neighbors within the GATT.

Privatization Funds

To assist ongoing Latin American privatization programs and spur new investment there, Bush pledged to support a new U.S. contribution of $100 million to a multilateral fund, to be administered by the Inter-American Development Bank (IDB) and to seek equivalent contributions from Japan and the European Economic Community. In addition to cofinancing with the IDB, Bush subsequently requested a five-year grant of $500 million to provide further support for investment reform, particularly privatization. Given the magnitude of Latin America's current capital requirements, the total sum in question (less than $1 billion) is relatively negligible. Still, as a symbolic gesture, the investment plank of the EAI signals a willingness on the part of the United States to lend an active hand in revitalizing the region and highlights its approval of the free market reforms undertaken there to date. It is significant too that part of these funds will be placed with the Inter-American Development Bank, which is now in a position to play a larger role in helping forge a Latin American proposal for regional recovery and expanded inter-American exchange.

Debt Relief

As for the crucial matter of debt relief, the Bush initiative of June 1990 calls for "write-offs" of some official development loans extended to Latin American nations in the past. Under the EAI, Bush promised to seek legislation that would reduce official Latin American debt owed to the United States. For some loans, the stock of debt would be significantly reduced, and interest payments on the amounts that remained could be paid in local currency and used by the debtor country in support of environmental projects. Since the lion's share of outstanding Latin American debt is held by commercial banks, the amount of relief offered by this program is comparatively modest — affecting only about $7 billion (less than 2 percent of Latin American external debt). In fact, some congressional advocates of debt relief for Latin America, while encouraged by the promise of official debt reduction, noted that the Bush initiative contained no mechanisms to put additional pressure on bank negotiators that would lead them to offer concessions on old debt or to resume loan flows to Latin America.

In this context, two points must be underscored. First, on the matter of debt the EAI is intended to complement the Brady Plan. Although the latter was not specifically introduced as an element of U.S. Latin American policy, the bulk of the debt relief for the major "middle-income" debtors of the Third World under the Brady Plan will occur in Latin America. In fact, the EAI speaks of the inclusion of IDB financial support for commercial debt reduction measures in concert with the Brady Plan. Second, by demonstrating U.S. willingness to go beyond the Brady Plan, the Bush initiative may provide backing for Latin American negotiators in their Brady Plan negotiations with commercial lenders.

Conditionality

On each of these fronts — trade, investment assistance, and debt relief — the EAI borrows a page from the IMF adjustment textbook. The assistance it promises is conditional upon the recipient nation following adjustment programs orchestrated by the IMF and IBRD and maintaining continued negotiations with commercial bank lenders. In all cases, the Bush proposal requires that Latin American nations continue with or institute movement toward market-oriented economies to remain eligible for assistance.

Although President Bush's EAI speech was barely publicized in the United States, it aroused keen interest in Latin America. Brazil and Argentina were among the first nations to issue informal official replies. Brazilian Economic Minister Zelia Cardoso de Mello greeted the announcement warmly, and the promise of official debt relief may have emboldened her in dealing with bank steering committees. Her Argentinean counterpart, Domingo Cavallo, reported a month later that both the foreign ministers and the economic ministers of Brazil, Uruguay, and Argentina were preparing a joint proposal for the practical implementation of the Bush initiative. In an article published in September, *The Wall Street Journal* noted that the ministers of economics (or finance) of Mexico, Chile, and Colombia had also greeted the EAI proposal as a constructive step on the part of the United States.[5] Nevertheless, as will be explained later in this book, Latin American enthusiasm for a regional free-trade agreement may not be an unadulterated blessing.

THE ENVIRONING FACTORS

A number of environing events led Bush to announce a fundamental shift in U.S. Latin American policy at that specific moment. At the end of 1989, he had attended a conference of Western Hemisphere leaders in Cartagena, Colombia. Although the conclave focused on narcotics trafficking, other issues were on the agenda. Upon his return from the Cartagena summit, Bush demonstrated his awareness that regional economic issues needed to be addressed. Days later, he asked the Treasury and State departments to work on a new Latin American policy. In the most direct sense, the EAI is the outcome of the efforts requested by Bush in the aftermath of Cartagena.

As is detailed in the next chapter, representatives of Mexican President Carlos Salinas approached the Bush administration in February 1990 to ask that prospects for a bilateral free-trade agreement (FTA) between the United States and Mexico be explored. With administration endorsement, the proposal is now much further developed than the EAI. Although a formal announcement about preliminary talks on the Mexican FTA was not issued until September 1990, word of the pending negotiations was already in widespread circulation. By lowering trade barriers between itself and Mexico, however, the United States would place exports from other Latin American nations at a comparative disadvantage. Thus, once it became evident that the United States intended to discriminate in favor of Mexico, some damage limitation was deemed necessary. The promise of hemispheric free trade helped reduce the negative ripples that a U.S.–Mexican FTA was bound to create in Latin America.

The announcement of the EAI took place as preparations were being made for the July 1990 G-7 summit of major developed country heads of state in Houston. In all probability, President Bush anticipated that the matter of development aid and debt relief for Eastern Europe would figure prominently at that conclave. Circumstantial evidence suggests that there was a linkage between the EAI, with its debt proposal, and G-7 debt relief for Eastern Europe. On June 26, just one day before the announcement of the EAI, the U.S. House Banking Committee reported favorably on a measure to provide $1.2 billion as a contribution toward the establishment of a development bank for Eastern Europe. At the same time, the committee both authorized $3.2 billion as a payment to low-income nations in Africa to deal with their debt crisis and called upon Secretary Brady to work with other Paris Club members on debt reduction. It is significant that while this debt relief measure was initially limited to sub-Saharan Africa, the committee amended the language of the bill to include low-income Latin American debtor nations.[6] Thus, there was undoubtedly some connection between debt relief and development assistance extended to Eastern Europe and Africa and Bush's decision to announce the EAI. Indeed, reacting to the president's Latin American initiative, Congressman Jim Leach stated frankly that "there is no moral imperative for Eastern Europe debt relief unless you have it for Latin America."[7]

Finally, at the time of the EAI proposal, a Bush tour of Latin America— including stops in Argentina, Brazil, Chile, Uruguay, and Venezuela—was scheduled for September. The trip was delayed by pressing events in the Persian Gulf until December 1990, but in making the EAI proposal at the start of the summer, Bush helped to prepare the way for his Latin excursion.

ROOTS OF THE EAI

Change in America's Strategic Perceptions

Underneath the considerations just reviewed were "deeper" reasons behind the EAI proposal. The end of the Reagan era brought a permanent break from the bipolar Cold War concept of Latin America as a pawn in the East-West power struggle that would be influenced by events in Eastern Europe. The peaceful replacement of the Sandinista regime in Nicaragua in February 1990 sounded the death knell of the Cold War in Latin America. All told, this was clearly a favorable development from the standpoint of the United States; but once the specter of a communist menace evaporated, the United States confronted a region beset by problems that could not be explained in Cold War terms.

It was a region where democracy was blossoming, although its prospects were clouded by huge social and economic problems. In fact, the United States had played a role in the process of democratization, even though the communist insurgencies it thwarted had been aimed with substantial justification against repressive right-wing military governments. In the past, the United States had alternately chastised and assisted Latin juntas, calling upon them to voluntarily loosen their strangleholds on political power. By 1990 — whether by choice, threat, or force — the traditional strongman dictatorship had vanished, replaced by fledgling democratic governments that were extremely fragile. Indeed, in elections held in 1989 and 1990, incumbent governments were being rejected in every election, sometimes by enormous margins. Latin American polities were at the crossroads, and the United States had been instrumental in getting them there. Arguably the United States was not only obligated to help them move further toward stable democratic regimes, but also strongly interested — the abortion of Latin American democracy could set the stage for a return to authoritarianism and thereby greatly reduce the region's prospective role as a commercial partner.

Direct Economic Factors

It should be recalled that the Brady Plan was launched just one year before the EAI proposal. In itself, the new debt strategy implicitly recognized that Latin America would not and could not simply grow out of its debt crisis, no matter how strenuous its adjustment efforts. The hostile reaction of commercial lenders to the Brady Plan demonstrated that the United States could no longer afford to leave the U.S. role in the debt strategy in the hands of bank steering committees. Moreover, the experience of the 1980s showed that debt overhang in Latin America and the adjustment programs marshaled to deal with it had profoundly negative side effects for the United States.

Even after a decade of adjustment and recession, Latin America was still a major U.S. export market at the end of the 1980s. In 1989 the value of U.S. shipments to Latin America was greater than that of U.S. exports to Japan and roughly equivalent to 57 percent of U.S. sales to the European Community. However, while the average annual growth rate of U.S. exports worldwide between 1981 and 1989 was 5.4 percent, the growth of U.S. exports to Latin America was only 1.8 percent. Consequently, the share of U.S. exports going to Latin America fell from 18 percent in 1981 to 13 percent in 1989. Moreover, the post-1983 recovery in U.S. exports to the region resulted primarily from growth in U.S. exports to a single country—Mexico. While U.S. exports to Mexico soared in the final years of the 1980s, deliveries to Latin America remained well below the pre-debt crisis peak of $18 billion registered in 1981.

At the same time, trade flows with Latin America became increasingly concentrated in a few countries, to the relative exclusion of others. Taken together, U.S. exports to Brazil, Venezuela, and, most important, Mexico, accounted for more than two-thirds of U.S. exports to Latin America in 1989. Similarly, in 1989 the United States bought 74 percent of its Latin American imports from the same three countries—a sharp increase from 58 percent in 1980. The same pattern has prevailed on the import side of U.S. trade with Latin America. U.S. imports from the region grew steadily during the 1980s, rising from $37 billion in 1980 to $57 billion in 1989. Most of this rise resulted from a spurt in purchases from Mexico. As for the remainder of Latin America, U.S. imports experienced only moderate growth.

Although the sharp drop in U.S. exports to Latin America can be explained by debt-adjustment-related recession, the relative lack of Latin American trade growth in U.S. markets must be ascribed to two factors. The first of these has been the continued decline in trade in commodities. Acknowledging this problem, Latin governments have encouraged the growth of nontraditional exports to the United States, manufactured goods increasing from less than one-quarter of the total value of Latin exports to America in 1980 to well over half by 1989. The second factor is the rise of U.S. nontariff barriers against manufactured goods of Latin American origin. Some growth of Latin exports to America and a broadening of this export basket has taken place, despite greater U.S. nontariff protectionism on both traditional exports and nontraditional manufactures, but the pace of increase is far less than might be expected, constricted by both relative prices and U.S. protectionism.

The most telling figure of all is the overall trade balance, and here the impact of debt and adjustment is unmistakable. The U.S. trade account with Latin America dropped from a surplus of $6 billion in 1981 to a deficit of $8 billion by the end of the lost decade. For the entire span, the cumulative U.S. trade deficit was about $93 billion. Daniel Benedict has calculated that by the end of 1989, Latin America's debt problem had cost the United States some $30 billion.[8]

What emerges from this accounting is a trade relationship that has lost its dynamic and fallen into a narrow, lopsided pattern. This was not always the case. During the late 1970s, Latin America was the fastest growing market for U.S. goods. Presumably, if Latin America can shed its debt-related doldrums and register output growth commensurate with its potential, the region could become a buoyant export market for the United States in the 1990s. In the 1990 edition of its *Economic and Social Progress in Latin America,* the IDB has optimistically projected that policy reforms instituted by governments in the region during the 1980s could pave the way for renewed Latin American economic growth. John Macomber, chairman and president of the U.S. Export-Import Bank (Eximbank), is certainly of this mind. He stated when the EAI was announced that "Latin America is going to prosper and the United States is going to prosper if we do it right."[9]

Clearly consumer demand in Latin America for U.S.-made goods is strong enough to warrant optimism. Latin American consumers are eager to purchase a wide range of U.S. products, from soft drinks to software. Latin America also desperately needs new transportation systems, mining and manufacturing equipment, and capital goods of all kinds. High-tech goods also have strong U.S. export potential. For example, a report recently issued by the Commerce Department estimates that Latin American markets for computer systems are now at $6 billion for hardware and $1 billion for software and that many of these markets are expected to grow at a rate between 10 and 20 percent a year in the 1990s.[10]

Along with the expansion of trade flows, the revival of growth in Latin America could lead to a resurgence of U.S. direct investment flows to that region. U.S. direct investment in Latin America has been growing at a sharp clip since 1989, rising some 20 percent a year. Some forward-thinking American multinationals have recognized Latin America's attractiveness as a production base and transferred resources there to take advantage of the low cost of production "at a time when other regions of the world, particularly Europe, are going to be high-cost production areas."[11] There has even been a modest resurgence in U.S. banking activity as money-center banks have expanded their presence there to better service American multinationals branching out in Latin America. Still, U.S. FDI in Latin America is confined to a comparatively small group of multinational conglomerates. Richard Crafton of Eximbank has openly wondered at the failure of American capital to seize opportunities in Chile, a nation that is both economically stable and open.[12]

America also retains a powerful stake in containing Japanese trade growth to and, above all, direct investment in Latin America. Japanese policy toward

Latin America was schizophrenic in the late 1980s and early 1990s, torn be-tween disdain for the region's debt payment record and zeal for trade, partic-ularly the attraction of direct investment coming into play through debt-equity swaps. When Latin American nations had active formal swap programs, Japan — unlike the United States — declared that it would not tax gains realized in debt swaps by Japanese corporations, thereby helping these deals along. At the 1988 annual World Bank and IMF meeting in Berlin, the Reagan ad-ministration blocked a plan by Tokyo to provide most of the Latin debtor countries with a multibillion-dollar investment pool. A year later, Tokyo tried to encourage fresh loans and investments from Japanese banks to Latin America government, and the Japanese followed suit to the Brady Plan by allowing their banks to boost their loan-loss provisions on developing country debt from 15 percent to 25 percent.

By 1990, however, as the big Latin American debtors started to back away from debt-equity swaps and as the results of the Brady Plan for Mexico and Venezuela were felt by its banking sector, the Japanese adopted a hardline toward debt reductions and new commercial loans for Latin America. While the Ministry of International Trade and Investment (MITI) sought to provide bank-loan guarantees and direct-investment insurance to Latin America, the Ministry of Finance (MoF) prohibited the banks from accessing these facilities. The MoF ruled that Brady Plan debt reductions should not be rewarded by the issuance of new credit to countries that did not meet their past obligations.

Even though Japanese banks and multinational corporations (MNCs) are under rein for now, Latin America is a natural direct investment location for Japan to access North American markets. The Japanese have been ex-panding overseas production in Mexico for some time now, and the prospect of a North American Free Trade Area (NAFTA) and of tariff-free entry to the United States of goods made by Japanese firms has accelerated the push. As the EAI opens trade between the United States and Latin America, Japan will have yet another back door for reexport of goods finished in Latin America to the north.

Adjustment

In Chapter 2 it is noted that most Latin American nations have undergone adjustment along orthodox lines leading to stabilization and liberalization. The late 1980s witnessed the adoption of a free market path by many gov-ernments, not only toward adjustment but also toward what remained of regional development plans. Some of these countries had turned to orthodox measures in the early 1980s as well, but these earlier reforms had been intended primarily to achieve fiscal and monetary stabilization. Only during the second half of the decade — with increasing momentum — were permanent structural changes undertaken. How well have the nations of Latin America carried out adjustment? For Mexico, that question is answered in Chapter 4, while Chapters 5 and 6 evaluate the performances of other Latin American economies. The dimension of external stabilization is covered in the discussion of debt (pp. 17–46). Setting aside foreign debt, while the range of adjustment performance in Latin America is broad, the extent of reform is still impressive.

The greatest degree of progress can be seen in external liberalization, the opening of trade and direct investment with the outside world and the adoption of realistic exchange rates. At the beginning of the 1980s, Latin America was closed to exports, and its isolation was reinforced by absurdly overvalued currencies. Two of its largest nations, Mexico and Venezuela, were not signatories to the GATT. Since 1986, virtually every nation in Latin America has undertaken unilateral trade liberalization, and both Mexico and Venezuela have joined the GATT. Brazil is now the only large economy with what could be called a protectionist trade regime. Nationalistic hostility toward foreign direct investment has waned, and discriminations against foreign ownership have been removed. Although debt-equity swaps were perceived as too costly to the home governments, all Latin American nations except Brazil now encourage direct investment in most sectors and provide substantive incentives in those geared toward export markets. Throughout the 1980s, most nations relied upon administered (and quite often multiple) exchange rates to deal with account deficits, compress imports, and ward off inflation. Invariably these devices proved futile and generated their own problems. By the end of the 1980s, most Latin exchange rates had been unified and were determined by market forces, albeit with help from central banks. That they were far more realistic can be seen in the revival of export growth.

Internal stabilization achieved in Latin America is much more variable. Some countries have carried out strenuous fiscal balancing acts, transforming operational government budget deficits into surpluses, as has been done in Mexico, Chile, Colombia, and Bolivia. The governments of Venezuela, Peru, and Argentina have a commitment to fiscal closure, but Argentina and Peru are still running large budget deficits, and Brazil has yet to begin serious adjustment on this front. Only a handful of nations, notably Mexico, Chile, and Bolivia, have significantly pared consumption subsidies. On the revenue side, tax bases have been broadened in some places, but reform has been slow in coming and subject to popular reversals.

Progress in domestic liberalization has been achieved in only a few countries. Although, administratively set interest rates were freed at the start of the 1980s, and Mexico has since denationalized the banks it took over at the start of the debt crisis, in Brazil and Argentina, governments have acted rashly by freezing or transmuting local savings into government credit. Privatization has been extensive in Chile, Mexico, and Venezuela; but throughout Latin America as a whole, the actual implementation of privatization has lagged well behind what might have been expected given the public-sector crisis that surfaced in the early 1980s. Virtually every government has paid lip-service to privatization, but dismantling the obsolete structures of these corporate states has proven an inordinately difficult task. Privatizations through debt-equity swaps rose during the 1987–1988 period but then fell as government interest in that form of conversion fell. Even if state-owned enterprises are transferred to the private sector, economies remain overregulated, with the exceptions of those of Mexico, Chile, and Bolivia.

Two distinct patterns emerge from this survey of adjustment: some nations have done far better than others; external liberalization has proven easier to accomplish than either domestic stabilization or domestic liberalization; there is a definite momentum sequence, a series of adjustment stages, as Marcelo Selowsky has observed, restructuring of the internal sector being the final phase. As nations have progressed along the path, their value to the United States as trading partners and investment outlets has risen accordingly. For this group of countries, the EAI offers an immediate reward. For Latin America as a whole, however, the general trend has been progressive, and this suggests that America will realize greater trade and investment growth in the future, thereby raising its stake in a dynamic Latin America. Moreover, by liberalizing trade and providing seed money for privatization, the EAI will enhance the region's commercial potential for the United States.

Political Factors

If President Bush had made the EAI proposal at the start of the debt crisis, it would have been met with skepticism or even hostility by Latin American leaders. But even more than the accomplishments registered to date suggest, a loose consensus has emerged among the region's leaders on the need for deregulation and privatization of state enterprises, realistic exchange rates, the phasing out of export taxes, reduction of tariffs and nontariff barriers to imports, maintenance of real positive interest rates, and the expansion of national tax systems from which loopholes favoring vested interests have been removed. It is this shift in thinking, coupled with concrete implementation by many countries, that made possible the warm reception accorded the EAI. In the past, it would have been seen as a Trojan Horse, a means for the United States to pry open Latin American markets and dominate them in a structure of dependency. Today, the governments of Latin America accept that the future cannot be built if the state shields business from contact with the outside world but must be formed through private enterprise (albeit with some guidance and help by government) interacting with foreign business.

This recognition marks a turning point in a Latin American development debate at least three decades old, a conflict between neoclassical orthodox capitalism, with its emphasis upon free exchange, and the structuralist-dependencía theories with their heterodox insistence that developing countries must control economic activity and protect themselves from vassalage to developed nations. Starting in the 1950s, Raul Prebisch, Hans Singer, and the Economic Commission for Latin America (ECLA) were the most prominent advocates of state expansion to accelerate development in the Third World. Because the private sector lacked resources and the structure of Latin American economies was weak and underdeveloped, the old school of development theory placed government at the forefront of economic progress and maintained that government should nurture indigenous industries until they could withstand competition from technologically superior First World rivals. Rather than advocating expanded exports of raw and semiprocessed commodities for manufactures from the industrialized countries, industrialization through import substitution was enshrined in structuralist theory. Export pessimism dominated, as Prebisch and his colleagues argued that the inevitable decline in terms of trade in traditional agrarian goods made it imperative that Latin America develop its own industrial base. As described in Chapter 2, by pursuing this path, Latin America saddled itself with a huge public production apparatus, a bias against exports, an inefficient private sector laboring under heavy regulation, and ultimately, a mountain of foreign debt.

Today, the structuralist argument is virtually absent, and the export pessimism that dominated so much of Latin American thinking after World War II has been jettisoned. The Latin Americans have learned—not only from reviewing their own hard experience but by comparing it with that of other developing nations like the NICs of the Far East—that an inward-looking development strategy discourages export development and weakens the base for supporting debt service.

Latin America has not yet accepted pure capitalism with the same enthusiasm as the developing nations of East Asia, but the notion that the state can substitute for the private sector as the economy's engine of growth as long as it is sealed from foreign penetration is no longer tenable. The structuralists have not endorsed the idea of an open economy driven by market forces as the only path to development. Indeed, Brazil's adherence to the vestiges of an import-substituting industrialization strategy remains a point of pride for the structuralist camp. Old-school representative Osvaldo Sunkel would go so far as to ascribe the demise of structuralism in Latin America to the neglect of structuralism in the curriculums of Latin American universities.[13] But very few Latin Americans, and none in power, see import substitution as the basis for national development.

To be sure, there are important variants within the new orthodoxy of Latin American economic thought, and many questions remain—even for those who accept the basic market-oriented approach to development. Today, there are two competing models for redesigning the Latin American developmental state. The first begins by stripping away public functions and confidently assigning them to the private sector and the market. This approach, which has been pursued in Chile, is associated with the laissez-faire philosophies of Ronald Reagan and, more cogent, Margaret Thatcher. Its demands upon government are few: set the right policies and incentives, behave consistently and credibly, move aside and allow the economy to resume growth of its own accord. The other follows the path through which East Asia has been able to post its development gains. It starts by confronting the central challenge of the public deficit. Once fiscal closure is at hand, the government orchestrates (but does not command or own) the activities of the private sector through an indicative or light industrial policy.

Despite these differences, both current approaches to development are compatible with the free market stance of the United States and highly favorable to U.S. commercial interests. Latin American ideology has moved toward U.S. capitalist and democratic philosophy to an extent that would have seemed implausible, if not impossible, a decade ago. In fact, the most significant change in Latin America during the 1980s was not directly related to foreign debt, macroeconomic stabilization, or structural adjustment. Instead, what the U.S. Department of State calls the "quiet revolution" proceeded with very little notice. Throughout the region, dictatorial regimes were replaced by democratic governments. In Brazil, Argentina, and Uruguay, control of national political life by a military-industrial elite has given way to popularly elected governance. Although General Pinochet looms in the background of Chilean politics, that nation now has a civilian president. Nominally a democracy, Mexico was dominated by a single party, the PRI, for most of the century. While that PRI remains the largest political faction in Mexico today, the 1988 presidential election was strongly contested at the ballot box by both conservative and liberal opposition. In 1989, General Alfredo Stroessner, president of Paraguay since 1954 and thus Latin America's longest-surviving dictator, was deposed. By March 1990 every country in South America had, for the first time in history, a democratically elected president.

Accompanying this tide of democracy has been a wholesale revision in Latin American ideas about the nature of government. The Latin American notion of the state dispensing of concessions has been replaced with one of government fostering private initiative. Today, the political leadership is following an ideology most frequently labeled *realism* or *pragmatism*. As IDB President Iglesias recently noted, "politicians who used to promote populistic policies are now taking a very tough and architectural approach to economic solutions."[14]

When the Latin debt crisis erupted, it was widely believed that adjustment sacrifices would cause a reversal in the incipient trend toward popularly based government. It was believed that only authoritarian regimes, such as Pinochet's Chile, would be able to impose adjustment burdens upon their people. But exceptions like Bolivia arose, and far from undermining democracy in Latin America, the debt problem seems to have accelerated the continent-wide shift away from authoritarianism.

Precisely why Latin American democracy has thrived in the face of debt and adjustment hardship is a matter of conjecture. One factor is undoubtedly that the traditional opposition to democratic government, the military, is still recuperating from the institutional damage resulting from recent episodes of authoritarian rule and does not want to assume responsibility for economic management in the face of current difficulties. More important, the power behind the military, Latin America's business elite, are weary of years of economic mismanagement by military establishments and are now ready to trade a stagnant system of privilege for an open and competent leadership in step with global economic realities.

But Latin American democracy is not secure, for many current leaders have been elected by espousing populist slogans and then surprised their constituents with orthodox adjustment programs. They are now trying to carry out free-market reforms without broad-based popular support, and only the disarray of the opposition and the diffidence of the military allow them to remain in office. Unless their mixture of adjustment and democracy starts yielding tangible benefits in the near future, some new form of demagoguery could well reverse not only adjustment but also democratization. To the extent that the United States has an interest in free-market *and* democratic principles, the EAI is a tool through which it can help support likeminded regimes in the Western Hemisphere.

In the 1990s, the issues at the heart of U.S.–Latin American relations will increasingly be "intermestic," that is, arising from the international spillover of domestic concerns and involving both international and domestic aspects and actors.[15] Examples of such issues are immigration, the environment, disease control, arms control, and guarantees of basic human rights. These shared problems may serve to divide the United States from its Latin American neighbors and may even impede negotiations pursuant to the EAI. In certain instances, these parallel issues may determine EAI outcomes: environmental issues have already played a role in the negotiation of a free trade area with Mexico as has the matter of narcotics control; differences about human rights have created a barrier between the United States and Chile; arms shipments to the Third World from Brazil and Argentina are contrary to U.S. policy; and the destruction of the Amazon Rain Forest in Brazil is a potential stumbling block to strengthening ties with that country.

But there is another way of looking at these shared issues in relation to the Bush proposal. By strengthening economic ties with Latin America, the United States can nurture both the good will and the institutional contacts that favor closer cooperation in dealing with these quandaries. Even before formal EAI negotiations begin, the benefits of participating in a hemispheric economic alliance should prompt Latin American governments to undertake unilateral steps in these areas and to engage in joint programs with the United States to deal with them.

As described in Chapter 2, many Latin nations experienced large-scale capital flight during the 1970s and 1980s. Plainly, these same countries have a major interest in creating incentives for its repatriation and in limiting future episodes of flight should their stabilization drives stall. Part of the problem can be addressed through the conclusion of tax treaties between Latin American capitals and Washington, under which the latter would undertake to withhold taxes due the former on investments in the United States of its nationals or to report earnings data on tax-free investments to Latin American source countries.

Several roadblocks have impeded progress on this front in the past. Many Latin American nations still lack any legislation to tax overseas investment earnings by their citizens, cleaving to an "origin" principle of taxation (which imposes levies only on activities taking place within their borders) as opposed to a "residence" principle (which taxes the investment income of nationals no matter where it is earned). For its part, consistent with its adherence to residence taxation, the United States has long exempted interest on bank deposits owned by nonresidents from taxation: it does not even impose a refundable withholding tax on these revenue streams. In 1984 it extended this treatment by exempting interest on Treasury securities held by nonresidents from withholding as well.[16]

Today, Latin American governments have a strong motivation to undertake tax treaties with the United States since cooperation on this count could provide them with a stream of tax revenues on overseas investments, reduce tax differential incentives to future capital flight, and increase incentives for the repatriation of flight capital. A broad-based deal in this area might involve acceptance of tax sparing by the United States in exchange for the adoption of a residence principle of taxation by Latin American governments. This would both substantially reduce Latin American tax burdens on U.S. MNCs and generate additional tax receipts for the United States. From Latin America's perspective, a compromise along these lines would be entirely congruent with its desire to attract direct investment by eliminating the burden of an onerous tax regime upon FDI outside of debt-equity swap programs. Since Latin American flight capital will return home if the region's economies show stabilization and growth and since America has a broad commercial stake in the revitalization of those economies, the United States should move to manage the reflux with Latin governments in a manner that allows for an orderly repatriation rather than stop-and-go spurts. Again, while the EAI is silent on the flight capital question, the conclusion of trade and investment treaties with individual Latin American nations would stimulate U.S.–Latin cooperation in this field.

Institutional Factors

Changes in the policies of international financial institutions clearly favor the implementation of the EAI proposal. Until the end of the 1980s, the International Monetary Fund was widely perceived in the indebted developing nations as an enforcer for developed country banks and governments. When the World Bank introduced higher conditionality into its loan programs, as both its insistence on adjustment and its policy prescription for adjustment began to converge with those of the IMF, it too was seen as a debt collector intent upon liberalizing heavily borrowed countries so that they would remain subordinated to the world's industrialized powers. For both bodies, the argument was fleshed out by the growth-retarding properties of the stabilization policies these organizations recommended for (or imposed upon) debtor economies, by their refusal to accept temporary heterodox deviations from the standard adjustment recipe, and by the notion that the IMF and IBRD were usurping sovereign functions.

As early as 1988, and certainly by the time the Brady Plan was announced, a major change occurred in the IMF–World Bank strategy for revitalizing deeply indebted developing economies, one that pivoted upon the recognition of a need for debt reduction. Not only did the IMF and the Bank endorse the Brady blueprint, they made funds available to put it into operation in Mexico, Venezuela, and Costa Rica; they approved loans to nations in arrears to commercial banks and without formal commercial debt rescheduling in progress; and they became more understanding about the use of emergency heterodox adjustment measures, such as wage-price controls to reverse inertial inflation. Since April 1989, after nearly a decade in which relations between the IMF and the Bank and Latin American debtor governments became increasingly strained, a cordial, pragmatic, and mutual enlightenment now marks exchanges between these global institutions and their Latin American members. Even in second-tier countries like Brazil, Argentina, and Peru that were highly critical of the IMF and IBRD, fell from compliance with Fund-supervised adjustment programs, and fell in arrears to foreign debtors (including the Fund and the Bank), current IMF Managing Director Michel Camdessus has found ground for compromise. Brazil, Argentina, and Peru all had serious IMF programs in operation by mid-1991.

The positive course of Latin American relations with these pivotal international bodies in the late 1980s and early 1990s bodes well for the EAI blueprint. Simply the fact that Latin American governments have a much more accommodating attitude toward the Fund and the Bank suggests the extent of their realistic acceptance of orthodox adjustment. At the same time, the fact that these bodies have expanded their financial support to debt-reduction exercises through the Brady Plan enhances prospects that Latin America can again become a growth market for U.S. exports and a favorable environment for U.S. direct investment. Moreover, as animosity toward the IMF has subsided in Latin America, the perception that the United States is using it as a debt collector or instrument of dependency creation has begun to evaporate as well.

Another institutional development that provides ancillary support for the EAI is the growing role of the Inter-American Development Bank, which has an explicit part in President Bush's proposal as an administrator of privatization seed money. By 1988, the IDB had found its lending resources stretched thin. In that year, the regional bank was unable to borrow on capital markets for relending to Latin American nations because its level of debt was greater than its callable capital. Two weeks after the announcement of the Brady debt-reduction plan, a series of tense negotiations conducted in Amsterdam concluded when IDB member countries agreed on a seventh replenishment of the regional bank's resources, bolstering its capital resources by $26.5 billion.

According to IDB President Enrique Iglesias, the seventh replenishment suggests a revised and expanded role for the IDB and, with it, the restoration of Latin American growth.[17] The role of the IDB in an EAI process extends beyond recycling its seventh replenishment contributions. While both the IMF and the World Bank withdrew from some Latin nations during the 1980s (e.g., Bolivia, Peru, Argentina, and Brazil), the IDB maintained a presence in these countries. Because of its status as a Latin American institution, popular perceptions of the IDB have remained positive. At the same time, IDB project lending policies have moved in the direction of IMF and IBRD conditional loan programs, with borrowers required to undertake or continue orthodox stabilization and liberalization measures. For the United States seeking to implement the EAI, the Inter-American Development Bank affords both an institutional bridge and a source of additional capital transfers to America's prospective Latin partners. With its loanable assets restored through 1992, the IDB can enlarge its role in the revitalization of Latin America. The IDB also shares the basic compromise realism that underlies the Brady program, the revised policies of the IMF and the World Bank, and the Enterprise for the Americas Initiative itself.

THE LACK OF AN INTEGRATIVE MECHANISM IN LATIN AMERICA

Another side of the EAI proposal that can be viewed as either a hurdle or an opportunity concerns its implicit vision of a unified free trade region, as opposed to a series of bilateral free trade agreements between the United States and the nations of Latin America taken individually. In the wake of the debt crisis, intraregional trade underwent a greater decline in volume and value than did Latin American worldwide trade. Moreover, intraregional trade in manufactures dropped further than total trade among Latin American economies. Despite the sharp growth of trade between Mexico and the United States in both directions, Mexican trade with other Latin American countries amounts to little more than 3 percent of its total trade. Since debt and adjustment have had a depressive impact on virtually all Latin American economies, it is not surprising to see exchanges of products and services within the region follow a downhill trend.

On the other hand, a number of regional trade organizations were established in the 1960s, including the Latin American Free Trade Association (LAFTA), the Central American Common Market (CACM), and the Andean Pact, when Latin American growth rates were among the highest in the world. None of these arrangements has proven durable. Although the Andean Pact lingers on, LAFTA is now a skeletal body, and CACM virtually collapsed with commodity prices in the late 1970s. These compacts, all based on the now defunct import-substitution development strategy of the time, were intended not so much to expand trade within the region as to present a unified block *against* trade and direct investment flows from outside the region. Latin American countries have yet to demonstrate a capacity to take part in mutually beneficial trade enlargement. On the other hand, the EAI would fill the institutional void of Latin American integration created by the effective demise of LAFTA and CACM. This in turn would create an institutional apparatus to further U.S. commercial interests by impeding a return to a closed Latin America.

There may, in fact, be a problem here for the EAI as it takes its final form. Heartened by the Bush proposal and waiting for the United States to complete its FTA with Mexico, several Latin American nations are now working to reduce barriers to trade they have erected between themselves. There are two separate axes discernible at this time. The first includes Argentina and Brazil. Once these two nations agreed to eliminate all tariffs between one another by 1995, Argentina's exports to Brazil doubled between 1989 and 1991. As initial trade liberalization has taken place between Argentina and Brazil, the scope of their agreement has expanded to the establishment of a common market based on the EC model, with a membership that also includes Chile, Uruguay, and Paraguay. In 1991, these five countries endorsed the idea of an Andean FTA, and it is expected that they will adopt a uniform commercial policy by the end of 1994.

A second axis is centered in Mexico. In January 1991, the presidents of Mexico and four Central American republics met to discuss a common market. Mexico has already offered free trade and low-cost oil to five Central American nations with the expectation that the arrangement would begin by 1996 and extend, eventually, to Colombia and Venezuela as well. In addition, Mexican President Salinas met personally with the presidents of the Andean Pact axis in October 1990. While he did not suggest that Mexico would join their common market, in each session, the Mexican leader advocated lowering commercial barriers among Latin American countries.

For the United States, with its EAI vision of a hemispheric alliance, the existence of subregional common markets within Latin America serving as rivals to the EAI would generate some significant drawbacks. These alternative associations might be used as bargaining chips in bilateral EAI negotiations with the United States. Nations that join a subregional pact may liberalize trade among themselves but raise barriers to trade with other nations, including the United States. Consequently, the emergence of these competitive subregional groupings puts pressure on the United States to move rapidly in securing its vision of a hemispheric free trade agreement before it is upstaged. More specifically, what the Bush administration seeks to avoid is a trade alliance featuring the big two second-tier nations, Brazil and Argentina, that would attract a first-tier country like Chile or Venezuela into the ranks of a subregional free trade group. In such circumstances, the United States would be forced to terminate its EAI plans with a qualified candidate nation or risk indirect exploitation—a back door for tariff-free exports to the United States by nations that still hold on to protectionist trade and investment regimes. Clearly, Latin America can benefit from economic integration, but the form and the auspices under which integration occurs are of compelling importance both to the United States and to Latin America's own long-term well-being.

The Need for U.S. Adjustment

As conditioned as Americans are by cultural and economic hubris when the topic of economic integration with Latin America surfaces, one of the first questions asked is this: Are the nations of Latin America advanced enough to participate in a partnership with the United States? The question is valid, taking initial force from the fact that Latin American per capita income (while varying from nation to nation) is about one-tenth that of the United States. But when we turn to the more complex yardstick of readiness, inquiry must cut two ways. Seen from this perspective a valid and straight-forward inquiry arises: Is the United States ready to put *its* house in order and to create conditions necessary for *it* to achieve sustainable fiscal convergence and a more outward-looking orientation with *its* more disciplined Latin American partners (of the future)? In other words, how well has the United States done in handling its external debt problem and the accompanying need for adjustment?

From the start, although foreign financing has been sufficient to cover America's current account deficits in the 1980s, the United States has become the world's largest debtor nation in a very short time, and its accumulated foreign debt continues to grow. Unlike that of Latin America, this debt does not take the form of sovereign bank loans; it is chiefly debt paper sold to private individuals and institutions abroad. Although there is now a wide-spread view that America is excessively dependent upon foreign capital, very little of substance has been done to reduce this dependency. Should current trends continue, the United States will begin to feel the ripples emanating from its increasing unstable external accounts.

With respect to external liberalization, the United States has an open direct investment regime, and the value of its currency is determined primarily by the free play of market forces. In the area of trade, however, America is now struggling to close the gap between imports and exports that grew to alarming proportions during the mid-1980s as foreign capital streamed into the U.S. economy in search of high yields and furnished the wherewithal for the import binge of the Reagan years. During the late 1980s, substantial progress was registered on this front, and the sharp improvement in the U.S. trade balance that occurred in the 1988–1990 period is expected to continue into the early 1990s. In 1990, the disequilibrium of America's trade account declined by about $8 billion, leaving an annual trade deficit of around $100 billion.

Much of the improvement in America's trade balance came from a renewal of exports, which grew by some $30 billion in 1990. On the other hand, while imports also grew in 1990, it appears that purchases of foreign goods and services in the United States were heavily repressed by the growth of nontariff barriers. On the whole, in terms of trade liberalization, the United States has moved against the grain of orthodox adjustment. Apprehensive about the trade imbalance, the Congress pushed President Reagan and is now pressuring President Bush to "get tough" with nations penetrating U.S. markets and increasing their income through what are seen as unfair trading practices. Plainly this more aggressive posture is a strong factor behind America's adoption of a polylateral foreign economic policy. According to a growing chorus of critics, "the United States has retreated farther from free trade during the 1980s than in any comparable period since World War II."[18] This retrenchment has taken the form of nontariff barriers. Tariff protection of U.S. producers has remained about the same since the Tokyo Round or even declined in relative terms, but voluntary export restraints (VERs) or import quotas now constitute the core of American protectionism. President Bush has tried to hold back the protectionist tide in Congress. In 1990, he not only vetoed a bill that called for a tightening of quotas on foreign-made textiles and clothing but also discouraged the filing of unfair trade practice cases to avoid antagonizing trade partners while negotiations were in progress at the GATT Uruguay Round. Still, U.S. trade policy has generally drifted toward general growth in quantitative restrictions on imports and the use of explicit sanctions to pry open foreign markets.

A disproportionate share of the impact of this hardline stance on imports has been borne by Third World exporters, particularly Latin American nations. The negative effect of tighter U.S. quotas on developing country exports has been especially harsh because the United States has historically taken a far greater share of their exports than have Japan or Western Europe. In many instances, it now appears that the United States is using ancillary issues like human rights as a pretext for continuing, or even extending, trade barriers to Latin American exports of agricultural produce, semiprocessed commodities, and light manufactures. As time elapses, it has become increasingly difficult for the United States to maintain its demand for the opening of Latin American markets while simultaneously constructing higher and thicker walls against Latin American imports.

On the surface, in terms of domestic liberalization, the United States appears to require only fine tuning. Unlike Latin economies, with their relatively inefficient SOEs, America has refrained from the expansion of the government into productive functions. In fact, during the 1980s, the Reagan administration partially dismantled the nation's regulatory apparatus, although the social regulation of economic activities by federal and state governments has increased of late. The United States also has a liberal financial sector (albeit cushioned by government bailouts), with market-determined lending and deposit interest rates.

On the other hand, despite a drop in interest rates during the first two years of the 1990s, real interest rates in the United States have remained high by historical standards ever since the early 1980s. Plainly, although inadequate domestic savings rates have contributed to this, high rates are mainly the result of poor macroeconomic management, which creates a need for tight monetary policies by the Federal Reserve Board. The crux of the problem is, of course, the federal deficit and the growth of public domestic debt. The government has paid lip service to budget balancing, but progress has been painfully slow and subject to periodic reversals. During the 1980s, it took the United States seven years to reduce the deficit from 6 percent of GNP to below 4 percent. Again, there is a vast discrepancy between a United States urging Latin American governments to put their fiscal houses in order while its own domestic stabilization effort is sluggish and suspect.

Judging adjustment in the United States in light of adjustment in Mexico and the first-tier EAI Latin economies surveyed in Chapter 5, one must conclude that several prospective U.S. trade partners in Latin America have outperformed America in terms of adjustment, especially in the dimensions of external liberalization and internal stabilization.

One concern voiced about the Brady debt-reduction plan is that once heavily indebted developing countries pare back their foreign debt burdens and the pernicious impact of debt overhang abates, incentives toward maintaining IMF- and IBRD-supervised adjustment programs will wane accordingly. As this occurs, pressure to abandon current stabilization and liberalization plans may increase, and political pressures to return to the state-driven, closed development strategy of the past may arise. As mentioned earlier, the EAI proposal tacitly acknowledges this, it contains an element of conditionality as a prerequisite to participation; and the obvious inference is that further external liberalization must occur for a hemispheric free trade area to come into existence. On the other hand, insofar as trade policy is concerned, an EAI will necessarily require the United States to reverse its drift toward reliance upon protectionist devices, at least with regard to its fellow EAI member states. In the long run, for the United States to hold up its end of a truly equitable EAI arrangement, substantially greater progress must take place on both the external stabilization and foreign liberalization fronts. Hence, one final benefit of an EAI for the United States is that it will compel partial adjustment of the U.S. economy along free-market lines, function as a barometer of same, and, by specifying the features of acceptable Latin economic partners, highlight the central role of fiscal closure in putting the U.S. economy on a sound growth trajectory.

CHAPTER 4

The United States–Mexico Free Trade Agreement and the Mexican Economy

HISTORICAL EVOLUTION

Given the condescending arrogance of traditional U.S. policy toward Latin America as a whole and the resentment it has engendered south of the Rio Grande, the notion of a free trade agreement between the United States and Mexico was clearly *not* on the U.S. agenda during the 1980s. To be sure, some far-thinking leaders spoke the need for a wholesale redefinition of U.S.-Mexican ties at the start of the Latin American debt crisis. Congressman Bill Richardson of New Mexico, for one, claims that he first proposed a U.S.-Mexico FTA in 1982 but met with the derision of his colleagues at that time. The simultaneous election of George Bush as a U.S. president from Texas and Carlos Salinas de Gortari, with a Ph.D. from Harvard, as president of Mexico that afforded a unique opportunity to put U.S.-Mexican relations on a wholly new footing. Along with Bush, Commerce Secretary Robert Mosbacher and Secretary of State James Baker, both Texans, all have close personal ties with members of the Salinas cabinet.

Even before his inauguration, President Bush gave several signals that he would seek to improve U.S. relations with Mexico upon taking his post at the White House. He conferred with Salinas in Houston in December 1988; and both men pledged vigorous new efforts to build bilateral cooperation on a broad roster of shared concerns.

Prior to work on the FTA, the United States extended its firmest support to Mexico through the Brady Plan and through U.S. support for the seventh replenishment of the IDB. In fact, Bush pushed Mexico's commercial debt renegotiation through in 1989 and, along with Treasury Secretary Brady, exerted pressure on reluctant banks to compel their support of Mexico's Brady Plan treatment. The growing importance of Mexico to the Bush administration was highlighted in August 1989, when half the Cabinet traveled to Mexico for a working session of the U.S.-Mexico bilateral commission.

Yet even in the fall of 1989, the notion of a U.S.-Mexico free trade agreement was still not on the drawing board. Some steps were taken. For example, as a result of the U.S.-Mexico presidential Washington summit of October 1989, Secretary of Commerce Robert Mosbacher and Mexican Secretary of Commerce Dr. Jaime Serra Puche established a U.S.-Mexico Joint Committee for Investment and Trade (JCTI), setting up a formal mechanism to coordinate U.S.-Mexican business development activities. Official statements issued after the session suggested that trade liberalization between the two countries would occur incrementally. President Salinas signed a memorandum of understanding with U.S. Special Trade Representative Carla Hills. Pressed to describe the scope of this agreement, Hills cautioned that follow-up negotiations would concentrate on measures to open trade between the two countries sector by sector and were *not* aimed at reaching a free trade agreement.[1]

There is no reason to believe that Hills's admonition was intentionally misleading or that the United States harbored a secret plan to spring a free trade agreement on an unsuspecting public. That work toward a U.S.-Mexico FTA began only six months later testifies to the rapid tempo of events in the interim and to the fact that the impetus behind the proposal came mainly from the Mexican side.

Indeed, the pace of movement toward closer U.S.-Mexican cooperation has been largely set by President Salinas. Ignoring or overcoming previous nationalist restraints, he accelerated the program of external structural reform or liberalization initiated in 1985 by President Miguel de la Madrid. Under Salinas, Mexico undertook unilateral steps to attract U.S. investment and to reduce trade barriers. He also stepped up Mexican efforts to protect the environment and made unprecedented efforts both to curb the narcotics traffic and to confront official corruption. Salinas orchestrated a major public relations campaign to convince public opinion in the United States of the value of a closer bilateral relationship and backed it up with bold substantive measures.

Once Mexico's political leadership decided to hold firm to the structural reforms of the late 1980s and adopted unilateral trade and direct investment liberalization reforms, chances for an FTA with the United States improved dramatically. Mexico experienced a major current-account drain and significant production and labor dislocations as a consequence of this opening to the North, with U.S. exports streaming south and thereby injuring domestic producers. However, Salinas's attempt to integrate the Mexican economy with the U.S. economy took on real weight when he also tried unsuccessfully to broaden his country's trade ties with Western Europe. In February 1990, Salinas traveled to the European Community, where he met with the leaders of Great Britain, West Germany, Belgium, Switzerland, and Portugal. Prime Minister Margaret Thatcher gave him some words of encouragement and praised Mexico's adjustment, but other European heads of state issued a disheartening message. Although they admired his market-oriented strategy to modernize Mexico, they intended to make Europe the focus of their capital investment and commercial activities. In their schedule, the EC-92 program (for closer economic, political, and social integration among the community's member states) and assistance to Eastern Europe were higher priorities; aiding Mexican emergence from its debt-related recession was not even on the list. Salinas realized that European investment capital would either stay within the EC or be transferred to Eastern Europe. On the other, he saw that European nations that started from an economic base only slightly higher than that of his nation could benefit from integration with more advanced partners. Commenting upon the rise of Spain's fortunes since the EC's Iberian enlargement, Salinas admitted, "When I read that Spain, with a socialist government, gets $10 billion a year in foreign investment, I ask myself if we are not missing anything."[2]

The cordial rebuff Salinas encountered in Western Europe only reinforced his belief that Mexico had to work with a dynamic trading partner in order to avoid becoming a stagnant backwater. The United States, with its geographic proximity and well-established economic ties, was the obvious choice. After his return from the EC in February 1990, Salinas sent top aides to Washington to propose free-trade talks with the United States. This was an extraordinarily courageous step, given the customary Mexican enmity toward and suspicion of America and its high-handed, exploitative motives. The taboo on entanglements with the "Colossus of the North" had become an article of faith within "nationalist" and "revolutionary" Mexico. In May 1990, Salinas nevertheless informed his countrymen that he favored a free trade agreement with the United States.

After testing the political waters for four months, Salinas told President Bush in September that he wanted to begin talks in earnest. Less than a week later, the U.S. president formally asked Congress for an extension of fast-track authority to his trade representatives. While the immediate cause of the request was to give U.S. GATT negotiators additional leverage in Geneva as part of the Uruguay Round, Bush also needed the extension so that his trade representatives could later negotiate a credible pact with Mexico.

The president originally intended to notify the relevant congressional committees of his intention to enter into FTA talks with Mexico in the fall of 1990 and request fast-track authority for the negotiators. A Canadian request to be included in the bargaining, however, temporarily derailed Bush's plans. Although Canadian-Mexican trade and investment flows were minuscule, the Canadians were understandably concerned that a U.S.-Mexican FTA might diminish Canadian gains under the previously negotiated free trade pact between Canada and the United States. Although U.S. representatives were initially apprehensive about the increased complexity of three-way negotiations and the possibility that the Mulroney government might somehow upset the talks, Ottawa clearly demonstrated its diplomatic *bona fides* by firmly supporting U.S. policy in the Persian Gulf. The United States accordingly dropped its original intention to exclude Canada from the talks, and a compromise was reached. The Canadians would have the equivalent of observer status: they could monitor the discussions, voicing recommendations and even objections, but they would not be allowed to veto, or even vote on, the issues under negotiation. If the Canadian presence at the negotiating table proved too disruptive to the active parties in the bilateral talks, then Canadian representatives would withdraw. On February 5, 1991, the presidents of the United States and Mexico and the prime minister of Canada announced their intention to begin negotiations on a North American Free Trade Agreement (NAFTA).

Once the Canadian request had been resolved and the Persian Gulf War had ended, Bush resurrected the idea of a U.S.–Mexican FTA. At a meeting with President Salinas in Houston on 7 April 1991, Bush held a press conference on the matter. At that session, the president painted a picture of free trade with Mexico in glowing terms.

The United States has embarked on a historic task with Mexico and Canada, a creation of a trilateral free-trade agreement, which would establish the largest free-trade area in the world. It would involve some 360 million people and a total of $6 trillion in combined annual output. President Salinas and I are certain that this FTA, this trade agreement, will create jobs and provide opportunities for the citizens of both our countries.[3]

During the remainder of the month, the president's agenda was dominated by his efforts on behalf of the U.S.–Mexican FTA. Bush visited Hispanic-American communities along the border to drum up support for the pact. He sent Carla Hills to Congress to explain its provisions to key Democrats. He even called his chief GATT spokesman, Rufus Yerxa, back from Geneva to Washington to lobby Democrats on behalf of the FTA. Bush himself spoke personally with several Democratic congressmen. Most important, he showed a willingness to compromise with potential opposition by crafting an "action plan" filled with pledges addressing the particular concerns of special interest groups.

Fast-Track Authority and Bush's Action Plan

The first hurdle was extension of fast-track authority due to expire before U.S.–Mexican negotiations could be completed. Fresh from serving a commander-in-chief of an extremely popular and militarily successful Persian Gulf campaign, Bush spent large chunks of his accumulated political capital lobbying for the fast-track authority extension that would further the negotiations and greatly increase the chances that an agreement would be passed by Congress once it had been reached between negotiators for the two countries. Bush transformed the technical battle for fast-track extension into an intense personal crusade in which he put both his own prestige and that of his office at stake, carrying through on his April 7 joint news conference claim that: "The credibility of the United States as a trading partner is on the line here."[4]

What President Bush wanted was an extension of the 1988 U.S. Trade Act's fast-track procedures for congressional approval (or disapproval) of any deal negotiated by trade envoys of the two nations. Congress had already extended the procedure in the 1988 act until 1991. Under section 1103 of the 1988 act and section 151 of the 1974 Trade Act, the mechanics of the fast track are designed both to expedite negotiations and to assure a foreign signatory that Congress will not seek to amend the agreement. The fast-track process begins when the president notifies the Senate Finance Committee and the House Ways and Means Committee that he is ready to begin trade negotiations. These committees may disapprove within sixty days, in which case fast-track provisions are laid aside; but if they do not disapprove, the committees will later be limited in the amount of time they can spend deliberating over the resulting trade pact. Amendments to that pact from the floor of the Congress are also not permitted, leaving the legislators to take it or leave it as it is presented to them. In exchange for expedited consideration of the final agreement, the administration undertakes frequent in-depth consultations with Congress throughout the process, even before negotiations begin.

Opposition to the extension was concentrated among organized labor lobbyists and a hard-core group of pro-labor, farm-state, and textile-state lawmakers. They argued that the fast track would prevent Congress from amending trade agreements to protect U.S. jobs, the environment, and whole industries threatened by liberalized trade. In this initial skirmish, Bush's opposition was at a considerable disadvantage on two fronts. First, many legislators who actually opposed the U.S.–Mexican FTA were nevertheless compelled to extend fast-track authority to the chief executive in order to furnish U.S. representatives in Geneva with negotiating clout in the stormy Uruguay Round of GATT talks. At the same time, others feared that their opposition to the fast-track extension would be used to paint them as protectionist or even isolationist at a time when America was redefining its role in the world economy. In view of the opposition of many leading Democrats to Bush's Persian Gulf policy, this would lead to the perception that the Democrats were intent upon retreatism, a public view that they wanted to avoid, given the popularity of the president's activist policies in both the Persian Gulf and the Middle East as a whole.

With his opposition in disarray and hamstrung by circumstance, the president held the trump cards. On 18 May 1991, both the House Ways and Means Committee and the Senate Finance Committee overwhelmingly rejected parallel measures introduced by Representative Byron Dorgan and Senator Ernest Hollings that would have deprived the Bush administration of fast-track trade authority. One week later, Congress confirmed the committee's report, the House voting 192 to 231 against the Dorgan resolution and the Senate rejecting the Hollings resolution 36 to 59. Thus, fast-track authority was extended through 1992, providing ample time for the completion of a free trade accord with Mexico.

What sealed the victory was President Bush's "action plan." Instead of dismissing concerns about job loss, environmental consequences, and the like, Bush outlined a series of steps his administration would take to prevent or mitigate fallout from the FTA in these areas. By sweetening the FTA proposal with action-plan provisos, the president won over key Democratic leaders such as Majority Leader Richard Gephardt, House Ways and Means Committee Chairman Dan Rostenkowski, Senate Finance Committee Chairman Lloyd Bensten, and House Speaker Thomas Foley. Although a hard core of congressional opposition to the FTA was unmoved (some 60 Rust Belt Democrats worried about the "jobs" issue), fence-sitters came into line, and even stalwart supporters of organized labor began to waver.

The most politically significant plank in the action plan addressed concerns that American workers would lose jobs as industries were forced to compete with liberalized Mexican exports or as U.S. producers shifted operations to Mexico to take advantage of factor-cost advantages and shipped a portion of their output to the United States. Under the action plan, Bush promised that American workers laid off as a result of plant closings connected with the FTA would be retrained under the Economic Dislocation and Worker Adjustment Act. In an alternative put forth in the Democratic version of this FTA job cushion, such workers would be assisted through direct cash payments under the provisions of the Trade Adjustment Assistance Program. While it is not clear which form of compensation will prevail, the action plan pledged that something would be done. At the same time, the president also vowed not to negotiate any lowering of U.S. occupational health and safety regulations and to protect American consumers by refusing to accept any Mexican products that do not meet U.S. health standards.

The action plan contained another provision to help U.S. labor and industry both cope with the impact of increased competition from Mexican goods. In the event of an import surge from Mexico that threatened American industry, the provisions of the FTA would be temporarily suspended through a "snap-back" clause similar to that contained in the U.S.–Canadian FTA.

Many environmental groups initially opposed the FTA, noting that Mexico had far less stringent enforcement of pollution regulations than America and that the FTA would lead to the establishment of plants along the border that would generate unacceptable levels of air and water pollution and thus despoil the environment. While broad environmental issues will not be an integral part of the FTA negotiation, under the action plan the administration promised parallel steps to design and implement a joint U.S.–Mexican environmental plan. By promising to work with Mexico on environmental issues, to study the impact of the FTA on the border environment, and to include officials from environmental organizations in the panels advising U.S. Trade Representative Carla Hills, Bush won their cautious support.

CONTENTS

When talks do begin between representatives of the United States and Mexico (with Canadian delegates observing), at least six major issue areas must be addressed: (1) tariffs, (2) nontariff barriers (harmonization of technical standards and public procurement), (3) rules of origin, (4) antidumping provisions, (5) intellectual property protection, and (6) the status of Mexican restrictions on U.S. direct investment. In addition, several ancillary social issues will be covered in parallel talks as suggested under President Bush's action plan. These include questions concerning immigration, the environment, and narcotics.

The most straightforward facet of the U.S.–Mexican FTA will be the mutual phased reduction of tariff rates. The schedule for trade liberalization on this count will be similar to that governing the U.S.–Canadian FTA. Tariff rates on some goods already at zero will remain there, and other tariffs will come down over three, five, or ten years, depending upon the degree of anticipated dislocation. Thus, as with all barriers to trade exchanges between the two economies, it is anticipated that Mexican and U.S. tariff rates will be lowered gradually and that the longest transition periods will be granted to industries that are likely to be hurt by competition from Mexico — enterprises like fruit and vegetable production. Under the action plan, should liberalization cause too much disruption in import-substituting sectors like agriculture, a snap-back clause will allow the temporary imposition of an additional levy (or possibly a quota). This will enable producers harmed by competition to boost their competitiveness or to reduce or withdraw from product lines in which they can no longer compete.

The NAFTA accord must also address the issue of nontariff barriers. On the Mexican side, this will include the phased elimination of remaining import license requirements affecting U.S. goods. On the U.S. side, current quotas regulating textile and apparel imports from Mexico under the MFA will be relaxed and then lifted altogether. Perhaps the most difficult negotiations will concern the establishment of uniform, or at least compatible, product standards. Health and safety consumer regulations in Mexico are not as exacting as they are north of the border. Indeed, such safety features as automobile seat belts are seen by Mexican producers as "imports from neurotic cultures."[5] Reconciling these outlooks and expressing them in product standards will occupy a considerable part of the negotiating agenda at the technical level, as will the establishment of a mechanism for certification of products that meet these standards. Absent the establishment of common product standards and certification procedures, the anticipated mutual gains from tariff reduction will not be fully realized, while complaints and disputes stemming from the accord will be unnecessarily numerous and burdensome.

Another matter that will require attention are "rules-of-origin" clauses. Under anticipated local-content requirements, goods may move across the Rio Grande under the FTA only when a proportion of their value was created within Mexico or the United States. Otherwise, either country (but particularly Mexico), could function as a back door, allowing third-party multinationals (Asian direct investors, for example), to manufacture goods elsewhere, ship them to Mexico, perform some marginal finishing work upon them, and then ship them to the United States or Canada, without paying tariffs. To meet the demands of midwestern congressmen that Mexico could not become a duty-free staging area targeted at American markets for Japanese and other exporters, as part of his action plan, President Bush assured Congress that the prospective FTA with Mexico would contain a local-content requirement. With reference to automotive products, a sector in which the potential for misuse of the FTA as a back door is high, only products containing 50 percent North American production inputs would be eligible for entry into the United States without the imposition of tariffs or quotas.

Some Mexican producers have been named in antidumping suits brought by American firms in the recent past. The plaintiffs claim that Mexican producers have shipped products to the United States where they are priced at levels below those charged to Mexican distributors with the intention of unfairly competing against their U.S. rivals by using loss-leaders to expand their market shares. In a case involving the Mexican firm Cemex heard in the summer of 1990, the Mexican cement-maker was slapped with a 58 percent countervailing duty for dumping its output in the United States. The case illustrates the definitional and technical problems involved in creating protection against dumping. Cemex argued that it was selling its product in the United States at a rate equivalent to that being charged in its home market; U.S. competitors argued that the effective rate was lower since the same charges were being billed to U.S. distributors despite the added transportation costs involved in exporting the cement. The Cemex case highlights the fact that agreeing on a definition of dumping will be a knotty issue facing the FTA negotiators.

At the GATT, the United States has been especially concerned about the inadequacy of intellectual property protection in the developing world. Testifying on the proposed U.S.–Mexican free trade agreement, U.S. Special Trade Representative Carla Hills, while a strong supporter of the pact, has already expressed strong reservations about the adequacy of Mexican legal protection for patents, trademarks, copyrights, computer software, industrial designs, trade secrets, and other forms of intellectual property.[6] Prior to the announcement of preliminary work on the FTA, to avoid sanctions under the 1988 U.S. Trade Act, the Mexican government promised to extend patent protection to twenty years and to accelerate the phasing-in of expanded intellectual property protection that had been planned for full implementation by 1997. Following the release of plans for the FTA, the Salinas administration pledged its commitment to providing basic protection of intellectual property rights before the start of negotiations.

In Mexico, national oil reserves are held by the state-run enterprise PEMEX. Indeed, foreign ownership of energy resources is specifically prohibited by the Mexican constitution. When the prospect of the FTA was first raised, the issue of U.S. direct investment in PEMEX oil and gas holdings was cordoned off because it is too politically controversial to alter, and the Bush administration indicated that it would not press on this issue. After the Salinas-Bush meeting late in 1990, PEMEX received $1.6 billion from the U.S. Export-Import Bank as a "tied" concessional loan linked to PEMEX purchase of oil and gas equipment and services in the United States. Such steps may presage the fall of the current ban on U.S. participation in the exploration and development of Mexican petroleum. For their part, the Mexicans can use the "oil card" to gain U.S. concessions in other areas, but selling American participation in the core of the Mexican energy sector to his people will not be an easy undertaking for Salinas. In camera talks may occur on this front, but it is likely that substantial liberalization will take place only after other provisions of the FTA have been in place for some time.

DIRECT COMMERCIAL GAINS

From a purely commercial standpoint, the principal motive behind the proposed free trade agreement is that existing trade and direct investment flows between the two economies are already large, that they have grown by leaps and bounds during the Bush-Salinas era, and that considerably greater exchanges would take place should tariff and formal nontariff barriers be lowered or eliminated altogether.

Trade

In 1989, some $52 billion in two-way trade passed between Mexico and the United States. This flow increased to nearly $60 billion the following year, and in 1991 trade between the two reached $67 billion. American exports to Mexico are substantial. In 1989, Mexican consumers purchased goods and service valued at $26 billion, making Mexico the third largest export market for the United States and leaving Mexico accounting for about one-half of all U.S. exports to Latin America. Indeed, between 1986 and 1990, U.S. exports to Mexico more than doubled, growing from $12.4 billion in 1986 to $28.4 billion in 1990, with $34 billion as the final tally for 1991.

This surge of exports has affected all segments of U.S. shipments to its southern neighbor. Agricultural exports totaled $2.5 billion in 1990, making Mexico our third largest market for farm products. Exports of consumer goods have tripled, from $1 billion to $3 billion. Capital goods went from $5 billion in 1986 to $9.5 billion in 1990. On a per capita basis, Mexico imported $295 from the United States in 1990, compared with $266 for the European Community and just $9 for Eastern Europe.

For Mexico, the U.S. market is even more crucial. The United States still accounts for nearly 70 percent of Mexican exports. In 1990, Mexico sold some $30.2 billion in goods to the United States. Although the pace of Mexican export growth to its principal trading partner has begun to slow as the peso has appreciated, that figure is projected to rise by some 8 to 10 percent in 1991 to around $33 billion.

Although the United States experienced a modest deficit (less than $2 billion) in its trade with Mexico in 1990, that imbalance is expected to shrink as growth in U.S. exports outpaces imports. Even the current pattern of trade approximates an equilibrium that stands in sharp contrast with U.S.–Japanese trade imbalances. With U.S. purchases of Mexican oil removed from the ledger, U.S. nonoil trade has swung from a deficit of $1.2 billion in 1986 to a surplus of $2.1 billion in 1989. According to President Salinas, his administration's unilateral trade liberalization has already created thousands of jobs in the United States.[7] Using the latest rule of thumb ($1 million of net exports supports 30 jobs), one private analyst has calculated that the swing in the bilateral trade balance between 1986 and 1990 has led to the creation of more than 100,000 jobs in the United States. While developing countries in Asia tend to use their trade revenues from the United States to purchase government bonds, thereby supporting the U.S. deficit, Mexicans use their export receipts from the United States to buy U.S.-made goods and services.

Recent trends in the sectoral composition of two-way trade between United States and Mexico testify to the maturation of the latter's export sector. Between 1984 and 1988, bilateral trade exchanges of manufactured goods and services tripled. Within this category, trade in high-technology products with Mexico accounted for about 20 percent of both exports to and imports from Mexico in 1988. Communications equipment and electronic components are by far the largest category of U.S. high-tech trade with Mexico — about 50 percent of U.S. high-tech exports and 70 percent of imports. Today, mainly as a result of direct investment production and cross-border reexport, nearly 40 percent of U.S. trade in manufactures with Mexico takes place between related parties, such as subsidiaries of the same multinational corporations; and, about 70 percent of all bilateral trade is intraindustry, that is, exports and imports tend to be in the same product category.

Turning to specific industries, a large share of Mexican deliveries to the United States consists of energy. In 1989, oil and petroleum products accounted for about 16 percent of total U.S. imports from Mexico, making Mexico the fourth largest supplier of petroleum to the United States. With petroleum heading the list, in value terms the ten top U.S. imports from Mexico in 1990 were (in U.S. dollar billions):

1. crude petroleum (4.0b)
2. equipment for distributing electricity (1.5b)
3. autos (1.2b)
4. motor vehicle parts (1.1b)
5. telecommunications equipment and parts (1.0b)
6. electrical switchgear apparatus (0.9b)
7. television receivers (0.9b)
8. internal combustion engines (0.8b)
9. radio receivers (0.7b)
10. fresh/frozen vegetables (0.7b).

Except for petroleum, considerable duplication is seen in the ten top U.S. exports to Mexico in 1990:

1. motor vehicle parts (2.0b)
2. telecommunications equipment and parts (1.0b)
3. electrical switchgear apparatus (0.9b)
4. equipment for distributing electricity (0.9b)
5. cathode valves, television tubes, etc. (0.6b)
6. measuring and checking instruments (0.5b)
7. internal combustion engines (0.5b)
8. ADP parts (0.5b)
9. base-metal manufactures (0.5b)
10. corn (0.5b).

It is anticipated that after a free trade agreement is reached this same basic trading pattern, with its large component of intrasectoral and intraindustry trade, will remain in place. U.S. imports of Mexican agricultural products should rise substantially, as should Mexican purchase of U.S. petroleum technology, telecommunications wares, and antipollution devices.[9]

As is implied by the growth of U.S. exports to Mexico since 1986 and as is further detailed later in this chapter, the completion of a free trade agreement provides the United States with a means to reward the Mexicans for the trade liberalization they have undertaken to date. Testifying before the House Ways and Means Subcommittee on Trade in June 1990, Carla Hills spoke of a "sea change" in Mexico's trading regime during the late 1980s. She specifically noted that during this brief period (1) Mexico reduced its tariff rates from 100 percent to 20 percent (partially because of its entrance into the

GATT) and (2) today, the system of import licenses that the Mexican government once used to stem the flow of U.S. goods now covers only about 7 percent of all U.S. shipments to Mexico in value terms.

Nevertheless, and also arguing on behalf of a free trade arrangement, liberalization of exchanges between the United States and Mexico is not only incomplete but is far more restricted on both sides than trade between the United States and Canada before their agreement. Hence, the FTA with Mexico is likely to yield a further increase in the size and the range of bilateral trade. Better still, the United States, Canada, and Mexico are not usually direct competitors in the same products. Contrary to the arguments advanced by U.S. organized labor, a recent study by the U.S. International Trade Commission concludes that widespread increases in imports in direct competition with U.S. production would be unlikely should a NAFTA arrangement be implemented.[10]

From the U.S. standpoint, as the Mexican domestic economy recovers from its debt overhang, free access to a market that already consists of some 85 million consumers and is projected to reach 100 million by 2000 is plainly of interest. Even after the trade liberalization of the late 1980s, Mexican tariffs are still higher (10 percent on average) than the average tariff of 4 percent imposed on Mexican exports to the United States. In some product categories, Mexican tariffs are as high as 20 percent, while import licensing still affects 40 percent of U.S. agricultural shipment to Mexico. Following the Canadian–U.S. FTA pattern, remaining Mexican duties on U.S. goods would be phased out, as would NTBs like import licensing requirements. By the same token, in the absence of an agreement, Mexico would be free to raise all its tariffs to 50 percent, its GATT-bound level.

Tariff elimination will enhance U.S. competitiveness at home and abroad, providing American companies the opportunity to realize significant cost savings through economies of scale and scope. Two recent analyses by the U.S. International Trade Commission and KPMG Peat Marwick indicate that the overall impact of a North American FTA on U.S. employment would be positive.

Although the average U.S. tariff on Mexican exports is only 4 percent, Mexico could also expect to experience trade gains under the prospective FTA. The United States currently imposes NTBs in the form of quotas and outright prohibitions on some Mexican-made wares and agricultural products. Even as U.S. shipments to Mexico surged some 30 percent during the six months after the Mexican trade liberalization of 1989, Mexican deliveries to the United States rose only 8 percent in value; and growth in textiles and steel was virtually nonexistent because of U.S. quotas. Cement is another product category in which the Mexicans continue to feel the impact of U.S. protectionism. Cemex, the country's largest cement producer, has been forced to cut its shipments to the United States in half (and pay a hefty fine) as part of an antidumping judgment rendered against it on dubious grounds by the U.S. International Trade Commission.

Nowhere are U.S. restrictions on Mexican exports more comprehensive than in the agricultural sector. The United States currently bans Mexican poultry; and while Mexico grows more avocadoes than any other country, it sells none to the United States because protectionist rules favor California growers and allegations have been made that Mexican avocadoes are infested with worms.

Under an FTA, U.S. nontariff barriers to trade in steel, textiles, and cement would be reduced and gradually eliminated. As the two nations work together to establish and implement a common set of health standards, the Mexicans can anticipate that nontariff restrictions on their agricultural output will also be dismantled. While reports prepared by the United States government imply that America would be the big winner in securing free trade with Mexico, in the long term, Mexican trade gains under the FTA may be more substantial. One former Mexican cabinet minister stated in 1989 that the Americans "might accept a deal now, but not in 10 years' time because by then our industries will be able to flood their market, and not vice versa."[11]

Foreign Direct Investment

Mexico is already an important direct investment outlet for the United States. At last count (1989), the value of American direct investment was $7.1 billion, and multinationals headquartered in the United States held 62 percent of all foreign direct investment. Since 1989, anecdotal evidence suggests that both the value and the share of American direct investment has risen, the former more sharply than the latter. The big three U.S. automakers are extremely prominent—all have subsidiaries in Mexico, and there is an active trade in parts and supplies manufactured on both sides of the border. In fact, General Motors Corporation is the largest private employer in Mexico.

One important area for U.S. investment in Mexico has been the long-established *maquiladora* or in-bond industries, mostly grouped along the border, where Mexican restrictions were waived for 100 percent investment ventures. These assembly plants are often foreign-owned and produce goods for export. As of 1990, some 1,936 *maquiladoras* employed an aggregate Mexican labor force of nearly a half million. Annually, about $3 billion in trade that flows across the Rio Grande is *maquiladora* traffic.

The Mexican government established its liberalized direct-investment rules for *maquiladoras* as a temporary regime. From the Mexican standpoint, they are not an ideal form of direct investment. To begin with, they have very few linkages to the Mexican domestic economy—almost all materials and components are imported for assembly by low-wage Mexican workers and reexported to the United States. The *maquiladoras* buy 97 percent of their parts from the United States and sell next to nothing inside Mexico. At the same time, they offer only low-wage, low-skill, "screwdriver" jobs to the Mexican nationals they employ; and therefore they do little to enhance the nation's vocational skill profile.

Ironically, recent moves by the Salinas government to liberalize direct investment as a whole are likely to have an adverse impact upon the *maquiladoras*. Their success has depended on their exemption from the kind of regulated trade environment that the Salinas is now dismantling. Consequently, many observers question their future.[12] A Proctor & Gamble executive serving as CEO of that firm's Mexican subsidiary has observed, "as a result of the economic opening-up, their days are past. Anyone here can now become a *maquila* without restrictions on local sales."[13]

In the immediate future, should a free trade agreement be concluded with Mexico, U.S. direct investment will undoubtedly expand further. However, in sharp relief to the *maquiladora* pattern, new American investment is likely to display far less geographical concentration, and, much more important, to demonstrate deeper and fuller integration into the Mexican economy. As this takes place, exploitation of wage differentials by MNCs will take on progressively less importance in their FDI decisions concerning Mexico. Instead, these decisions will turn increasingly on local conditions favoring the introduction of new production technologies, on the adequacy of transportation and infrastructure, and on the existence of distribution networks on both sides of the border.

Although a U.S.–Mexican FTA will prompt greater American direct investment, the Mexican Foreign Investment Commission stated in 1989 that in the long-term Europe and Japan are also likely to expand their relative share of foreign direct investment in order to gain proximity not only to the Mexican domestic market but more crucially to the United States.[14]

The Potential for U.S. Investment in the Mexican Oil Industry

One of the principal attractions for the United States of the FTA with Mexico is that nation's substantial petroleum reserves. The state-owned oil conglomerate PEMEX has proven hydrocarbon reserves of 66.5 billion barrels, 85 percent in oil and 15 percent in natural gas. Its proven crude reserves are sufficient to maintain current production levels for more than 50 years, well above the world average. Its massive existing reserves and capital plant are worth about $45 billion, making PEMEX the fourth largest oil company and tenth largest industrial firm in the world in terms of assets. PEMEX's best customer is the United States, which buys half its crude output. Nearly half of the oil stored in the United States Strategic Petroleum Reserve was purchased under contracts with PEMEX. At the same time, in 1989 alone PEMEX and private Mexican firms purchased $1 billion-worth of oil equipment and services from U.S. suppliers.

Despite its latent wealth, PEMEX (and, indeed, the entire Mexican oil sector) suffers from idle capacity—the result of past neglect and a current lack of working capital. In response to the Iraqi invasion of Kuwait, President Salinas promised more oil shipments, but PEMEX was able to boost its export volume of 1.3 million barrels per day by only 12 percent because of production constraints. This was not a complete surprise. During the first part of 1989, PEMEX earned $4.82 billion but was obliged to spend $1 billion importing petroleum from the United States to fulfill contract requirements.

The problems besetting PEMEX are comparatively long standing. Between 1982 and 1988, as the ratio of Mexican public-sector revenue to GDP rose a minuscule 1 percent, government oil export revenues declined by 5 percent. Although sales and earnings rebounded substantially in the second half of 1989 and through 1990, PEMEX nevertheless still suffers from a triple burden: anemic investment since the early 1980s; higher taxes on energy; and internal demand for petroleum products that advances faster than its obsolete facilities can handle. The result has been a decline in reserves, production, and exports. If the current trend continues, Mexico will become a net oil importer by 2004.[15]

The Mexican oil sector accordingly seems ripe for partnership with American capital. Analyzing PEMEX's undercapitalization, one Mexican financial consultant has predicted that "eventually, PEMEX has to go on the market," joining the list of state-owned enterprises privatized or partially privatized by the Mexican government.[16]

Mexico is a major oil producer with the potential to boost both its oil output, currently 2.6 million barrels a day, and its exports to the U.S. This potential is hobbled, however, by a constitutional bar that has excluded private enterprise, Mexican or foreign, from oil exploration and production ever since Mexico nationalized oil companies, mostly American-owned in 1938.[17]

During his initial talks with President Bush, President Salinas emphasized that his country would maintain curbs on U.S. direct investment in Mexican resources. Under the aegis of the JCTI, a U.S. mission expects to invest some $3 billion on the periphery of the Mexican oil sector by 1995. This hints that Salinas may yet allow U.S. direct investment into the core of the oil sector. Some private analysts in Mexico have said that oil will be used as a bargaining chip in FTA talks.

U.S. Investment: Regionalization and Production Sharing

Despite its name, the proposed U.S.-Mexican free trade agreement is not only, or even primarily, concerned with free trade. Among other matters, it deals with the regionalization of production, notably U.S. foreign direct investment; and here its global significance becomes substantially clearer. On a technical level, however much Mexico may have liberalized its economy, there remain barriers to U.S. direct investment in some Mexican industries, such as financial services. For existing U.S.-owned entities in Mexico, performance requirements associated with investments continue to distort export opportunities for U.S. products, while local content requirements bar U.S. part suppliers from directly supplying Mexican manufacturers. Plainly, the United States has a major stake in removing these sorts of impediments to cross-border factor and product flows.

It is expected that the completion of the FTA will prompt U.S. firms to move production sites south of the border. It is also clear that the FTA would spark a second wave of U.S. investment, far beyond the investment in *maquiladoras* clustered along the border. Dozens of major manufacturers, including auto, electronics, and appliance makers, already have moved some assembly of components to the border region; and Ford Motor Co. and Chrysler Corp. even assemble complete vehicles there. Now the trend is toward more engine plants and complete supplier bases, concentrating labor-intensive operations mostly in Mexico. Economy cars, appliances, and other manufactured goods with tight margins and fierce competition will be assembled in Mexico.

For this reason, organized labor groups are in the vanguard of the opposition to the pact. However, as former Congressman Charles Vanik stated before the House Ways and Means Committee, the FTA would decidedly be the lesser of two evils. Vanik once opposed a free trade deal with Mexico because of the potential for U.S. job loss, but he now supports the treaty, since the alternative would create "incentives" for offshore sourcing in the Pacific Rim.[18] Given the production cost advantages that prevail in the Far East, U.S. firms in labor-intensive industries have little choice but to shift production there if they hope to compete in global markets. Most of the jobs lost to U.S. direct investment and offshore sourcing in the 1980s went to Asian NICs.

In light of the inexorable movement of production toward low-cost areas, the United States has an interest in influencing where the recipients of U.S. direct investment are located. Advocates of a free trade agreement with Mexico note that when U.S. direct investment money moves there it creates jobs and income in Mexico with potentially significant multiplier effects for the U.S. economy. As the Mexican economy grows, both its capacity and its propensity to purchase U.S.-made goods and services grows accordingly. As Rudiger Dornbusch has stated, U.S. "interests would be better served if production went to Mexico than if it went to Thailand or Indonesia."[19]

The Japanese have an ambivalent role in the administration's vision of Mexico after trade liberalization with the United States is completed. Mexico is now a high priority for the Japanese who are already operating sixty-five *maquiladoras*. A U.S.–Mexican FTA would only serve as a further catalyst for Japanese investment. Japanese companies are quietly stepping up operations as the free trade agreement with the United States beckons them to expand and deepen their production presence. For example, shortly after learning about the proposed FTA, executives at Nissan Motor Co. unveiled plans for a $1-billion auto-assembly plant in Aguascalientes. If local content requirements can be satisfied, cars and trucks from that facility may be shipped across the border duty-free. In light of the gains the Japanese would realize by having this "side-door" to American markets, it is by no means surprising that their government has become increasingly generous toward Mexico. On a recent visit to Mexico City, Japanese Prime Minister Toshiki Kaifu brought word of a $2.5-billion financial aid package from the Japanese Export-Import Bank.

Witnessing the growth of Japanese-Mexican ties, the Bush administration has mixed feelings. On the one hand, the United States must clearly applaud direct investment inflows to Mexico, whatever the source. The original Department of Commerce study predicted as one consequence of a U.S.-Mexican FTA that "the newly industrialized economies of the Far East would probably lose investors to Mexico."[20] In fact, the prospect of additional direct investment going to Mexico rather than the Far East is by no means unwelcome in Washington. This would slow Asian export drives aimed at the United States; and unlike Mexico, Asian NICs have little outstanding commercial or official debt to be repaid to the United States. On the other hand, the Bush administration realizes that in addition to bringing sorely needed capital to Mexico (and diverting it from the Pacific region), the Japanese will also bring their production competitiveness and acquire a staging platform from which to launch export campaigns at U.S. markets. Obviously, Washington wants U.S. companies to get the jump on the Japanese in establishing an enlarged production presence in Mexico, and a free trade agreement would further that goal.

In the broadest analytical frame, the FTA would vastly enhance the leverage of its members—the United States, Mexico, and Canada—in an increasingly regionalized world. If Mexico joins the United States and Canada to create a unified free trade area, this will lead to a single North American market with a population of over 400 million—larger than the current twelve-nation EC. With a combined economic size of $6 trillion, an American bloc would outstrip the ECs ($4.8 trillion) by about 20 to 25 percent and would add around 0.5 percent to the continent's economic growth.[21] As Richard Schulze has observed: "A united North American continent would clearly increase our leverage (with) a united Europe and with the Pacific Rim."[22] Having seen his bid for stronger trade and investment ties with the EC come to nothing, President Salinas is clearly aware that the FTA is important in a global context. On his visits to the United States and Canada, Salinas has consistently reiterated that a single North American market is necessary to offset not only the competitive advantages European producers will realize when the full effect of the EC-92 program comes into force but also the current advantages the dynamic Pacific Basin economies already possess. President Salinas bluntly stated at the 1991 Houston Summit with President Bush that

What is truly at stake is that a decision is being made as to what will happen with North America by the end of this century or the beginning of the coming century. We have to be competitive vis-à-vis Europe and the Pacific basin, and the only way of doing so is by being together. And otherwise, it is not a matter of losing jobs to Mexico but spending the rest of your life buying Japanese and European products.[23]

A U.S.-Mexican free trade agreement could also function as a pry bar in America's dealings with Japan, since the Japanese "would fear that, if it did not make accommodations, opportunities to participate fully in this huge, booming area would be diminished."[24] Finally, it would also preempt or diminish Mexico's announced alternative plan to join a planned Pacific Basin economic alliance.

The Performance of the Mexican Economy under Adjustment

The impact of adjustment can be seen in Mexico's recent economic performance. Mexican GDP rose 2.9 percent in 1989 and 2.5 percent the following year. It was expected to reach 3.0 percent when the figures for 1991 were tallied. Output growth, still negative or flat in per capita terms, has been better than expected; and all parts of the Mexican economy except agriculture and a few manufacturing industries have taken part in it, with the manufacturing sector leading the way. Even under high lending rates, gross fixed investment is growing at a double-digit pace. While high real rates of interest remain, the decline in the overall government budget deficit from 16 percent of GDP in 1987 to 4.3 percent in 1990 should reduce the crowding out of the private sector in the nation's credit markets. Inflation is still high by North American standards. While consumer prices dropped from 160 percent annual inflation in 1987 to 20 percent in 1989, a modest upward spike was experienced in 1990 as inflation reached 26.7 percent. Inflation was expected to resume a downward course in 1991 as the government reduced its domestic credit needs and the peso's value remained fairly high.

In a variation on the typical adjustment pattern of Latin America in the late 1980s and early 1990s, Mexico's trade and current account balances have not shown superior progress to domestic accounts. Even though nonoil exports grew in 1989, the current account registered a deficit of $5 billion. A goodly portion of this deterioration was the result of import inventory accumulation by firms reacting either to the novelty of import liberalization or to the belief that import liberalization measures would not be permanent. William Cline has estimated that Mexico's current account deficit will hover at about $6 billion annually during the first half of the 1990s, assuming (somewhat optimistically) that annual GDP growth rises to a level between 5 percent and 6 percent.[25]

Much to the elation of U.S. exporters, there has been a surge in Mexican imports from the United States as lower tariff rates and a more liberal trade regime has been put into place. In 1988, merchandise imports came in at $19 billion, up from $12 billion in 1987. The growth in imports, dominated by capital goods, resulted in a sharp reduction of the trade surplus to $1.8 billion in 1988. Import growth has continued as further liberalization has occurred. Since pent-up demand for U.S. goods has already been met, the rapid expansion of imports has led to public expectations that trade liberalization is exacting its toll and that sooner or later an abrupt devaluation will become necessary. In another sense, however, the results of trade liberalization have been positive. Few Mexican firms have succumbed to foreign competition, while domestic production costs were greatly lowered through reduced costs on imported production inputs and capital goods. More important, Mexico has experienced a compensatory growth in nonoil exports, helping to mitigate the growth-inhibiting effects of continued fiscal austerity.

Mexican nonoil exports have more than tripled since 1983 to nearly $15 billion, largely in manufactured goods. In 1980, only 35 percent of Mexico's exports were manufactures; but by 1990, contrary to the traditional bilateral trade pattern between a developing country and a dominant industrialized trading partner, this share had increased to 75 percent.

ADJUSTMENT GAINS

Is Mexico economically prepared to participate in a free trade agreement with the United States, and how attractive a trading and investment partner is Mexico likely to be? Toward the end of this chapter a brief summary of recent Mexican economic performance is presented. Overall, it shows an economy beginning to resume growth after a decade-long hiatus, with both trade and investment starting to pick up once again. This transitional status, however, does not answer the questions raised above. Instead, it is not so much where Mexico is today as how far it has traveled to get there that supports an affirmative answer on both points. The general trajectory of adjustment in Mexico is traced in this section, and each of the four dimensions of adjustment (internal, external, stabilization, and liberalization) is investigated in closer detail.

The General Course of Adjustment

Mexico entered the lost decade of the 1980s with every confidence that its newly found oil wealth, multiplied by OPEC's second price hike, would furnish the wherewithal to withstand any external shocks. At the start of the decade, President Lopez-Portillo contrasted the Mexican economic outlook to that of other Latin American LDCs, publicly declaring: "There are two classes of countries, those that have oil and those that don't; we have it."[26] Thus, when Mexican oil riches proved insufficient to support a bloated government budget at a time when international interest rates were soaring, his successor, Miguel de la Madrid, was compelled to hastily formulate a makeshift stabilization program and work toward a permanent alteration in development strategy. Under de la Madrid, adjustment was not a smooth process. Changing public perceptions about Mexican oil insulation from external shock required time; and in the course of de la Madrid's administration, still more shocks rocked Mexico, among them a 30 percent deterioration in terms of trade between 1983 and 1988 as global oil prices dropped. While Mexico's initial approach to adjustment was to rely upon public-sector control of the economy, after 1983 the Mexican government shifted toward structural liberalization. Even as new shocks were encountered, including a virtual shutdown in international lending to Mexico, de la Madrid stayed the course, integrating the Mexican economy with the outside world and freeing the private sector from government control. With the election of Carlos Salinas to the Mexican presidency in 1988, this process was broadened and deepened.

In August 1982, President Lopez-Portillo had stunned the international financial community by announcing that Mexico lacked the requisite foreign-exchange holdings to make its scheduled payments to commercial lenders. Although the Lopez-Portillo administration was prepared to adjust, its version of adjustment ran counter to orthodox reliance on market mechanisms and included such heterodox elements as the intensification of import controls, the use of exchange controls, and the nationalization of private Mexican banks. Paradoxically, there was little concern for the real culprit behind Mexico's economic woes at the start of the 1980s, a public sector that was too large to support itself. True, the initial adjustment strategy contained some orthodox elements, and the primary public deficit (that is, without interest payments on foreign and domestic debt) of 7.4 percent of GDP in 1982 was converted into a primary surplus of 4.2 percent by 1983. This was accomplished by a sharp cut in public-sector investment, since it was easier for the government to slash capital expenditures than to cut operating outlays. As for current expenses, they were protected by political considerations, chiefly the political fallout that was bound to occur if public employment were pared or consumption subsidies reduced. Thus, despite a sharp cut in the overall budget deficit, the losses of the inefficient state-owned enterprises combined with repayment pressures from domestic and foreign debt led the Lopez-Portillo government to follow an inflationary path to adjustment.

By 1983, with Mexican GDP dropping some 4.2 percent, Mexico could not grow its way out of its current account squeeze since a positive transfer of resources to foreign lenders was required, even under rescheduled debt repayment schedules. The only place from which this could be obtained was the trade account. Rather than create incentives to expand exports, de la Madrid's initial approach was to erect barriers to imports. Thus, instead of becoming more outward oriented, as orthodox adjustment theory recommends, Mexico chose the short-run solution of further regulating market exchanges with other nations, particularly the United States.

At the start of 1984, government-induced recession was leading to popular unrest, and the de la Madrid regime allowed some reflation of the domestic economy. A vicious cycle arose: monetization of the government's domestic debt crowded private investment out of credit markets; in order to provide some liquidity, the government engaged in still more credit creation. In this manner, the government delayed a domestic liquidity crisis, but its international reserves were drained. Interest rates were forced up sharply as the government issued expensive domestic debt to repay relatively cheap foreign debt obligations; the peso appreciated; and domestic inflation continued upward.

In the second half of 1985, the shortcomings of this improvised approach created an impasse. The government could no longer raise dollars from the private sector by offering abnormally high interest rates on still more public debt offerings. De la Madrid instituted serious fiscal and monetary austerity measures at this time, but it was perhaps more important that he advocated the first measures in what would become the liberalization of the Mexican trade regime. The government found that its drive to compress imports through administrative mechanisms actually undermined export expansion, notably by raising the cost of both the capital goods and the intermediate inputs required for the production of tradeables. It also found that using a fixed exchange rate to curb inflation was self-defeating. Although high positive interest rates helped maintain an overvalued currency, ultimately confidence in the peso plummeted; and by 1985, every indication was that the day of reckoning was at hand.

In September 1985, a different kind of shock literally rocked Mexico and figuratively shocked its adjustment program. A massive earthquake devastated the capital city. To deal with the immediate costs of the disaster, the government was forced to abandon its fiscal stabilization objectives. It nevertheless continued its liberalization program in the nation's external sector. A year later, an external shock rippled through the Mexican economy as Saudi Arabia flooded world oil markets and sent Mexican oil prices into a tailspin. By the end of 1986, the government had engineered a real devaluation of 30 percent; and under these circumstances, further trade liberalization was deferred.

Recovery began across the board in 1987 as international oil prices moved up. During that year, the central bank accumulated almost $7 billion in foreign reserves, and the condition of Mexican business improved. Ironically, the immediate problem became the overheating of the domestic economy. As inflation rose once again, the Mexican exchange rate was used as an inflation-dampening device. This course showed its shortcomings throughout the year: an overvalued peso inhibited Mexican nonoil exports and did little good in holding prices down. The collapse of the American stock market in 1987 exacerbated this situation as the main export market for Mexican goods weakened substantially. Moreover, although the terms of a debt rescheduling plan with foreign banks covering private Mexican debt offered a repayment bargain (with a 1988 deadline) they brought a sharp rise in private demand for credit.

Under these circumstances, President de la Madrid took a bold step that became a political watershed in Mexican economic adjustment. His government, along with representatives of business and labor, entered into an economic solidarity pact in December 1987. This agreement contains a mutual acknowledgment that orthodox adjustment, including both stabilization and liberalization measures, is necessary for the long-term well-being of the national economy. In exchange for this endorsement, the government allowed that certain heterodox components like wage-price freezes, may be necessary from time to time to cushion policy impacts, reverse public expectations, and the like. While the broad course of Mexican development must adhere to the straight and narrow road of reliance upon the free play of market forces upheld by government discipline, negotiated temporary deviations from this path were permitted.

Each of the four dimensions of adjustment under President Salinas is examined in the following section. Under his administration, the restructuring of the national economy initiated by de la Madrid has been intensified and deepened. Salinas's first comprehensive economic program, covering 1989–1992, places particularly strong emphasis on domestic stabilization policies. Salinas has obtained an extension of the economic solidarity pact and, congruent with its spirit, has employed an income policy to break inertial inflation. Indeed, the four dimensions of adjustment as they now stand suggest that the progress achieved in the 1980s is being used as a platform for further gains in the 1990s by the Salinas government.

External Stabilization

In terms of external stabilization, Mexican foreign debt is obviously the most crucial component. In handling outstanding external obligations, the Mexican government adopted a succession of stances toward its creditors, none as confrontational in its approach as that of Peru under Garcia or of Brazil under Sarney. Until Mexico completed its 1989–1990 Brady Plan agreement, the repayment of its foreign debt was in some doubt. Today, it is almost certain that Mexico's reduced foreign debt will be serviced as scheduled. At the same time, for Mexico to meet its external financing needs, new sources of capital must be tapped. The lenders of the past, however, particularly international commercial banks, remain reluctant to furnish the Mexican government with fresh loans.

After experiencing balance-of-payments difficulties in 1976, the Mexican economy rebounded in the 1978–1981 period, with prices rising on energy exports and oil production expanding in response. Unfortunately, the oil bonanza stimulated a vast expansion in public-sector spending which, coupled with recession in developed-country export markets, created large fiscal and current-account imbalances. These were initially financed by foreign borrowing from commercial banks, with net external public debt rising by $20 billion, or 60 percent, in 1981 alone. Prior to the Brady Plan workout of 1989–1990, the nominal amount of Mexican external debt remained fairly constant at around $100 billion, $70 billion of it from banks, most of that being medium- and long-term bank credits (a portion of these were originally short term, transmuted into lengthier maturities in successive reschedulings).

In 1982, when Mexican President Lopez-Portillo told the world that his nation would be indefinitely suspending payments on principal to foreign banks, the latter insisted that his government turn to the International Monetary Fund for conditional adjustment financing. Mexico did just that, entering into an extended IMF arrangement late in 1982 for the years 1983 through 1985. The existence of an IMF program for Mexico cleared the way for its rescheduling of debt with both the banks and official credit sources. The IMF program called for fiscal discipline, liberalization of exchange controls, and a large initial devaluation of the peso followed by frequent adjustments in the exchange rate. Some improvement was registered, but within little more than a year, Mexico fell out of compliance with its IMF program. While the de la Madrid government continued to make interest payments on both official and commercial loans, the mid-1980s saw a virtually complete shutdown on new credits. A stalemate ensued, with very little change taking place in Mexico's debt status between 1985 and 1988.

Early in 1988, the Mexican government, with the help of Morgan Guaranty, sought a major conversion of existing debt into the alternative payment instrument of bonds. Mexico drew down on the reserves it had accumulated in 1987 to purchase zero-coupon U.S. Treasury securities. It used the Federal "zeros" as a credit enhancement to back the principal of the bonds it issued in exchange for debt. While Mexico converted $3.6 billion into $2.5 billion in new bonds, for a modest debt-service savings, sales of the enhanced Mexican bonds were much smaller than expected, presumably because the interest payments were not guaranteed and the promise to pay interest on the bonds was no more credible than the promise to pay interest on the debt. On its own, Mexico might chip away at its outstanding debt and reduce its debt service through such transactions; but its capacity to purchase credit enhancement was limited, as was the willingness of the banks to discount old debt for new. Mexico entered into a formal rescheduling agreement with its bank creditors, but this plan was criticized for the meager concessions it granted to the debtor.

The Morgan-assisted debt conversion had fallen short of the mark, and Mexico's 1988 rescheduling with the banks had been a disappointment. Plainly something more comprehensive and radical was required. In the first few months of 1989, the newly elected Salinas government pressed for a multiyear financing package with the commercial banks that would involve debt and debt-service reduction operations large enough to produce a substantial decline in the country's external debt. Bank steering committees were willing to enter into a new round of talks, and the sessions were scheduled for the spring of 1989. Just how fruitful the restructuring could be—coming on the heels of 1988's disappointing experience—was questionable.

At that moment, and by no means by coincidence, the Mexican debt outlook brightened considerably with the announcement of the Brady Plan in March 1989. Formal negotiations were initiated with the bank creditors in April 1989. In the following month, the IMF approved a three-year extended arrangement to provide support for debt and debt-service reduction operations. Shortly after the IMF accord, Paris Club official creditors agreed to reschedule $2.6 billion in debt service falling due between 1989 and 1991, while the World Bank approved structural adjustment loans of almost $2 billion and, in January 1990, an additional $1.26 billion for financing debt and debt-service operations. In all, some $7 billion was required for enhancing the debt exchanges under the 1989–1990 workout, with the IMF, the World Bank, and the Export-Import Bank of Japan chipping in about $2 billion each and the remainder coming from Mexico's own foreign-exchange reserves.

With this $7 billion in hand, the Mexican government took steps to provide commercial bank creditors with enhancements, in the form of payment guarantees backed by thirty-year U.S. Treasury zero-coupon bonds, for all principal obligations on debt converted into bonds, as well as a rolling guarantee for part of the interest stream. Should Mexico meet all contractual payments on the bonds or retire them prior to maturity, the accrued value of these zero-coupon bonds would accrue back to Mexico. Armed with these resources, Mexico reached an agreement in principle with its bank lenders on 23 July 1989.

This brief synopsis may imply that the 1989–1990 plan worked like a charm, with each party faithfully carrying out its assigned role as envisioned by the Mexicans and Secretary Brady. But the agreement of July 1989 was reached with the fifteen-member bank advisory committee, and the task of getting each of the 540 banks owed money by Mexico to choose one of the three options proved arduous. Indeed, even coming to an understanding with the fifteen-member steering committee required substantial arm-twisting on the part of the United States government, which was intent upon carrying out the debut of the Brady Plan. In fact, none of the banks that took part in the Mexican Brady Plan treatment was pleased with any of the three main options on the menu. They reckoned that if they all chose the bond option, it would be equivalent to a subsidy for Mexico of some $15 billion.[27]

The Mexican negotiators solved the "free rider" problem of individual bank lenders refusing to extend new money but benefiting from an improvement in Mexican credit standing by insisting that creditors who did not take part in the accord would lose everything. In effect, Mexico refused to honor the old loans: the bankers either accepted one of the three options offered or lost their money. Mexico was able to get away with this step only because it had the backing of the U.S. government and other official creditors. In the end, the Mexican government was not thrilled with the result. The debt and debt-service reduction was significantly less than it had sought. As for new money, Angel Gurria, chief Mexican debt negotiator, originally insisted on $4.5 billion in new money from the banks; later he revised this figure down to $2 billion; ultimately, Mexico received less than $1 billion in new loan commitments.

Under Mexico's Brady Plan treatment, creditor banks were given three financing options:

1. An exchange of claims for thirty-year discount bonds (at 65 percent of face value) carrying a market interest rate (with a spread of 0.8125 percent over the London Interbank Offered Rate [LIBOR]), full guarantee of principal to be paid back in one installment after thirty years, and eighteen months guarantee on interest;
2. conversion of claims into thirty-year par bonds with below-market fixed interest rates (6.25 percent) and the same maturity and guarantee structure as that of the discount bonds; or,
3. provision of net "new money" (i.e., new loan facilities) for 1989–1992 amounting to 25 percent of eligible claims, repayable over fifteen years, including 7 years' grace.

As a concession to the banks, the package incorporated a new $3.5-billion debt-equity program and a "value recovery clause" that enables them to receive higher payments from Mexico if, starting in 1996, oil prices exceed the threshold level of $14 a barrel after adjusting for inflation.

After almost a year of negotiations, Mexican representatives signed the first comprehensive debt relief package under the Brady Plan debt strategy on 4 February 1990. The final package covered $48 billion of Mexico's $95 billion in external indebtedness (as of end 1989). However, the banks' choices from among the options available to them were far different from those envisioned by the Mexican negotiating team. Only Mexico's largest commercial creditor, Citibank, opted to furnish Mexico with new loans to satisfy its obligations under the workout. Virtually all the other U.S. banks, large money-market-center institutions and regionals alike, along with the Japanese and European banks, opted for an immediate "hit" on principal (option 1) or interest payments (option 2). All told, the 1989–1990 Brady Plan treatment cut Mexican debt by some $15 billion (16 percent of Mexico's external debt), but because Mexico must repay the IMF, IBRD, and the Export-Import Bank of Japan for their stake (about $5.7 billion in concessional loans), real net debt reduction amounted to about $10 billion. As for annual debt service, it was cut by nearly 15 percent, that is, about $4 billion a year between 1989 and 1994.[28]

Reviewing the outcome, many independent observers were critical of the

Brady Plan debut. Debt had been cut by just about 10 percent, debt-service by little more than 15 percent, new money commitments fell far short of expectations, and the package included a debt-equity swap program about which the Mexicans were none too keen, given that they are still in the midst of a stabilization drive. Others saw the agreement in a more positive light. William Cline, for example, noted that the banks actually met Mexico two-thirds of the way (35 percent debt or interest reduction versus an original request of 55 percent; or new money refinancing 60 percent of interest versus an original request of 80 percent).[29] Cline has also stated that holding out for better terms would have yielded little additional debt relief and risked an outright break with the banks. There were fears that creditors would capture the lion's share of the gains from debt conversion. Before the deal, the debt covered by the package traded at $19 billion on the secondary market; but after the deal, it was worth between $19.1 billion and $19.9 billion. This suggests that most of the debt-relief money went to Mexico rather than the banks.

But the true value of the Brady treatment for Mexico cannot be judged on the basis of the rescheduling exercise's outcome in a narrow context. While Mexico's annual debt service was reduced by no more than $4 billion, the completed deal proved a tonic for the Mexican private sector and general confidence in the Mexican economy. Two important events took place as the Brady Plan treatment took effect. First, interest rates on Mexican debt issues and domestic bank loans dropped in nominal terms by some 8 percent to 13 percent. Second, after the announcement of the package, some $10 billion in Mexican flight capital was repatriated. In addition, the completion of the commercial debt reduction package set the stage for a major restructuring of debt payments owed by Mexico to the official creditors of the Paris Club. Taking all this into account, there can be little doubt that Mexico is in much better shape in terms of its external stabilization goals today than it was before it underwent Brady Plan treatment.

Even with debt-service reductions and $1 billion in new money coming to Mexico by virtue of the Citicorp commitment, in the foreseeable future, Mexico will be paying out far more to its commercial bank creditors than it will receive from them. This by no means is a departure from the general pattern of the lost decade. Between 1985 and 1989, new financing from Mexico's commercial bank creditors was less than 20 percent of that nation's interest payments to them. Mexico may also enjoy some reduction in official debt service and even some fresh bilateral or multilateral assistance. But Mexico has about reached its IMF and World Bank borrowing ceilings, and the net transfer of funds between Mexico and concessional lenders is also likely to be outward. Given that foreign direct investment will not generate a large usable stream of tax revenue and that unassisted debt conversions on the secondary market carry substantial drawbacks in an economy characterized by inflation and domestic debt, the question naturally becomes one of where Mexico will get the foreign exchange to meet its remaining debt repayment needs.

Part of the answer lies in the trade account, but this sector cannot be expected to generate $6 billion to $7 billion a year, the amount Mexico will need to meet its current-account requirements. Two other sources of external capital may play a stronger part: the international capital markets and the continued repatriation of flight capital.

Some private Mexican firms have been able to raise foreign exchange loans quite readily. In 1990, for example, Cemex successfully issued a convertible Eurobond offering of $100 million through its subsidiary, Sunbelt Enterprises. A year later, Cemex had increased its Eurobond offering to $425 million to meet market demand. PEMEX was also able to tap the Eurobond market in the wake of Mexico's Brady Plan agreement, becoming the first agency of the Mexican government to return to voluntary international capital markets.

External Liberalization

From the external restructuring of the Mexican economy, it is evident that a wholesale change has taken place in its stance of exchanges with the outside world as a whole and the United States in particular. In 1982, the weighted-average tariff stood at around 25 percent and nearly all product categories were covered by import permit requirements or official import prices. Moreover, decades of protectionism allowed, and perhaps even provoked, a number of trade practices that eventually became codified in both written and unwritten rules. Although profitable for some, these rules caused inefficiencies in many industries, notably trucking, finance, and petrochemicals.

Change began to occur in 1985 with the implementation of trade liberalization measures that were kept in place despite the external shocks that followed. In 1986, Mexico took a major step toward permanent trade liberalization by becoming a GATT signatory. Since joining the GATT, Mexico has lowered tariffs from nearly 25 percent in 1985 to about 10 percent in 1991. Even more important, Mexico under Salinas has reduced import tariffs *unilaterally,* that is, beyond its GATT obligations and without compensatory tariff reductions by its trading partners. Once almost impenetrable, Mexico's NTBs have also been lowered or dismantled in their entirety. By 1987, import licensing applied to less than 20 percent of goods, while official import prices were eliminated altogether. However, some tariff and NTB hurdles to increased U.S.–Mexican trade remain. In some product categories, high tariffs persist; and in others, quotas remain in place. Particularly vexing are Mexican local-content requirements which effectively inhibit trade flows from the United States in such areas as pharmaceuticals and electronic hardware.

Many Mexican observers feel that unilateral liberalization of trade under de la Madrid and Salinas has gone too far and too fast.[30] As Mexico has loosened its trade regime, especially under Salinas, the economy has sucked in imports from the United States. The pace of Mexican trade liberalization may have been intended to mobilize an export lobby within Mexico that would support still more trade reforms. At the same time, there can be little doubt that the current rate of trade liberalization has been part of an effort by the Salinas government to convince the United States of its commitment to free trade in general. Mexico has bent over backwards to provide an inviting atmosphere for the U.S. commercial interests. Clearly, U.S. exporters have benefited from this relaxation of constraints on their products. However, if Salinas has been playing to the United States on the trade front, he cannot be especially pleased at the audience response. In 1989, after the latest round of Mexican tariff and NTB cuts, Mexican exports to the United States increased by only 8 percent. In certain sectors, notably textiles and steel, American reciprocation has been frustratingly slow in coming.

Complementing liberalization of trade, in 1989 Mexico instituted major changes in its rules for foreign investment, providing greater transparency, increased foreign participation, and greater efficiency in the application process. These reforms offered foreign investors access to previously protected and highly profitable areas such as telecommunications, chemicals, and even the Mexican stock market. A year later, the Salinas administration moved still further, allowing non-Mexicans to own 100 percent of enterprises valued up to $100 million without prior approval from the National Foreign Investment Commission if certain conditions on location and net foreign exchange needs are satisfied. On proposed projects larger than $100 million, the approval of the commission is still required, but the commission must issue a ruling within forty-five days. There are still some significant barriers stemming from the remnants of Mexico's highly restrictive 1973 FDI law. As noted earlier, the Salinas government has insisted that foreign capital be kept from energy exploration and production activities, while Mexican local-content requirements in some sectors act to deny U.S. part suppliers the opportunity to deal directly with Mexican manufacturers.

Part of the direct investment boom has stemmed from a formal debt-equity swap program set up by the de la Madrid government in 1987. This program was suspended by Mexico a year later. Initial analysis suggested that the decision to end the program was based on the potential inflationary impact of large-scale debt-equity swaps on the Mexican economy, but many observers now believe that the program was ditched because the government wanted the plan it preferred — the Morgan zero-interest bond plan — to have no competition.[31] Approaching the Brady Plan workout, Mexico's foreign bankers expressed irritation with the Salinas administration's current cool attitude toward swaps. They pressed for and got a new program with a total value of $3.5 billion. This proved extremely attractive to foreign investors seeking a debt-equity swap bargain. When the government auctioned $1 billion in swap rights in July 1990, the offering met with almost $20 billion in bids. Clearly, the Salinas government is more reluctant than its predecessor to stimulate FDI with swaps, preferring foreign equity investments at market rather than debt-discount value.

In order to maintain trade and direct investment liberalization and keep Mexican products competitive on world markets, Mexico has been compelled to do what many other indebted LDCs have been most loath to do—devalue its national currency. Trade liberalization during the 1980s was accompanied by large devaluations aimed at maintaining external competitiveness. Today, Mexico's real exchange rate is at least 20 to 25 percent more competitive than it was at the start of the decade.[32]

Two potential problems could eventually lead to a need for a further realignment of the peso. First, an undervalued peso contributes to inflation by effectively raising both the cost of imported goods, including capital equipment and intermediate inputs, and the cost of servicing external debt. Hence, there is a crucial tradeoff between competitiveness and domestic inflation. Second, although domestic interest rates have fallen since the Brady Plan accord, they are still high in real terms. As investors shift to the peso to take advantage of these rates, the cross-currency value of the peso necessarily increases. In the near term, an overvalued peso makes U.S. imports a bargain for consumers, but in the long run, it could serve to undermine Mexican adjustment and threaten the buoyancy of the Mexican economy as an export outlet.

Domestic Stabilization

The structural liberalization of the Mexican external sector has been accompanied by stabilization and structural reform in Mexico's domestic economy. In terms of fiscal balance, the public sector has been pared down dramatically since the start of the debt crisis. Many state-owned enterprises have been privatized, and productive activities still in government hands have become far more efficient. The massive budget deficit that Mexico registered at the start of the debt crisis has been transformed into a primary fiscal surplus equal to 8 percent of GDP. Under de la Madrid, noninterest government spending dropped from 37 percent of GNP in 1981–1982 to 27 percent in 1986–1987. All this has taken place under adverse circumstances, such as the external shock of rapid declines in the price of oil on global markets in 1986.

Adjustment in other parts of the Mexican economy has in some instances assisted the goal of fiscal closure. For example, the substitution of tariffs for quantitative trade restrictions boosted central government revenues. In other instances, pursuit of fiscal stabilization has been impaired by structural liberalization, as the freeing of interest rates increased both the size of the domestic debt and the cost of servicing it. Thus, while there was a surplus in the primary budget of the central government in 1988, the operational deficit (with interest payments factored in) deteriorated from a surplus equal to 1.8 percent of GDP in 1987 to a deficit of 3.5 percent in 1988. During 1988, real interest payments on public domestic debt were about twice those paid on foreign debt, even though the former is worth only half as much as the latter. To meet both external and domestic obligations without monetizing its debt, the central government must maintain a primary surplus of 6 to 7 percent of GDP. Assuming reasonable access to foreign funds (i.e., just enough to keep the real value of the foreign debt constant) a public-sector surplus of this magnitude would give the Salinas government the margin it needs to service its foreign and domestic debts without resorting to inflationary financing.[33]

The sharp cuts in public expenditures demanded by fiscal adjustment have led to deterioration in Mexico's physical infrastructure and neglect of social welfare. By the end of the 1980s, Mexican public investment was at its lowest level since World War II. The effects of putting off investment in infrastructure can be seen in the deterioration of highways, water systems, telecommunications, ports, and the like. This neglect, of course, hampers private-sector efficiency and productivity gains and tends to deter additional foreign direct investment. At the same time, antipoverty programs and other types of social expenditure, particularly in health and education, have been sorely neglected. On both counts, an economic cost is about to come due; and with regard to welfare outlays, a social and political bill also looms increasingly large.

Although considerable room for improvement remains, Mexico has made great strides in cutting domestic inflation. At start of the debt crisis, the Mexican inflation rate was 100 percent a year, and little progress was made to reduce it until the economic solidarity pact of 1987, which immediately generated favorable results. In a few months, inflation dropped from 7 percent a month to 1 percent a month. The objective of stable prices was furthered by the Brady Plan, which helped reduce consumer uncertainty.

To accomplish their fiscal goals, the de la Madrid and Salinas governments have expanded the nation's tax base—reducing loopholes, tightening enforcement, and bringing new sectors into its fold. Tax reform was undertaken in 1987 and accelerated in 1989 and 1990 by significant expansion of base and a reduction in marginal tax rates. The most significant of these measures was a complementary tax on corporate assets first introduced in 1989, establishing a lower bound for corporate tax liabilities. The effect was to eliminate some important loopholes and to increase corporate income tax revenues by more than 30 percent during the first half of 1989. This was accomplished even as corporate tax rates were reduced from 40 percent to about 36 percent. The government has also reformed the personal income tax, reducing the top rate from 50 percent in 1986 to 35 percent in 1991. Here there has been strong emphasis on enforcement. As Mexican tax authorities have observed, between 1921 and 1988 Mexico put just two tax evaders in jail, whereas under Salinas, the new tax collector has already imprisoned forty.

Domestic Liberalization

The domestic economy has also undergone considerable structural reform in the related areas of financial liberalization, privatization of state-owned enterprises, and general deregulation of the economy. Throughout the 1980s, Mexicans learned that interest rates cannot be kept negative in real terms, and since the failure at administering domestic interest rates in 1985, rate determination has taken place through market mechanisms. In March 1989, the process of liberalization was completed when the Salinas government eliminated all controls on bank-deposit and lending rates. The 1989 reform was helped along by the prospect of a major foreign-debt rescheduling and comprehensive debt and debt-service reductions under Mexico's Brady Plan treatment. In 1989, nominal interest rates declined by between 8 and 13 percent after the announcement of the July accord, leading to a 40 percent drop in total interest charges paid by the government on its domestic debt. As with inflation, Mexico still has some way to go on this front. With one-month commercial debt paper still paying about 20 percent a year, the cost of funds to investors remains high.

Emblematic of the turnabout in Mexico's economic thinking is the extensive privatization that has taken many SOEs out of the public sector. The change is more significant because the Mexican government cultivated a socialist image for nearly half a century, making privatization politically risky. The policy of privatization has, in fact, undermined the dominant Popular Revolutionary Party's (PRI's) power base and its range of instruments for political mobilization. The ongoing divestiture of state-owned companies is in itself a reflection of a new conception of the state's role in the economy, a more pragmatic line of thinking that favors an active but streamlined role for government.

Although a few individual cases of privatization have received much publicity, the growth of this trend can be seen in the fact that of the 1,155 entities owned by the government at the beginning of 1983, only 350 remained in the public sector by 1990. Critics have cautioned that there is less here than meets the eye, that many nominal divestitures entailed liquidation, transfer to state or local government, or merger with other state-owned enterprises.[34] The government has responded that the biggest privatizations have had to be deferred until the economy was in better shape. In fact, recent divestitures, which have targeted some of the biggest SOEs, have been true transfers to the private sector. These included the partial privatization of the national telephone company, Telmex. After the government sold about half its stake in Telmex to private investors, operating revenue for the first nine months of 1990 increased by 63 percent, creating more favorable conditions for the government to sell the rest. The international capital markets responded favorably. In May 1991, the privatization of Telmex was completed as it issued $2 billion in shares abroad that investors bought up rapidly. In addition, under 1990's privatization campaign, regulations affecting the petroleum sector were altered to allow some private domestic capital participation in activities previously reserved to PEMEX. The most important and dramatic privatization move in symbolic terms occurred in May 1990, when the Mexican Congress approved a constitutional amendment that returned two-thirds of the equity in eighteen banks nationalized in 1982 to private hands. The sale will eventually generate $6 billion earmarked for housing, education, recreation, health, and other social needs. Just as important, this move represents a clean break from policy at the start of the debt crisis and a further step in the direction of financial and interest rate liberalization.

Efficiency gains under privatization can be garnered only if divestiture is accompanied by deregulation. Here Mexico has also accomplished much. Measures to remove barriers to entry into certain sectors and to promote a more competitive business framework on the whole have been rapidly introduced, with some impressive results. At one time, through a labyrinth licensing arrangement, fifteen families controlled the Mexican trucking industry. Exemplary deregulation opened up the trucking industry, dispersed ownership, and increased effective trucking capacity by about 10 percent overnight. Similarly, as a result of the reclassification of petrochemical products, private firms are now allowed to perform functions formerly reserved for PEMEX. This has resulted in several billion dollars in badly needed investment capital flowing into the nation's energy sector.

POLITICAL GAINS

According to long-time Mexico-watcher Riordan Roett, "Salinas has made some very daring assumptions about the rebuilding of relations with the United States — he's putting his eggs in one basket. . . . The Bush administration will have to show [that] its political commitment to Mexico is backed by financial resources, otherwise it will go up in flames."[35] To economist James K. Galbraith, the central purpose of pact is primarily to stabilize Salinas and reinforce the structural changes going on in the Mexican economy.[36] The Bush administration has backed the FTA with Mexico and solidly supported the current Mexican regime in order to maintain the free-market orientation of the Mexican economy. Since President Salinas is constitutionally limited to a single term, a free trade agreement would strengthen his market-oriented reforms and virtually eliminate the possibility that his successor, who will take office late in 1994, could dismantle them. Thus, independent of Mexico's substantial adjustment and modestly improved economic performance, a free trade agreement with the United States will influence, and in turn be influenced by, developments within the Mexican political scene. President Salinas is committed both to the continuation of free-market adjustment and a trade pact with America, while the Bush administration sees a free trade agreement as vital both to Salinas's political fortunes and to prospects for further adjustment south of the Rio Grande.

Salinas was fortunate in being the PRI candidate in the 1988 Mexican presidential election. He benefited from his PRI predecessor de la Madrid's successful negotiation of the economic solidarity pact and from its positive effect on the Mexican economy. Nevertheless, Salinas won the 1989 election from his nearest rival, Cuauhtemoc Cardenas of the left-wing Party of the Democratic Revolution, by only a slight margin, with many political opponents charging that the difference between the two was the result of PRI electoral fraud. Cardenas remains very much a force on the Mexican political scene, campaigning in state and local elections held in the summer of 1991 on an anti-free trade platform and calling for a reversal in the liberalization of the Mexican economy through a return to the nationalist economic policies of the past.

The Mexican public's perception of Salinas's style may ultimately undermine both his political power and the prospects for a free trade agreement. Salinas is viewed by many of his countrymen as an authoritarian figure, bent upon imposing his free-market vision of Mexico, including a trade pact with the United States, independent of popular opinion. As a rule, Salinas has responded to public pressure for political reforms with incremental changes. In the now commonplace analogy, he has emphasized *perestroika* before *glasnost*. Moreover, campaigning as a populist, Salinas jilted organized labor in favor of the nation's wealthy industrialists. Many on the left of the Mexican political spectrum see Salinas as a yuppie with a Ph.D. from Harvard surrounded by an Ivy League–educated clique of advisors.

As has been the case during the last several decades during which the PRI has remained in power, perennial charges of fraud have followed Salinas, both concerning his own election and concerning balloting for state offices since then. These charges are now being echoed by opponents of the proposed FTA in the United States, and such criticism could embolden President Salinas's domestic foes and test the depth of his commitment to social justice and fairer voting procedures. It is ironic that the strength of Salinas's party has been reduced by the adjustments it has carried out, since opportunities for patronage appointments and special government favors have declined with the contraction of the state's economic apparatus.

Salinas's greatest challenges are caught up with the future of the Mexican economy and of the FTA with the United States. He has led Mexicans to expect a tidal wave of foreign investment and growth once the free-trade deal is in the works. Anticipating this, the Mexican stock market soared during the first few months of 1989. Salinas promised a return to vigorous growth after the Brady Plan agreement was in place. While some progress is in evidence, the results have yet to trickle down to the man in the street. This in turn has undercut the credibility of the glowing promises of economic gain that have accompanied President Salinas's public relations campaign on behalf of the FTA. If the pact fails to materialize, Salinas could find himself in major trouble with the Mexican electorate. Equally worrisome, if the FTA is put into place and its results fall substantially short of public expectations, not only Salinas but the FTA and Mexico's adjustment drive as a whole could be undone or reversed by a nationalist successor.

Parallelism in the Bush Action Plan

The parallelism of the Bush action plan refers to talks on increased cooperation between the two countries in such areas as the environment, immigration, narcotics, electoral reform, and human rights protection. Presumably, not only would U.S.-Mexican FTA talks demand some further action on these fronts and serve as an incentive for Mexico (and, to a lesser extent, for the United States) to undertake unilateral policy measures in these crucial "intermestic" areas, they would also facilitate permanent institutional linkages between the two nations to deal with these shared problems. In addition, by strengthening the economic ties joining the United States with Mexico, a free trade treaty could magnify the need for further policy coordination. The following sections examine in greater detail the strong interests shared by the United States and Mexico in the fields of immigration policy, environmental protection, the enforcement of narcotics laws, the enhancement of human rights, and the management of a flight capital reflux from the United States back to Mexico that is already under way.

Immigration

Just as Mexico removed the issue of U.S. direct investment in its energy sector from the negotiating agenda, the United States has insisted that so-called "labor exports," that is, totally free immigration from Mexico to the United States, will not be on the FTA agenda. In fact, one of the factors accounting for U.S. opposition to the FTA is undoubtedly the prospect of unlimited migration across the Rio Grande. This issue has nevertheless played a part in the preliminary campaign for a U.S.-Mexican FTA. On the one hand, President Salinas has noted that absent a free trade agreement with the United States depressed economic conditions in Mexico would prompt more workers to cross the border illegally. This, of course, creates a secondary incentive to reach an accord that will contribute to the well-being of the Mexican economy. At the same time, there are now more than twenty million Hispanic-Americans in the United States, making them the fastest-growing ethnic and cultural group in the country. About half of public school students in Los Angeles County and in four southwestern states are of Latino origin; and Hispanic voters in California, Texas, and Florida already exercise strong influence on political decisions.[37] The large number of Hispanic-American voters in the United States serves as a strong nucleus of support for a U.S.-Mexican FTA both in the preliminary stages and when the final pact is brought before Congress for approval sometime between 1993 and 1995.

The Environment

The environment is an ancillary area that will spill over into the proposed FTA negotiations and affect their reception in the legislatures of both nations. Prior to the announcement of the action plan, many environmental groups in the United States opposed an FTA with Mexico. They warned that Mexico had far less stringent enforcement of pollution regulations and that the FTA would lead to the establishment of plants along the border that would generate unacceptable levels of air and water pollution and despoil the environment. Only by promising to work with Mexico on these concerns, to study the impact of the FTA on the border environment, and to include officials from environmental organizations in the panels advising U.S. Trade Representative Carla Hills could President Bush win their cautious support.

On the Mexican side, the Salinas administration helped Bush by improving Mexico's environmental image. In preparation for the U.S.-Mexican FTA, the government increased the budget of SEDUE (a Mexican environmental agency) some sevenfold in 1991 and simultaneously announced a five-year program to reduce pollution in Mexico City. It carried a pricetag of $2.5 billion, a projected cost later increased to $4.6 billion. Named as one of Mexico's worst polluters, PEMEX has also shown willingness to come to grips with the pollution issue. It is now committed to a program of processing petroleum, gas, and petrochemicals in a cleaner, more efficient manner and has budgeted an additional $3 billion toward that end. In its plans to upgrade its environmental record, PEMEX has been under strong pressure from the central government. In March 1991, without previous planning, Salinas shut down Mexico City's oil refinery (the largest single source of industrial pollution) at a cost of $500 million and 5,000 jobs. Mexico's *maquiladora* assembly lines represent another environmental sore spot. Indeed, critics charge that one reason for U.S. direct investment in this reexport conclave is to circumvent far more stringent U.S. environmental laws.[38] Should some *maquiladoras* survive their loss of competitive advantages under a program of general direct-investment liberalization, their costs are bound to rise as the Mexican government also applies more uniform and more uniformly stringent environmental protection regulations to them.

Narcotics Traffic

As both source and transshipment point, Mexico has been important in the flow of illegal drugs into the United States. U.S.-Mexican cooperation in the interdiction of narcotics has been less than exemplary, the U.S. side complaining of local Mexican law-enforcement corruption, and the Mexicans observing that the root of the problem is demand for narcotics by U.S. consumers. Some U.S. congressmen have voiced reservations because of the reduction of border controls that is likely to accompany the implementation of a free trade agreement. Charles Rangel, for one, has expressed concern on these grounds. In June 1990, he observed that cocaine shipments to the United States from Mexico had more than doubled in two years. He later admonished that a U.S.-Mexican FTA "would make it more difficult to keep contraband from entering the United States."[39]

Human Rights

Finally, although Mexico has made enormous strides toward a full democratic regime, individual civil liberties in that country are not yet as fully protected as they are in the United States. Recognizing this factor and its potential negative influence on U.S.-Mexican relations (including the passage of a free trade agreement), President Salinas created the National Commission on Human Rights in May 1990. Stronger U.S.-Mexican economic ties through a free trade accord would provide further impetus for the Mexican government to accelerate progress in the area of individual rights.

Orderly Management of Flight Capital Reflux

From the Mexican standpoint, the FTA would probably stimulate a reflux of some of the $50 billion to $80 billion in flight capital that private Mexican citizens have shifted outside the country. After the completion of Mexico's Brady Plan commercial-debt rescheduling, brightening prospects for the Mexican economy spurred flight capital holders to repatriate more than $10 billion. Early in 1990, Mexico signed a tax-information-sharing agreement with the United States, under which the U.S. Internal Revenue Service will, on request, furnish Mexican tax authorities with information on the receipts of specified individuals from specific sources. Since the agreement does not provide a mechanism for routinely furnishing Mexican authorities with information on the receipts of all Mexican residents, it is unlikely to end tax evasion; but it is at least a first step toward enforcement. More important, since the FTA would also boost Mexico's prospects in the eyes of its investment community, it would lead to a return of flight capital.

A massive reflux of capital from U.S. banks to Mexico would have conflicting consequences for the United States. On the one hand, a large flow would create a source of further deficit in the U.S. capital-account balance. On the other, while this money would migrate from accounts at U.S. banks and brokerage houses, it would also boost the Mexican debt-service capacity and with it the quality (and secondary market value) of outstanding U.S. bank loans to both public and private Mexican creditors. In the long run, both the United States and Mexico might benefit from a treaty on cross-border taxation and information sharing.

ADVOCATES AND OPPONENTS

On both sides of the Rio Grande, the proposed U.S.–Mexican FTA has powerful advocates and opponents. In the North, the strongest pro and con lobbying groups are located within the private economic sector, while in Mexico this same range of opinion is to be found in a specifically political arena. Although the extension of fast-track authority by the U.S. Congress to President Bush eliminated a major hurdle in the path of its eventual signing, opposition forces could still derail the FTA during congressional consideration of the terms reached in bilateral negotiations. It is unlikely that President Salinas will encounter a roadblock in the form of a conflict between the Mexican executive and legislative branches, but it is possible that opposition to a free trade agreement with the United States could topple Salinas and his dominant PRI political party. Thus, opposition to the FTA is a rallying point for the opposition that carries greater dangers for President Salinas than endorsement bears for the political fortunes of the U.S. president and his party.

Among the strongest proponents of a free trade agreement are local and national politicians from the American Southwest. There is a marked geographical division within the United States on this issue since many of the gains that have occurred even without the pact are concentrated near the Mexican border and completion of the FTA would raise economic activity there at the expense of other regions of the country. To date, a driving force behind the FTA has moved at the state and regional levels. Governors of Mexican states have been negotiating with their American counterparts to spur cross-border trade. Granted, the full impact of these deals will be felt only if an agreement is struck at the national level. Nevertheless, the Southwest has a strong vested interest in seeing the FTA move forward.

The mainstay of U.S. support for the FTA can be found among U.S. businessmen, especially executives and investors in U.S. multinational corporations. Although the National Association of Manufacturers (NAM) has been cautious about lending its approval to a U.S.–Mexican FTA, the Business Roundtable has extended its wholehearted support to the pact.[40] It is from organizations representing major American firms and their individual members that the core argument on behalf of the FTA has been most powerfully and finely articulated. This group has stated its conviction that a NAFTA will help keep jobs in the United States by strengthening the ability of U.S. firms to compete against Asian and European companies.[41] In support of this position, many American manufacturers have noted that joint production arrangements with Mexico have both saved U.S. jobs and created new ones. Summarizing this viewpoint, a 1988 study conducted by the U.S. International Trade Commission reported that the vast majority of some nine hundred firms surveyed felt that assembly in Mexico had improved their overall international competitiveness. By extension, this same group believes that being allowed to operate on a continental scale under a NAFTA will enhance their capacity to defend American jobs against European and Asian competition.[42] Most of the corporations taking part in this study indicated that the alternative to moving part of their labor-intensive operations to Mexico (where a substantial amount of U.S. components are used) is to move their entire operations to Asia, causing the purchase of fewer U.S. components and less machinery and, ultimately leading to loss of U.S. jobs.[43]

In an in-depth case study of the Zenith Corporation's experience submitted by members of the U.S. multinational community, a concrete example of the relative advantages of a U.S.–Mexico FTA were brought to the fore. By establishing operations in Mexico instead of the Far East, Zenith was able to keep intellectual property development and associated technical jobs in the United States. At the same time, because of cost-competitive Mexican operations, Zenith has been able to enter several new businesses, each of which has added jobs in the United States, both at Zenith and among its vendors. Moreover, by moving some production facilities to Mexico, Zenith was able to save U.S. jobs related to its picture tube, plastic molding, and final assembly operations in the United States. In the aggregate, Zenith officials maintain that the firm's Mexican operations have helped to preserve about eight thousand jobs at Zenith itself as well as thousands of more jobs among the vendors of packaging, glass, printed circuit boards, and other components who supply Zenith.[44] In making a case for the free trade agreement, American big business clearly has a persuasive argument because it can calculate the effects of alternative choices to location in Mexico and thereby demonstrate the advantages of a free trade pact with reference to specific cases.

Aside from general nationalist or racist Mexophobia, American opposition to the FTA has crystallized around lobbying groups for organized labor and for certain trade associations. Most of the political forces arrayed against the proposed agreement are attached either to trade unions or to industry associations that would face heightened competition. The FTA issue has generated a schism within the American Democratic party along both ideological (free trade versus protectionist) and regional (West versus Midwest and East) lines. As for producer opposition, it is concentrated in sectors and industries likely to see their market share in the United States reduced as a consequence of intensified competition from Mexican exports but unlikely to receive a compensatory advantage by shifting portions of their production activities to Mexico. These prospective American losers definitely include textile and apparel manufacturers, steel and cement companies, makers of inexpensive glassware, and some fruit and vegetable farmers.

The chief argument against the FTA is that it will prompt manufacturers to shift operations to Mexico to take advantage of low-cost labor. Critics charge that this will expose American industries in specific sectors to heightened competition once tariff and nontariff barriers to Mexican exports are lowered or removed. This is, of course, the jobs issue, and it is by no means a coincidence that the sharpest criticism of the proposed trade pact has issued from the ranks of U.S. unions where hard-core adversaries to the proposed pact are concentrated. Their objections have been recognized, but by no means accepted, by President Bush. In his joint press conference with President Salinas in April 1991, he vowed:

We have some tough opponents in this country. Some elements in organized labor are fighting it, and they are wrong, and I'm going to take them on head on because I know that this is in the best interest of our country.[45]

Opposition has also formed around organizational satellites of the trade unions, particularly in the midwestern rust belt. The Religion & Labor Council (Kansas City) and Federation for Industrial Retention & Renewal (Chicago) are offshoots of a grassroots, union-backed industrial retention movement that have expressed their strident opposition to the U.S.–Mexican FTA.[46]

Union opposition has focused on the gap in manufacturing wages, which average $1.90 an hour in Mexico and $14.50 in the United States. This differential would afford firms operating in Mexico a labor-cost advantage against which American outfits could not compete, providing powerful incentives for some of those same U.S. companies to move production to Mexico. In the vanguard of the opposition to the FTA, Representative Frank Guarini has cited labor union estimates that the United States would lose some 400,000 jobs should such a pact come into being.[47] Mark Anderson, an economist for the AFL-CIO, has sharply criticized the U.S.–Mexican FTA from the standpoint of both jobs and social welfare. Testifying before Congress at the end of June 1990, Anderson warned that: "A free-trade agreement with Mexico, a country where wages and social protection are almost nonexistent when compared to our own, simply invites disaster for U.S. workers."[48]

In making its case against the U.S.–Mexican FTA, the union movement has tried to build bridges with industry and environmental groups. Labor spokesmen have asserted that regulations on environmental damage, workplace safety, and exposure to hazardous waste—far more stringent in the United States than in Mexico—must be built into the final price of U.S.-made wares, leaving them at a competitive disadvantage vis-à-vis goods produced in Mexico. American labor opposition has also extended its hand to Mexico's political opposition. Some union officials have gone so far as to question the legitimacy of the Salinas government, noting that Salinas's election was accompanied by widespread charges of fraud and abuse (brought mostly by the political opposition).[49]

Within Mexico the bulk of support for the free trade agreement comes from five overlapping interest groups: (1) the Salinas administration itself, and the incumbent PRI party; (2) large Mexican firms that are close to achieving authentic multinational status; (3) current or potential exporters to the United States who anticipate growing sales in U.S. markets if a free trade accord can be reached; (4) Mexican producers that use U.S. intermediate production inputs or capital goods; and finally (5) consumers. As mentioned earlier, the Salinas government now has a compelling interest in seeing *its* free trade overtures to the Bush administration bear fruit. The results of FTA talks will undoubtedly influence local and state elections within Mexico, affect chances for the PRI to retain the Mexican presidency after Salinas's term ends in 1993, and, most crucial, promote or constrain President Salinas's policy, power, and latitude during the remainder of his tenure. Large Mexican firms, including some recently privatized SOEs, would plainly benefit from a further opening of U.S. markets. Equally important, a signed trade agreement would boost their ability to mobilize capital from domestic and international sources and (perhaps more significant) create opportunities for joint-venture production with strong and technologically sophisticated U.S. firms. That Mexican corporations, small production entities, and labor (at least in those sectors that can naturally expect increased export revenues, the FTA) are interested in its realization is self-evident. The same is true of Mexican companies that rely on U.S. sources for production inputs or equipment, since the FTA would effectively reduce the cost of these goods by lowering Mexican tariff and nontariff barriers to them. Consumers, of course, would presumably benefit from the reduced price of U.S. wares and the impact of competition on the pricing policies of domestic import-substitute producers.

Mexican opposition to the FTA has come from intellectuals, journalists, and elements of organized labor. They have argued that free trade with the Colossus of the North will bankrupt less efficient firms, exacerbate unemployment in a nation with one million new laborers a year, and compromise national sovereignty. Within this sector, one Mexican economist has remarked that the time is not ripe for the FTA. He asserts that because of cumbersome Mexican labor legislation, only a few local industries will be able to adjust to a competitive regime. When compared to U.S. labor federations, Mexican labor unions have adopted a low profile. The Confederation of Mexican Workers, Mexico's largest trade union federation, is a formal element of the PRI party. Thus, at Salinas's urging, the confederation grudgingly rubberstamped a bilateral trade agreement with the United States. Still, dissidents within the confederation and in other Mexican labor organizations have argued that the agreement will be used to defeat unionism in North America.

The heart of Mexican resistance to the FTA can be found among that nation's political opposition parties, for in Mexico the FTA is a much more crucial political issue than it is in the United States so far. The son of former President Lazaro Cardenas (who nationalized the Mexican oil industry during the 1930s), Cuauhtemoc Cardenas, who heads the Party of the Democratic Revolution, campaigned on anti-free trade platform in the summer of 1991. Far to the left of Salinas, the younger Cardenas has also opposed the Mexican president's acceleration of external and domestic liberalization. Apart from criticizing the proposed U.S.–Mexican FTA, Cardenas has transformed Salinas's handling of the matter into a broader attack both on the Mexican president and the PRI's longstanding monopoly over political power. Even those who do not support Cardenas or advocate a return to the anti-American socialist and "revolutionary" Mexico of the past have complained that Salinas has undertaken adjustment without due consideration of Mexico's social development.[50] Salinas's decision to undertake free trade talks with the United States is viewed even by probusiness elements as presumptuous. Opposition politicians have complained that Salinas's supporters in the ineffectual Mexican Congress have worked to keep the free-trade hearings off the floor and have banned hearings on the subject. Luis H. Alvarez, president of the conservative National Action Party has complained, "We don't even have access to information on what's going on," in initial FTA parlays.[51] Thus, aside from the free-trade issue itself, opposition to the FTA by diverse wings of the Mexican political spectrum is seen as a means of weakening President Salinas and the PRI.

One final source of opposition to the FTA from both Mexico and the United States comes from those who see it as a challenge to the multilateral trading system at stake in the Uruguay Round. It is something of a paradox that free-trade purists within the Bush administration object to the proposal on the grounds that any bilateral agreement is bound to distract attention from the Uruguay Round of negotiations on the GATT and that bilateral deals can artificially divert trade from its most efficient patterns. These opponents have been joined by others, notably spokesmen for the EC. Hence, when the idea of another U.S. free trade agreement reached their desks, editors at the U.K.-based *Economist* claimed that it would undermine multilateralism via GATT,[52] and later that the Bush administration was using the FTA with Mexico as a bargaining chip to push the Uruguay Round ahead in much the same way that the 1985 U.S.–Israeli FTA was used to prod the EC into an eighth GATT round.[53]

Apart from the fact that the EC itself is the major regional exception to GATT multilateralism, supporters of the U.S.–Mexican FTA have correctly observed that the pact is permitted under the GATT. Bilateral free-trade agreements are within both the letter and the spirit of the GATT so long as they conform to that organization's Article 24, that is they cover most sorts of trade, not just trade in one or two goods, and avoid tariff and nontariff barrier increases to trade with other countries. Canadian Trade Minister John Crosbie has tried to assuage fears of this sort.

Some fear that these new trading arrangements are in conflict with the multilateral system. This confuses the purposes of today's arrangements with the unfortunate commercial policy of the 1930s. During the 1930s the approach to preferential arrangements was not to reduce barriers but rather to increase barriers on non-preferred commerce, so that instead of trade creation, the outcome was trade destruction.[54]

It is ironic, then, that in addition to traditional protectionist groups like organized labor in the United States and left-wing nationalists in Mexico, the FTA has been opposed by champions of free trade.

THE CURRENT OUTLOOK

Can a free trade agreement between the United States and Mexico come about and achieve its intended goals? No definitive answer to this question can be rendered, chiefly because the proposed agreement is virtually unprecedented in the annals of global economic policy. Although the U.S. FTAs with Israel and Canada furnish immediate forerunners to a U.S.-Mexican free trade deal, "the implications of this agreement will be unlike any the world has seen before."[55] The creation of a North American free trade area with Mexico would mark the first time that an industrialized country has joined a Third World nation in a massive free-trade area.

Critics of the proposal have projected that even if a formal agreement is signed the Mexican market is unlikely to yield long-term U.S. export growth when over half of Mexico's nearly 90 million people are undernourished, 17 million live in extreme poverty, and 40 percent of the total workforce earns less than the minimum wage of U.S. $3.25 a day. Mexico is demographically young, with some one million labor-force entrants a year into an economy that is not growing rapidly enough to absorb them and already features perennial double-digit unemployment rates. Deficiencies in infrastructure, the remnant of the bureaucracy, and the infamous Mexican legal system will also inhibit the growth of U.S. exports and of direct investment in Mexico. Despite the fact that President Bush engineered an extension of the fast-track authority needed to begin negotiation of the FTA, further congressional approval will be required for the agreement to be finalized. Should Bush's popularity erode or the U.S. economy continue to languish, prospects for congressional approval would diminish rapidly. The same comments are true of Salinas's handling of the Mexican economy.

From the other side, the economic and political factors beneath the FTA are cited to support the case for a successful signing of the agreement and positive results stemming from it. At the same time, more optimistic observers believe the disadvantages of the FTA have been grossly exaggerated. In the United States, labor productivity has begun to pick up, and in baseline terms (depending on the yardstick used), output per employed person is roughly five or six times that of Mexican workers. Hence, the comparative Mexican labor-cost advantage should be counterbalanced by the enormous U.S. capital and technological edges.

At the same time, political scientists note that in addition to the foreign relations gain that the FTA would bring, the announcement of the program by President Bush has created a situation in which a unilateral abandonment of the plan would be a political disaster for U.S.-Mexican and, indeed, U.S.-

Latin American relations. As for the capacity of congressional opponents to block passage of the FTA, even the staunchest adversaries concede that it will be difficult to overturn a free trade treaty negotiated between the United States and Mexico once it arrives on Capitol Hill bearing the signatures of Bush and Salinas.

The most compelling reason for optimism about both the completion of a free trade agreement with Mexico and its positive influence on the Mexican economy, however, comes from the activities that U.S. corporations and investors have already undertaken in anticipation of its becoming a reality. According to Nicholas Scheele, president of Ford's Mexican subsidiary: "We're going to see investment pouring in here. The dollar numbers are going to make people's heads spin."[56] General Electric, one of the first American firms to restructure its U.S. and Canadian industrial strategy to take advantage of impending free trade, has already announced plans to open new consumer appliance assembly facilities in Mexico to supply U.S. and Canadian markets. Analogous to the EC-92 program in Western Europe, as American firms develop strategies and make concrete moves to take advantage of a free trade agreement with Mexico, something of a self-fulfilling prophecy unfolds as it becomes progressively more costly to reverse these moves.

CHAPTER 5

First-Tier EAI Candidates: Chile, Venezuela, Colombia, and Bolivia

By virtue of the adjustment progress that its economy has accomplished to date, Mexico can be considered a first-tier country in the framework of a broader hemispheric economic alliance with the United States and Canada. Granted, Mexico is a special case, but other economies in Latin America have equalled its adjustment record and, like Mexico, have economic and political assets that argue for closer economic integration with the United States at this time.

In terms of stabilization and liberalization, Chile stands at the head of this group; in fact, Chile is thus far the only major Latin American country to qualify for EAI privatization loans. The principal roadblock to a bilateral accord between Chile and the United States is the checkered history of political relations between the two nations during the Pinochet regime and the spectral presence of General Pinochet himself as a Chilean grey eminence.

Less substantial political barriers separate the United States from Venezuela. Like Mexico, Venezuela has large petroleum reserves within an energy-export sector that could arguably benefit from increased foreign autonomous and direct-investment capital flows. The problem with Venezuela is that, while some adjustment has been registered, the incumbent Perez regime has only begun to reverse decades of economic statism and the initial popular response to his adjustment program has been disheartening.

A quiet model of policy discipline within Latin America during the 1980s, Colombia has had little need for additional stabilization programs. Nevertheless, Colombia remains comparatively closed to trade and investment under an inward-looking and nationalist development strategy. Some departure from this stance can be seen in the policies of the current regime, and President César Gaviria reacted positively to President Bush's EAI overture.

Still, whether Colombia would be willing to undertake further reforms and thus become eligible for EAI participation is problematical.

In a purely normative sense, no nation deserves more recognition for its adjustment accomplishments in the 1980s than Bolivia. Under President Paz, and without the benefit of Brady Plan assistance, Bolivia has made a complete about-face and undergone the most drastic restructuring of a national economy along free market lines in Latin America. The problem here, of course, is that Bolivia is a small and still woefully underdeveloped nation, with a narrow export sector, a limited potential for import absorption, and a relatively poor direct investment environment.

CHILE

The adjustment experience in Chile differs from that elsewhere in Latin America in three key ways which, taken collectively, carry a sobering lesson about the limitations of stabilization and liberalization in ensuring national economic well-being. First, by the time of the Latin American debt crisis, Chile was already an open economy committed to fiscal and monetary discipline. Second, the debt crisis in Chile was not associated with overborrowing by the central government in international or domestic credit markets. Instead, it came about as a consequence of overborrowing by the private sector and by Chilean parastatals, with the central government forced to pick up the tab through bankruptcies and forced socialization of debt. Third, although the Pinochet regime probably made substantial policy errors during the debt crisis, its experience demonstrates that capitalist restructuring and a generally sound fiscal and monetary course do not make a country immune to the debilitation of external debt. Moreover, while Chile was absolutely scrupulous, even maniacal, in its commitment to repay foreign commercial creditors, neither its reputational collateral nor its strenuous adjustment was rewarded by the international banking community with fresh voluntary loans.

The General Course of Adjustment

The Chilean debt crisis began in 1981 as a result of external shocks, notably the rise in real global interest rates and a dramatic plunge in the price of its chief export, copper, from 99 U.S. cents per pound to 79 cents in a single year. Faced with these conditions, the administration of General Augusto Pinochet heeded the advice of its Chicago-school economic team, which explicitly recommended a do-nothing policy. Both Pinochet and his consultants were shocked when foreign commercial bank flows were shut down in 1982, the bankers seeing this increased need for credit as being no different from that of other Latin American governments (Chile suffering from regional contamination) and interpreting the decline in Chilean terms of trade as a lasting, secular phenomenon.

Determined to play by the book, Pinochet took the orthodox, recessionary path to adjustment and instituted a steep nominal and real devaluation of the Chilean peso. The resulting sharp contraction of output and the sudden withdrawal of foreign credit created serious problems for both the real and the financial sector. Many private debtors could not service their foreign debts at the new exchange rates, while others could not pay the higher interest rates on their domestic-currency debts. The result could only be an increasing volume of bad loans in the banking system. By 1982, as commercial bankruptcies tripled, Chile was in the midst of a domestic debt crisis far more significant than its external repayment woes. With its intimate linkages to the financial sector, the Pinochet regime bailed out the commercial banks by offering them both foreign exchange at a preferential rate and domestic credit subsidies. Between 1982 and 1985, the cost of the subsidized exchange rate to the central banking system averaged more than $700 million a year, an enormous sum given that Chilean GDP during this time was barely $20 billion.

In 1984 and the first half of 1985, continued recession proved politically unacceptable. The Pinochet government briefly reflated the economy and allowed the peso to appreciate. While this stemmed the outflow of foreign exchange reserves, which had declined by more than $1.5 billion in 1982 and 1983, it caused a further deterioration in Chile's current and trade accounts, the trade surplus dropping from nearly $1 billion in 1983 to less than $300 million in 1984 as a consequence of a less competitive exchange rate.

By 1985, with yet another team of American-trained economists at helm, the Pinochet government acknowledged the need to restore fiscal austerity and to complement stabilization with long-term structural reforms. Another major devaluation was undertaken, and export incentives were put into place on the premise that the external sector could act as the economy's main engine of growth. Structural liberalization was pursued with a vengeance in the final four years of the Pinochet government. There was one further significant departure from orthodox adjustment at the end of that period. In an effort to win public support for its candidates in the 1988–1989 elections, the Pinochet regime abandoned monetary discipline. The growth of credit led to a 13 percent rise in domestic demand in 1989 and generated inflationary pressures in its wake.

Shortly after defeating General Pinochet in the 1989 presidential election, newly installed head of state Patricio Aylwin took the unpopular step of mopping up excess liquidity by tightening credit and cutting government outlays. Economic activity dropped from high, but unsustainable, double-digit expansion in 1989 to GDP growth of less than 2 percent in 1990. Believing that the sins of the recent past had been counterbalanced and that price stability was restored, the central bank loosened monetary policy in 1990 but was forced to tighten it again as the crisis in the Persian Gulf sent energy-importing Chile into an inflationary spiral. Since then, Aylwin has basically continued his predecessor's orthodox adjustment approach, but has shown considerably greater sensitivity toward the plight of the nation's poor.

Despite his iron-handed rule, Pinochet left Aylwin with an economy that was widely hailed as a model for the region, including a balanced budget, greatly reduced foreign debt, a dynamic export sector, and substantial foreign exchange reserves. For the time being, this free market approach enjoys support from virtually all segments of Chilean society, including business, the military, and the working class. Despite all this, the Chilean approach to adjustment has been criticized for using overkill, with output growth depressed below equilibrium and the interests of both foreign and domestic investors and creditors placed well ahead of the needs of the Chilean people.

External Stabilization

No country in Latin America has gone further toward relieving itself of the burden of external debt than has Chile. While outstanding foreign debt at the end of Pinochet's tenure was still high, with interest payments to external creditors alone amounting to 9 percent of GDP, its net interest payment ratio was pared from nearly 40 percent in 1981 to around 30 percent in 1987 and 1988. After further progress during Aylwin's first year in office, Chile's total external debt stood at $16.3 billion by the end of May 1990, more than 16 percent below the peak level of $19.5 billion in 1986. Much of this debt reduction came about as a result of conversions on the secondary market, notably an aggressive debt-equity swap program. If anything, this drive to pare debt overhang was intensified by Aylwin. In 1990, by using its export receipts and still more swaps, Chile reduced its external debt by $10 billion. With current commercial debt at less than $5 billion and the discount on Chilean paper in secondary market shrinking to less than 10 percent, Chile has about reached the end of its debt conversion drive. Most of the remaining debt is in short-term maturities, and while Chile faces a bunching of debt payments on principal in the 1991–1993 period, its growing export receipts should allow it to overcome this amortization hump.

The Chilean approach to debt repayment was admirable. Patricio Meller, among others, has characterized it as "investing in reputation."[1] After the 1982 debt crisis and the sudden decrease in commercial bank credits, two principles guided the Chilean government's attitude. The first was the non-confrontation principle. In response to bank steering-committee demands, the Chilean government "voluntarily" guaranteed private external debt. Moreover, throughout the 1980s, Chile maintained full and punctual interest payments on the external debt, while rescheduling a large share of the amortization payments on that debt. Ironically, Chile was the one country to flirt with the straightforward capitalist solution of allowing its private citizens to default on their loans to foreign creditors and resolving individual cases through bankruptcy proceedings. The banks, however, rejected this conventional commercial approach, and by threatening to withdraw all trade credits, forced Pinochet's government to vouchsafe the repayment of debt that it never contracted in the first place. Despite this rough handling, when Chile subscribed to IMF standby programs in 1983 and 1984, the highest priority in its letter of intent to the Fund was faithful servicing of its external debt obligations.

The second cardinal tenet of Chilean debt policy is that sound macroeconomic policies and serious adjustment efforts will attract voluntary foreign financing. In practice, this rule has not panned out. In 1984, Chile briefly departed from its orthodox adjustment path. Yet in 1985, the bankers furnished Chile with the same amount of new money as they had before the lapse. Worse, after Chile got back on track, and even intensified its adjustment efforts, the banks actually reduced their remaining lines of credit to the "model" debtor. By contrast, Chile did receive substantial assistance from the IMF, the World Bank, and the IDB, which taken collectively financed some 40 percent of Chile's interest payments to its commercial creditors.

Today, Chile is paying off its debts without a Brady-style reduction. Because its paper is trading on the secondary market near par, Chile's positive repayment record has left it practically ineligible to benefit from a Brady Plan workout. When Aylwin first assumed office, his finance minister, Alejandro Foxley, spoke of a major rescheduling of Chile's remaining foreign bank debt by the end of 1990, one that would include new money commitments and an extended grace period. This would allow Chile to overcome its temporary public and corporate cash flow problems. In exchange for the agreement, Chile would pledge to continue its current debt-equity swap program.

Although Aylwin's political opponents charged that he wanted to postpone foreign debt repayment to avoid damaging his chances for reelection in December 1993,[2] no agreement was reached with the banks. Miffed at the burden of the Brady Plan, the bankers insisted on both a comparatively high spread for new financing and the Chilean government's assumption of still more private debt. This time, Chile was in a stronger position and could afford to wait its creditors out while continuing debt service payments to them.

One remaining problem is that Chile has virtually exhausted its concessional lines of credit from international organizations. The IMF provided Chile with about $300 million a year during the mid-1980s, while the World Bank, the IDB, and official bilateral credit agencies furnished around $500 million. In 1991, Chile began to make net positive transfers back to these institutions.

In facing their external financing needs, the Chileans have a number of strong cards to play. Import cover now stands at seven months, with government reserves equivalent to 25 percent of remaining foreign debt. While Chile has not been successful in contracting medium- or long-term loans from commercial creditors on reasonable terms, its trade and interbank credit lines are substantial, and there have been several voluntary long-term loans to Chilean companies. Most important, while Foxley had planned to enter into a commercial bank debt workout and then tap into international capital markets, that order has been reversed. In 1991, without a commercial rescheduling agreement completed, Chile's government tested the international waters with a $320-million Eurobond issue. Indeed, still other nonbank sources of private capital, such as mutual funds that specialize in Chilean investment, may enable it to circumvent banking intermediation altogether. Finally, though Chile is not a major capital flight nation, private citizens have acknowledged the upturn in their nation's fortunes, repatriating around $1.4 billion in 1989 and 1990.

External Liberalization

The structural adjustment of its external sector in terms of trade liberalization and the openness of its direct investment regime were largely in place during the 1970s, epitomized by Chile's homogeneous 10 percent tariff. Changes have been marginal and moving in a positive (free market) direction. Chile has a heavy weight of trade, the value of two-way flows being around $15 billion in 1990, equivalent to nearly 60 percent of GDP. This, in itself, indicates a higher degree of openness than can be found in most developing countries. Tariffs are low, and nontariff barriers are negligible.

Chile also has one of the most open and liberal foreign investment policies in the developing world. As embodied in its 1974 Foreign Investment Statute, commonly known as Decree Law 600, there are hardly any restrictions on investment by foreigners, and equal treatment with local businessmen is guaranteed.

Chile was the first Latin American country to introduce a debt-equity conversion program and has been the most successful in implementing it.[3] By the end of May 1990, $3.3 billion of face-value debt had been converted using Chapter 19 (Chile's debt-equity program, administered by the central bank) and $2.8 billion using Chapter 18 (domestic)—including other conversion methods and buybacks, a total of $9.4 billion of external debt has been extinguished.

The very success of the Chilean swap program now limits prospects for future conversions of foreign debt into equity. On the one hand, the secondary market price of Chilean debt paper has improved to around 90 cents on the dollar. This, in turn, limits the implicit subsidy to investors available by purchasing Chilean debt at a discount and the willingness of the Aylwin government to extinguish debt through any form of conversion that involves its direct or indirect purchase of foreign liabilities on the external market. Consequently, future debt-equity conversions featuring foreign participation will be limited to those that engage in export or import-substitution activities that the Chilean government has an interest in stimulating, apart from the broad aim of debt extinction.

In terms of its exchange-rate policy, while the Chilean government still manages the relative value of the peso, it employs a trotting-peg mechanism of exchange-rate determination that rests chiefly upon market forces rather than government fiat. Recent trade statistics suggest that the Chilean currency is now realistic and, in fact, highly competitive.

Domestic Stabilization

Chile's domestic stabilization record is extremely strong. Although the central government's extension of credit subsidies to its financial sector drove its fiscal balance off kilter in the first half of the 1980s, by the end of the decade, the budget deficit had been eliminated and public-sector savings reached 5 percent of GNP. Chile's pattern of public expenditure shows a substantial change between the Pinochet and Aylwin administrations. Under Pinochet, Chilean defense expenditures mushroomed from 3 percent of GDP in 1970 to around 7 percent in 1983. Inordinately high military outlays continued through the first stage of adjustment, even as the central government's wage bill was being slashed by nearly a third, public pensions were deindexed from price changes, and total public social expenditures were reduced by around 20 percent in per capita terms. According to Aylwin's Finance Minister Foxley, the quality and quantity of social services — sanitation, housing, etc. — has deteriorated substantially in the past 15 years and needs to be improved.[4] Aylwin's populist regime has committed itself to more equitable distribution of wealth and income. Between 1989 and 1991, expenditures on health, education, and housing grew some 20 percent in real terms.

While domestic inflation made a serious upturn in the first full year of Aylwin's regime (largely as a consequence of price increases on imported energy), like its predecessor, the current administration has followed a disciplined monetary policy. In fact, Aylwin has undertaken institutional reforms to guard against the temptations of using monetary policy as a means of debt disposal or political expediency. In December 1989, the Chilean central bank was declared autonomous, becoming the first independent central bank in Latin America, insulating it from political pressures. In order to enlarge its social welfare budget, the Aylwin government, with the concurrence of rightist National Renovation party, passed a tax reform law during its first year that raised corporate and value-added taxes and boosted government revenues by around 1.5 percent of domestic output.

Domestic Liberalization

Despite the fact that Chile had an open, market-based economy by the start of the debt crisis, further internal structural adjustment took place in the 1980s. If anything, financial liberalization was carried out too abruptly in the first part of the decade, since it created an underregulated network of commercial banks and finance companies charging a real domestic interest rate in excess of 35 percent annually. The bank bailout of 1983–1985 required the issuance of some $6 billion in government bonds to recapitalize the central bank. The financial crisis of this period prompted the establishment of a new regulatory system and establishment of safeguards against the abuses of the past.

Privatization is normally looked upon as a phenomenon of the 1980s in Latin America, but Chile's first divestitures took place a decade earlier when the Pinochet government reprivatizated some 250 SOEs and returned some 3,700 formerly private businesses that had been illegally seized by the Socialist Allende regime to their previous owners without cash payments to the new government. In an unfortunate postscript to this initial reprivatization effort, the credit crunch of the 1980s caused widespread bankruptcies of re-privatized financial institutions and costly government interventions to support enterprises that had been transferred back to the private sector after the Pinochet coup.

From 1986 onward, privatization focused upon the divestiture of traditional SOEs. This process encompassed public utilities (electricity, telephone, tele-communications) as well as the national airline and parastatals in other sectors. By the end of the Pinochet years, the total net worth of programmed SOE privatization reached approximately $3.6 billion. In the very last year of his rule, Pinochet accelerated the privatization process as just about everything in the public sector was placed on the auction block, including a large part of the national forests. Critics of the Pinochet government charged that the drive was intended to create supporters for progovernment candidates and to reduce the power of any future democratic government.[5]

Chile's privatization experience was lauded by conservative advocates of orthodox adjustment and castigated by their opponents, who have argued that neither fiscal nor efficiency arguments can be marshalled to justify the extent of the program. By the second half of the 1980s, in the wake of public-sector adjustment measures imposed earlier, the privatized SOEs generally had surpluses and had begun transferring resources to the central government, having already been structured so as to be self-financing. Since they were removed from the public sector in very short order, with no public debate on the matter and at a discount of around 50 percent on average, it is difficult to justify the pace and extent of Chilean privatization in the late 1980s.[6] Perhaps the most controversial facet of the divestiture program was the decision to allow foreign investors to participate. The latter could obtain an effective subsidy through purchase of external debt certificates at a 30 to 40 percent discount and a further subsidy by purchasing this paper after a major devaluation of the Chilean peso. This giveaway program prompted Chilean economist Patricio Meller to complain: "Does foreign investment require such large incentives to come to Chile?" adding that in the future, "the government should not play the role of Santa Claus to high-income groups and foreigners."[7]

In direct contrast to Latin America as a whole, the Pinochet regime controlled Chile's political and social life with a strong hand, but followed a laissez faire economic philosophy that limited government regulation of private enterprise to emergency interventions. Even among Chile's state-owned enterprises, "simulated privatization" has been implemented through the installation of monitoring and control systems ruled by performance criteria to compel publicly owned and managed firms to conform to private sector operating standards. Thus, Chile's huge copper industry, Codelco, differs from the vast majority of Latin parastatals in displaying all the dynamism of a privately managed company. If anything, the move toward privatization may have gone too far too fast, and under Aylwin regulatory oversight is being strengthened to avoid the recurrence of private-sector abuses.

RECENT ECONOMIC PERFORMANCE

Whatever its political and social shortcomings, adjustment under Pinochet and its continuance under Aylwin has placed the Chilean economy on a sounder footing than any other in the region. Through strong adjustment and sound macroeconomic policies, Chile's current economic problems are mild in comparison with those of other Latin American nations. A year after Aylwin assumed office, Chilean reserves stood near record levels, the central government budget showed a primary surplus, the external sector boasted a healthy trade surplus, and Chile enjoyed a foreign direct investment boom.

GDP growth in Chile is a yardstick of just how different its economy is from others in the region. Output growth in 1988 was actually higher and unemployment lower than in the precrisis year of 1981. Between 1987 and 1989, the Chilean economy expanded at a rapid clip, growing by some 6 percent annually. Overstimulation by the Pinochet government prior to national elections caused an unsustainable 10 percent GDP expansion in 1989, forcing the Aylwin government to reinforce austerity. Consequently, in 1990 and 1991, growth dropped to 2 percent. Nonetheless, Chile is entirely capable of registering output expansion well in excess of population growth, a feat that few other Latin American nations can equal. Inflation is a second temporary legacy of the 1989 reflation by Pinochet; in 1990, demand spillover from the prior year joined with sharp increases on imported energy to yield an inflation rate of 28 percent. Although low by Latin American standards, this rate should fall as the effects of Aylwin's belt-tightening measures move through the economy.

Aside from intentional stimulation, the growth surge of 1989 can be attributed to the return of foreign direct investment to Chile in copious sums. Given that gross fixed investment was cut in half during the initial stages of Chile's debt adjustment, it is not surprising that by 1988 gross fixed investment still had not recovered its 1981 level. In 1989 a direct investment boom started, occasioned in part by privatization and debt-equity swaps, but more significantly, without discount incentives in other sectors. Overall, investment rates in 1990 were expected to reach 22 percent of GDP, the highest rate in twenty-five years. In that year, the Chilean government approved close to $3 billion in new foreign investment applications, an amount equivalent to new direct investment between 1985 and 1988 as a whole. In 1990, actual foreign investment exceeded $1.2 billion, an all-time record and by far the best performance in Latin America. Even as debt-equity and privatization programs run their course, Chile's direct investment growth will continue, albeit at a slower pace.

The factors behind Chile's direct-investment magnetism are fairly straightforward. Chile maintains a world-class comparative advantage in certain natural-resource industries, especially mining, forestry, and agriculture, creating a strong and durable basis for attracting direct investment flows. With the passage of military rule, there is also growing interest in the country's tourism potential. Along with resource intensity, foreign direct investment in Chile is also labor-intensive, and with good cause. Chile has a deeply ingrained work ethic and a disciplined, nondisruptive labor force.[8] In addition, its reliance upon the private sector has nourished an indigenous entrepreneurial class unmatched in South America. Indeed, of 442 FDI projects surveyed by the government in 1989, 60 percent were joint ventures with foreign investors, 20 percent were entirely foreign, and 15 percent were public-sector.[9] The sole problem of this direct investment wave is that it has flooded Chile with U.S. dollars, making the control of monetary aggregates somewhat more difficult than in the past.

The real star of the Chilean economy has been its export sector. In the last part of the 1980s, its performance has improved while the basis for future expansion has been firmed. In the first half of the 1980s, most of the improvement in Chile's trade balance occurred as a result of devaluations and import compression. During this period—because of a substantial deterioration in terms of trade, chiefly a downturn on price for copper in global markets—exports showed almost no change in current dollars. After 1986, as terms of trade stabilized, export performance resumed a growth path. In 1987, the trade balance showed a surplus equal to nearly one-quarter of total exports; and in the following year, that ratio rose to nearly one-third. Since the mid-1980s, the value of Chile's total exports more than doubled, reaching roughly $8 billion in 1990 as exports rose another 10 percent in value terms. Exports were expected to grow even faster in 1991. More important than these short-term movements, the Chilean export basket has been diversified in the years since 1985. When Pinochet assumed power in 1973, copper accounted for more than four-fifths of Chilean export receipts. Today, it accounts for only two-fifths.

The Political Situation

Domestic. The biggest question mark in Chile today is not economic but political, and the nation's domestic political situation has exercised an inhibitory influence on the improvement of relations between it and the United States, even since the defeat of General Pinochet's party. After presiding over a decade of relative prosperity, Pinochet sought to strengthen and prolong his regime by allowing more leeway for opposition. He miscalculated, and his presidential candidate was overwhelmingly defeated in the free election of December 1989. Thus, after seventeen years, Chile returned to a democratic tradition extending almost unbroken for a century-and-a-half with inauguration of Patricio Aylwin Azocar as the candidate of the centrist Christian Democratic party on 11 March 1990.

The return of civilian government paved the way for Chile's restoration as a respected member of the international community. President Aylwin labored to shed his nation's pariah image by traveling abroad. Most democratic leaders in the Western Hemisphere had attended his inauguration ceremony, and Aylwin later visited both the EC and the United Nations, where he addressed a session of the General Assembly. Shortly after his assumption of the presidency, Aylwin was invited to join the informal association of Latin American Presidents known as the Rio Group, and other Chilean officials began to play important roles in international financial circles and multilateral institutions like the IDB.

Still, the transition to a popularly elected civilian government is not yet complete. Through arrangements established prior to the election of 1989, General Pinochet made sure of having a hand in each branch of Chile's government, whatever the ballot box results. In exchange for the first free elections in nearly two decades, Pinochet's opposition accepted his regime's timetable for a transition to civilian rule and a constitutional framework designed to limit civilian authority. Within that rigged framework, the outgoing regime was allowed to appoint nine of the forty-seven senators in the Chilean legislature, giving the Democratic Independent Union party the power to block legislation proposed by the governing coalition. Consequently, the government must always bargain with Pinochet's supporters or with the more moderate right-wing National Renovation party.[10]

During Pinochet's tenure, the Chilean Supreme Court accepted the regime's legitimacy without question and refused to hold the military accountable for repressive acts. Given this judicial legacy (on the part of a tribunal appointed by Pinochet), it is not surprising that in August 1990 the court unanimously upheld a 1978 statute protecting members of the security forces from prosecution for abuses. Within the executive, Pinochet himself remains the head of Chile's 53,000-man army and may legally keep his post until 1997. To enhance his position, Pinochet issued a series of decrees that bolster the autonomy of the armed forces. These included revoking the president's right to name and remove heads of military branches and shielding the defense budget by reserving 10 percent of copper export earnings for the armed forces. Last, before leaving office Pinochet placed the security forces under the organizational umbrella of the military. Pinochet currently influences national affairs outside the military through a shadow cabinet of high-ranking political advisors and sometimes threatens another military coup should Aylwin try to dismantle his power base.[11]

Despite all this, the outlook for civilian government is comparatively bright. Although many of the Aylwin policy initiatives have been stymied, government authority has not been seriously challenged by the armed forces, its public popularity is high, and its political opponents appear committed to democratic rule. It has been crucial to his success that Aylwin has sought alliances within the military and even defied Pinochet in this quarter by refusing to endorse his promotion of two generals. The basis of a genuine social consensus on Chilean economic development has been formed, as the nation's conservative business elite has shown a willingness to compromise with labor leaders. Some knotty issues remain—for example, the Aylwin government has been unable to overcome the opposition of conservative legislators to labor-code reforms, a principal demand of the major unions during the recent electoral campaign.

Relations with the United States. It is in the area of human rights that the most serious challenges to the Aylwin government and to improved relations with the United States arise. Pro-Pinochet senators have thwarted the government on human rights issues, watering down legislation proposed by the Chilean justice minister to investigate crimes committed during the military regime.

In 1990, the United States ran a trade surplus of $400 million with Chile, and much of Chile's direct investment surge has come from the United States. Judged in terms of their potential, however, bilateral trade flows are still low, and the United States is underinvested in Chile. Following Aylwin's election, the Chilean government believed that economic sanctions imposed by the United States during President Carter's human rights crusade would immediately be rescinded. This was not the case, tension remained between Santiago and Washington. U.S. reticence on this count created deep resentment in Chile. Worse, it gave Aylwin's rightist opponents the grounds to argue that democracy has failed to bring Chile the international rewards promised by anti-Pinochet leaders.

There was some movement on this front during Aylwin's first year. When he visited President Bush in September 1990, a long-standing ban on overseas private investment insurance (OPIC) in support of direct investment was lifted. After Chilean leaders mounted an intense lobbying effort, the Bush administration rescinded an arms-sale embargo in time for the U.S. president's trip to Chile in December 1990. Nonetheless, citing labor code violations (and backed by traditional protectionist forces), the Bush administration did not restore preferential trade status to Chile during Aylwin's first year as president. Chilean agricultural produce exports to the United States are still restricted by orderly marketing arrangements (quotas).

The chief symbolic source of U.S. displeasure with Chile is its handling of a criminal case dating from 1976. At that time, Chilean General Orlando Letelier and his American assistant Ronni Moffit were gunned down by Pinochet's security forces in Washington. To this day, the United States continues to demand that the former chief of Pinochet's secret police force, General Manuel Contreras, and a top aide be returned to Washington to face criminal charges for the assassination. The Chilean Supreme Court has refused to extradite the two, even though President Aylwin has expressed his commitment to their prosecution. Hamstrung by Pinochet forces ensconced in government, the Aylwin administration was chastised in an Amnesty International report on human rights abuses issued by the Rettig commission in early 1991. So long as political prisoners from the Pinochet years remain incarcerated, full-fledged partnership with Chile is politically unpalatable in the United States. Indeed, until a solution to Chile's quasi-democratic status is found, its human rights record may serve as a target for opponents of Bush's EAI proposal as a whole.

VENEZUELA

In terms of factor endowments, Venezuela is a prime candidate for inclusion in an EAI alliance with the United States. It boasts a modernized economy, a comparatively high per capita income, a skilled work force and, above all, considerable petroleum wealth. Herein lies the rub. Until the late 1980s, Venezuela was able to maintain macroeconomic stability without structural reforms because its oil revenues effectively cushioned the impact both of external shocks and of a growing external debt burden on the economy. Indeed, over several decades popular expectations rose regarding the limitless capacity of the state-run energy sector to overcome any temporary hardships Venezuela might experience. Consequently, deep adjustment in Venezuela was deferred until the late 1980s; and when it did take place under the Perez administration, it was virtually without popular support.

The General Course of Adjustment

Until 1983, Venezuela enjoyed a lengthy and enviable record of economic performance, GDP growth averaging some 6 percent over a four-decade span, and inflation holding at an inordinately low annual average rate of little more than 3 percent. What distinguished Venezuela from other economies in the region was its extensive oil holdings. Today, Venezuela still has 59 billion barrels of oil reserves, more than any country outside the Middle East.

The state-owned Petroleos Venezolanos (PDVSA) possesses more than a third of the Western Hemisphere's supply.

There was a downside to this legacy: the people turned to the central government to provide for their needs and expected the state to provide for those needs independent of external circumstances or budget constraints. The statist, oil-driven economy ran into stagflationary problems before the oil price decline of 1983–1984. By then, Venezuela was in need of an extremely large adjustment, but the government could not carry it out since the need was not felt by the population. Instead, the Venezuelan people received huge consumption subsidies financed by the use of accumulated international reserves. Consequently, the government avoided necessary adjustment until the situation was virtually unsustainable.

As international petroleum prices trended downward after the second OPEC oil shock, Venezuela experienced a balance-of-payments crisis in 1983. The government used the traditional but unorthodox Venezuelan adjustment measure of a multiple exchange-rate system to insulate the productive sector of the economy from the influence of speculative capital flows. As a subordinate measure, the government instituted modest fiscal austerity measures. However, when world petroleum prices firmed, belt-tightening seemed unnecessary; and planned public-sector investment doubled from 6 percent of GDP in 1985 to 12 percent in 1986. Just as the fiscal expansion started in January 1986, oil income fell by almost half, from an average of $13.9 billion for 1984 and 1985 to $7.6 billion in 1986. Still, the administration of President Jaime Luschini failed to react to the turnabout. Reserves dropped to $300 million, the central government's budget deficit rose to 12 percent of GDP, repressed inflation caused a collapse in the supply system, and artificially low interest rates determined by government fiat wreaked havoc upon the country's financial sector.

In sharp contrast to Aylwin, who enjoyed a positive inheritance from the authoritarian Pinochet regime, Carlos Andres Perez was heir to major economic problems and no popular consensus regarding how they should be handled upon his election to the Venezuelan presidency in 1988. Perez had little choice but to undertake a radically orthodox adjustment program, characterized as "one of the most aggressive . . . in Latin America."[12] In February 1989, he unveiled a six-point policy package that included unification and liberation of the exchange rate, major price hikes on gasoline, electricity, telephone, and other public-sector goods and services, elimination of price controls for most goods, significant trade liberalization, administered increases in bank lending rates, and an external debt-reduction campaign. Today, orthodox adjustment is taking place in Venezuela at a truly breathtaking pace. How long this can continue is problematical given popular resistance to the pangs of adjustment. When Perez first announced his program, it touched off riots in the streets of Caracas, and when he implemented a price increase on oil, a second wave of riots ensued, leaving some three hundred people dead. Venezuelans must be taught to understand that their reliance on revenues from energy exports in a highly volatile international market requires restructuring to enhance the economy's ability to move with rapid upward and downward price changes in global oil markets. Whether the political will to face that reality is present in Venezuela, however, remains in doubt.

External Stabilization

In terms of foreign debt, the Venezuelan experience shows some similarity to that of Chile. Many external liabilities were originally contracted by private borrowers; and like Chile, Venezuela was coerced into guaranteeing repayment. Unlike Chile, Venezuela was also plagued by inefficient state-operated enterprises, fiscal laxity, and extensive capital flight. Indeed, these external debt problems are largely the result of decisions made by private investors, who as a group took on too much foreign debt and then, when the current-account crisis of 1983 occurred, shipped dollars out the country. Government policies, notably maintaining both a grossly overvalued bolivar and deposit interest rates set at negative levels, helped to precipitate the flight of capital to haven economies. With no exchange or capital controls in place, private Venezuelan investors reacted to the perception that a major devaluation was at hand by all but wiping out the country's international reserves at the central bank.

But capital flight alone does not explain how an oil-rich country accumulated nearly $30 billion in foreign debt or how the government's even more onerous domestic debt arose. Another major part of the Venezuelan debt complex can be traced to the rapid expansion of state-owned enterprises during the 1970s and early 1980s. After the 1973 oil price rise, since private-sector trade unions were seen to be engaged in wasteful featherbedding, public-sector enterprises became fashionable. Hence, the growth of Venezuela's production Leviathan began as a reform movement underwritten by oil wealth. Although the central government itself was responsible for only $8 billion of Venezuela's outstanding foreign debt, it was forced to guarantee shaky commercial loans to inefficient SOEs. With the current account in deficit and foreign exchange reserves already decimated, the central government resorted to the issuance of debt in the domestic market, forcing the private sector to increase its short-term credit lines by nearly $5 billion. In effect, long-maturity sovereign external credit was serviced with much more expensive short-term, private-sector commercial debt and, when feasible, drawdowns on reserves.

Like Chile, Venezuela has received harsh treatment at the hands of international commercial creditors in the course of its debt reschedulings prior to a Brady Plan workout. In February 1986, the government signed a restructuring agreement with commercial banks, which came apart as oil prices collapsed. It included no new money, required a prepayment on principal, and extended no grace period for amortization. Under these terms, the public sector made net amortizations of $3.1 billion between 1986 and 1988.

The Perez administration assumed power with the intention of pursuing an international financial strategy based on reducing commercial debt and borrowing from multilateral agencies. By late 1989, as the recessionary impact of the domestic stabilization and restructuring program was felt within the economy, the outlook for timely service of foreign debt worsened and the price of Venezuelan debt paper on the secondary market dropped to one-third of issue price. The Brady Plan provided a mechanism for Venezuela to extricate itself from these difficulties. When the IMF approved a $3.7-billion three-year arrangement in June 1989, an additional $1 billion in Fund money, earmarked to support commercial debt reduction, was complemented by a three-year World Bank loan of $867 million.

Equipped with these resources, the Venezuelan government initiated negotiations with its commercial creditors on a Brady-style debt-reduction exercise in March 1990, and a final agreement was reached in December of that year. As was not the case in the Brady workout with Mexico, very few banks opted to leave Venezuela altogether by selling their paper at a 55 percent discount. Many elected to trade old debt for new low-interest bonds offered at 6.75 percent with guarantees. But much more important was the fact that nearly one-third of the debt renegotiated involved the attachment of credit enhancements to old debt paper in exchange for the provision of new money worth about 20 percent of current exposure. This should bring some $1.15 billion in fresh cash to Venezuela. The remaining creditors had two options. Some exchanged old debt for new bonds, with interest rates rising over six years if Venezuela's financial position improves. Others chose the less popular option of exchanging existing loans at a discount of 30 percent for paper paying interest at the LIBOR bank rate plus a margin of almost 1 percent. The Venezuelans were pleased with the agreement because it not only reduced their near-term debt burden but also furnished them with new loans disbursed through 1992. The bankers too were more satisfied than they were with the outcome of the Mexican Brady exercise. Seeing Venezuela as a better long-term bet than Mexico, they were more willing to extend fresh credit and consequently took less of an immediate knock on capital or interest. This positive outcome is even more heartening given that the commercial banks expressed extreme pessimism about the possibility of reaching an agreement during most of the bargaining process.[13]

During the early 1990s, the Venezuelans are planning to spend some $25 billion on new projects. Hence, aside from their foreign debt repayment needs, the Venezuelans require capital inflows to underwrite ambitious projects in their energy sector and infrastructural upgrades. In addition to foreign participation through direct investments, the Venezuelan government and its SOEs are trying to raise about $6 billion on international markets to support this program, with PDVSA testing these waters through an issue of some $130 million on the Eurobond market in October 1990.

Ideally, Venezuela could pay off its entire external debt and fund its capital improvement program through the repatriation of flight capital. While it is difficult to arrive at an exact dollar figure, many analysts believe that Venezuelan citizens shipped well more than the nation's $30 billion in foreign debt out of the country during the 1980s.[14] Government efforts to date to stem the flood of capital have been largely ineffectual. In 1981, the government freed interest rates in the hope that positive rates would help to keep capital in Venezuela. Capital flight subsided for a few months; but when the government came under pressure from the construction lobby and from weak banks to reimpose administrative controls on interest rates, a new wave ensued. Today, Venezuela lacks a mechanism for collecting taxes on income-earning assets held abroad by its citizens. In 1987, the Luschini government introduced legislation to tax foreign investment income; but in the absence of any enforcement mechanism, the tax yielded no revenue. In the interest of tax simplification, it was abolished in 1989 on the recommendation of the IMF. At bottom, both preventing future capital flight episodes and encouraging repatriation hinges upon fiscal closure, structural liberalization, and the foundation of a stable business environment driven by market forces. Evidence that the Perez reforms are a first step toward the attainment of these ends is seen in the return of some $2 billion in flight capital to Venezuela in 1989 and 1990.

External Liberalization

Venezuela is a latecomer to external-sector liberalization: under the Perez adjustment package, some progress has been made and is opening the economy to trade, capital, and direct-investment flows upheld by a realistic exchange rate. At the start of the Latin American debt crisis, Venezuelan trade policies amounted to a disarray of protectionist bulwarks. The disjointed tariff schedule ran as high as 1,000 percent for certain goods, and more than 60 percent of all imports required special government authorization. At the same time, tariff exonerations came in at 80 percent to 90 percent of gross receipts.[15]

The Perez government has adopted what must be considered by any standard a radical trade-liberalization policy. Measures to liberalize trade undertaken in Venezuela during the current administration include (1) elimination of nearly all quantitative restrictions and import prohibitions except for those on some symbolic luxury goods; (2) a 70 percent reduction in imports covered by special permits and a like cut in exonerations; (3) accession to the GATT; and (4) homogenization of and across-the-board cuts in tariff rates.

In June 1989, maximum tariff rates were reduced to 80 percent for consumer goods and 50 percent for industrial inputs. Nine months later, tariffs were respectively 50 percent and 30 percent; and by 1993, the maximum rate will decline to 20 percent. By 1991 the average tariff rate was 11 percent. Thus far, agricultural trade has been excluded from the process, but some liberalization has occurred in wheat and cotton. The key measure, as is discussed later, was the abandonment of a multiple exchange rate system in 1989, which eliminated the core of Venezuela's protectionist machinery.

How well the open Venezuelan trade regime will fare cannot be determined with any assurance since the current stabilization package has dampened import demand. Purchases from abroad are actually declining in the wake of trade liberalization. The outlook for permanent trade liberalization is clouded by the comparative disorganization of consumers and by the fact that it was instituted simultaneously with increases in various subsidized prices.

A stronger and more irreversible opening has taken place for direct investment. It is ironic that Venezuela loosened its national control of productive capital while pursuing an import-substitution industrialization strategy. In the 1960s, the government allowed foreign enterprises to be established and produce locally those goods that had previously been imported. Then Venezuelisation occurred in the early 1970s. This was not full nationalization but a series of discriminatory controls on foreign money and real assets. Bureaucratic gaggles blocked the efficient usage of external capital and swelled the government's wage bill to boot. Periodically, streamlining measures were implemented; but with a fragmented exchange system, complication was built into the direct-investment regime.

At the start of 1990, the Venezuelan Superintendency of Foreign Investment (SIEX) issued Decree 727. Sweeping changes were affected through it. All sectors of the economy, apart from life insurance and the media, were opened to 100 percent foreign ownership and all restrictions on earnings and capital repatriation were jettisoned. This regulation is sharply different from, and must not be confused with, Decree 86, governing Venezuela's debt-equity swap program, with its sharp curbs on short- and medium-term repatriations of profits and dividends. According to SIEX Superintendent Perozo, Decree 86 was intended as a limited-time measure for debt-equity swaps, but Decree 727 is Venezuela's "investment bible."[16]

In large part, Decree 727 is an enabling law pursuant to Venezuela's five-year, $21-billion oil-sector development plan, for which the government seeks foreign equity partners. A $3-billion Cristobal Colon liquid natural gas project, already in progress, is regarded as a major test of Venezuela's ability to draw foreign investors into its energy sector. A joint enterprise between PDVSA and Exxon, Shell, and Mitsubishi, the project waits approval by the Venezuelan Congress to go forward. Like Mexico, Venezuela is not yet ready to throw open its oil wells to foreign outfits. The government has allowed foreign telecommunications firms to submit bids for the purchase of a third of the government-owned telephone company, with remaining shares to be sold through the national stock exchange.

More to reduce debt than to stimulate greater direct investment inflows, the Luschini government undertook a debt-equity swap program in 1988. It was saddled from the start by the multiple exchange rate and the government's insistence that certificates be exchanged at the official (nonpreferential) rate. With the bolivar trading at 40 to the dollar in the parallel exchange market, the official rate for the Venezuelan swap debut of 14.5 bolivars to the dollar was enormously unappealing.

The Perez government has instituted a long-term debt-equity swap scheme, calling for a yearly total of $600 million in conversions through monthly auctions. The program, which is governed by Decree 86, features sharp curbs on short- and medium-term repatriations of profits and dividends. In 1990, debt-equity swaps activity ended halfway through the year when the government reached its quota of $600 million. The Perez administration is less than keen on these swaps, feeling that they substitute for direct investment that would be coming to Venezuela without the need for a discount through the secondary market and that current depressed prices on real assets offer too great a bargain to nonnational investors. In addition, should the government's plans for tapping into international capital markets prove out, it will provide a much cheaper source of investment funds and foreign exchange inflows to repay external debt than the swap program.

Venezuela's traditional approach to exchange-rate management has centered upon the fixed rate, which, when combined with low domestic inflation, translated into a stable real exchange rate. However, multiple exchange rates have been used to deal with balance of payments crises, and these have functioned to mask overvaluation and latent risk. In 1986, for example, the collapse of global oil prices compelled the government to undertake a 93 percent devaluation of the bolivar against the dollar. Faced with the prospect of a similar enormous devaluation, the Perez government decided to abandon the system and float the exchange rate. Given the exchange-rate differential of more than 150 percent between the official market and parallel markets, this constituted a major shock to the economy. In time, should price stability be maintained and monetary policy be insulated from political forces by institutional reform, Venezuela might do well in shifting to a trotting peg mechanism, while retaining rate unification.

Domestic Stabilization

Fiscal stabilization under the 1989 adjustment package has been severe. The Perez government achieved fiscal closure in 1989 and 1990 at the cost of output falling more than 10 percent. In the final years of the Luschini administration, investment spending was protected from budget cuts, while current spending (on education, health, maintenance of infrastructure, administration of justice, and the like) bore the brunt of the cuts. This led to the neglect of physical and human infrastructure, many projects abandoned before completion, and a significant social debt. Today, there is a growing consensus that higher priority should be accorded to health, education, and infrastructural needs.

Reform of Venezuela's tax structure is a key to long-term domestic stabilization, but the nation is an extreme case of tax disease arising from public-sector wealth. For many years, oil revenues were used to pay for public expenditures (at the height of the oil boom, oil contributed close to 80 percent of government revenue). Consequently, no serious effort was made to reform the tax system, which is plagued by high marginal rates, generalized evasion, little effort at enforcement, and double taxation of capital. The Perez administration plans to reform the tax structure through revision of the income tax and adoption of a value-added tax. Thus far, however, the legislature has been reluctant to eliminate loopholes that favor the wealthy or to impose new levies unless they are accompanied by still more special exemptions.

Domestic Liberalization

Domestic structural liberalization has also encountered some roadblocks, notably in the failed effort of the Perez administration to liberate interest rates, which have traditionally been fixed by the central bank. This has led to financial repression, with deeply negative rates when maxidevaluations boosted the cost of imports. This was the case until the Perez government raised interest rates from 13 percent to 28 percent and then freed them altogether, causing them to reach 42 percent by the end of 1989. Freeing interest rates created a political backlash, with the opposition bringing a successful suit against the central bank in the Supreme Court, forcing it to bring rates down by administrative order. The entire banking system is noncompetitive as a result of this legacy and is highly oligopolistic in structure, with more than 80 percent of the industry's profits concentrated in just four institutions.[17] Foreign penetration of the financial sector is virtually nonexistent: Citibank is now the sole purely foreign-owned bank in Venezuela, and it limits its activities to serving multinational clients.

Privatization is another area where a deep-rooted legacy, a late start, and political opposition have impeded domestic liberalization efforts. Privatization is an entirely new concept, an abrupt about-face from the 1970s when the watchword was nationalization. Parallel to the 1989 adjustment package, a privatization fund has been created with the initial task of selling off commercial banks, cement companies, sugar mills, hotels, and other public-sector assets. Privatization of other large concerns, such as airlines (the national airline Viasa) and a portion of the national phone company are under way.

Yet the immediate outlook is shrouded by depressed economic conditions under the stabilization program and by the widespread feeling that the government should delay further divestitures until growth conditions raise the selling price of its more attractive SOEs. Privatization is a controversial political issue in Venezuela, and the perception that it amounts to a giveaway could scuttle the current program. Last, deregulation efforts have been concentrated on the removal of price controls for all goods except some ten basic products, but these measures were instituted on the cutting edge of political turmoil.

Economic Performance

Between 1983 and 1988, the aggregate Venezuelan growth rate was negative, and the initial impact of the 1989 adjustment package was a further 10 percent contraction in the economy. A rebound took place in 1990, as the economy grew by about 4 percent with the recovery of global oil prices, and a GDP growth of 5 to 6 percent for 1991 seemed plausible if oil prices remained comparatively firm. Exchange-rate liberalization and uncertainty about the future course of structural reform have helped to keep inflation way above its customary level. In 1990, inflation came in at 40 percent, which was nevertheless a substantial improvement over the rate of more than 80 percent registered in Perez's first year.

In light of the suppression of imports through devaluation and domestic recession, the Venezuelan economy has posted major gains in its external accounts. In 1990, Venezuela logged a $6 billion current account surplus, with international reserves rising from $7.4 billion to $11.5 billion. Import compression has created a large bilateral trade imbalance between Venezuela and the United States, with the United States running a trade deficit of some $6.3 billion in 1990. Venezuelan imports were expected to increase 20 to 25 percent in 1991 over the $6.6 billion level of 1990, as economic activities accelerate. Capital goods imports by the oil industry alone were expected to exceed $1 billion in 1990.

POLITICAL FACTORS

Politically, the future of the Perez administration depends upon its capacity to stick with adjustment and make it work, both in substance and in the eyes of the Venezuelan people. When Perez assumed official in January 1989, the public was startled when the first action of its new president was to implement a drastic, comprehensive austerity program, including structural liberalization. To date, the administration's economic policy has received very little support from most sectors of society. Heated debates have erupted within the Venezuelan Congress over the scope and depth of economic reform, and the administration's relations with the legislature are strained to a degree never experienced before. Popular reaction against orthodox adjustment has been even more vehement, with Perez's popular approval rating plummeting down to 15 percent a full year after the start of adjustment.[18]

BOLIVIA

Bolivia does not possess a large vibrant economy or even the potential to develop one. Its categorization as a first-tier country is based primarily on the degree of adjustment it has accomplished to date. Beneath this, there is a moral dimension in advocating Bolivia's inclusion to the first tier of Latin American nations with which the United States might conclude a bilateral agreement congruent with the aims of the EAI. Bolivia's adjustment experience was pioneering, bold, and (initially at least) a solo flight. It was based securely on orthodox adjustment and undertaken when other Latin American nations were delaying or abandoning stabilization and liberalization reforms. The adjustment package instituted by President Paz Estenssoro in 1985 was planned and implemented with radically orthodox goals and methods. Bolivia set a precedent by being the first Latin American nation to reduce its debt overhang through a substantial buyback of commercial debt paper on the secondary market, long before the Brady Plan. Moreover, with some strong qualifications, the Bolivian program has been surprisingly successful. Most compelling of all, one reason for its popular acceptance was that Bolivian adjustment was charted and carried out without extensive support from multilateral financial institutions, which had formed the view that Bolivia was not serious about economic reform. Today, the Bolivian plan looks almost like a laboratory experiment of orthodox adjustment, with its homespun origin lending it political credibility.

ADJUSTMENT

The General Course of Adjustment

Prior to the 1985 program, Bolivia met with the standard Latin American debt crisis featuring the basic ingredients of overborrowing, a statist economy, policy mismanagement, deterioration in terms of trade, and skyrocketing interest payments on variable-rate foreign bank loans. The government was at a complete loss to deal with these shocks, and the Bolivian economy lurched into hyperinflation which reached an annualized rate of 24,000 percent in September 1985. The source of inflation, the monetization of domestic debt, can be traced to the tax system, with taxes equivalent to just 1 percent of GDP meeting only 3 percent of government spending and 75 percent of the expenditure financed by the central bank. Hyperinflation was not a structural problem but a fiscal crisis accommodated through the astronomical expansion of the monetary supply. The bulk of government expenditures took the form of direct and effective consumption subsidies. At the end of

1985, a dollar could fill two or three gas tanks, while through a "commissariat system," a Bolivian tin miner could purchase a kilogram of prime beef for the equivalent of 1 U.S. cent.[19]

In the summer of 1985, Victor Paz Estenssoro defeated conservative candidate Hugo Banzer in the Bolivian presidential election, and to many this appeared to seal Bolivia's doom. Paz was a populist directly associated with the creation of the very system of statist intervention that had brought Bolivia to its knees. It was a complete shock when, in a scenario that would be played out later in many Latin American countries, Paz proposed a radical yet orthodox adjustment, combining macroeconomic discipline and extensive structural reform. According to John Williamson, who witnessed the planning of the Bolivian austerity package, the program's goals were astounding: "In short, Paz's advisors planned the equivalent of about five GATT rounds, six Gramm-Rudmans, and more deregulation than had been accomplished by the Carter and Reagan administrations together, all overnight."[20] The only unorthodox element in the plan was that full, timely payment of external debt service was not a working objective. Under the adjustment program, debt-service payments were remitted to multilateral and bilateral organizations only; interest payments on obligations to foreign commercial banks were suspended. This turned out to be a politically shrewd exclusion: adjustment would be undertaken for its own sake, not for the sake of repaying foreign creditors.

After giving his now-famous inaugural "Bolivia is dying" speech, President Paz Estenssoro issued a single, 170-article decree. The contents of the mandate are described below, but its results were nothing short of phenomenal. On the domestic front, the adjustment measures had a dramatic and immediate impact on the financial condition of the central government and of the state-owned enterprises; it brought an end to hyperinflation, arrested decline in per-capita income, and pared debt overhang via a secondary-market buyback. In terms of external stabilization, within a year the measures achieved their objective of a net flow of funds into the country. Net resource transfer went from $ − 183.5 million in 1984 and $ − 139.4 million in 1985 to a positive $20.1 million in 1986 and $71.0 million in 1987.

The key to external stabilization was recognition of Bolivian adjustment by international financial institutions and a reflux of flight capital. In 1986, the World Bank announced its full support, although a whole year elapsed before its first loan was disbursed. Eventually, policy reform paved the way for multilateral official loans from the IBRD, during the 1986 to 1988 period, of approximately $350 million, while an agreement with the IMF also opened the door for official debt rescheduling through the Paris Club. Fortunately, credibility at home, which had boosted the stabilization measures, led to the repatriation of more than $260 million in flight capital.

However, two bold asterisks must be appended to the Bolivian adjustment miracle: the economy remained vulnerable to external shock, and output growth did not resume. Just as the Bolivian adjustment program was beginning to exercise a growth-promoting influence (after a preliminary contraction), the economy was rocked by a series of external shocks, including a fall of 54 percent in the global price of tin between mid-1985 and mid-1986 and Argentina's suspension of payments on Bolivian natural gas exports. Combined losses from these external shocks, which exceeded $150 million in 1987, were compounded by the domestic fallout stemming from export reeipt losses, notably the need to make emergency income assistance payments to tin miners idled by the collapse of the metal's price on world markets. More telling, domestic output remained flat, and private investment was meager.

External Stabilization

The Paz Estenssoro administration achieved stabilization of the country's external accounts in one fell swoop by placing commercial creditors on hold and repurchasing bank debt at a deep discount. By the time the adjustment program was announced, Bolivian debt repayment was a shambles, with no interest or amortizations payments being made to external lenders, and foreign banks stuck with some $670 million in nonperforming loans. Paz made the decision to renew debt service of official loans to bilateral and multilateral organizations while maintaining a moratorium on interest payments to the banks. This step was taken in contemplation of a commercial-debt rescheduling that would include the Third World's first comprehensive debt reduction through a secondary market conversion. Paradoxically, this drastic approach was feasible because the repayment status of Bolivian paper could hardly deteriorate any further and Bolivia's relations with the international financial community were already at a nadir. By the summer of 1985, the foreign banks had completely suspended loan flows to Bolivia, including lines of credit for trade financing and direct loans for trade transactions. Neither side had much to lose from trying something entirely new.

Prospects for a move of this sort working out were bolstered by the announcement of the Baker Plan, but the Paz Estenssoro government was not deemed eligible for assistance under it. Indeed, when Bolivia approached the United States for Baker Plan help, it was refused "on the grounds that the foreign commercial banks were not prepared to make fresh financing available."[21] It was from sheer desperation that Bolivia was forced to overcome its own problems independent of the IMF conditional financing. Bolivia had fallen out of compliance with its IMF standby, the central government budget was nowhere near equilibrium, and the Fund was still insisting upon the elimination of commercial debt arrears and a bank-rescheduling accord before it would lend its imprimatur to a Bolivian adjustment program. In a sense, the IMF had not caught up to Bolivia's assessment of its own debt repayment capacity and was still wedded to its narrow adjustment recipe. Jeffrey Sachs had to dissuade the IMF from demanding a Bolivian devaluation a month after the hyperinflation had been stabilized.[22] Eventually, Bolivia would receive crucial adjustment assistance from the Fund, the Bank, and, following Paris Club negotiations in 1986 and 1988, $215.8 million from various bilateral agencies — with the lion's share coming from Germany and Japan on concessional terms.

The Paz Estenssoro government cast aside the customary practice of lengthening maturities and repaying old debt with new loans and opted instead to open negotiations on repurchasing its debt. In March 1988, these negotiations culminated in the successful repurchase of about half the country's outstanding liabilities to foreign commercial banks at 11 cents on the dollar. The banks agreed to the scheme, since it had little impact at all on the market value of their Bolivian loans. Prior to the repurchase, Bolivia's $670 million in debt traded at 6 cents on the dollar and had a total market value of about $40 million. After Bolivia spent $34 million to buy back more than $300 million of its debt, the remainder traded at 11 cents on the dollar, giving it a total market valuation of nearly $40 million. What Bolivia got was a drastic cut in its scheduled bank debt service, while for the lenders the operation was essentially a wash. Bolivia garnered the wherewithal to carry out the buyback through its own foreign exchange reserves, supplemented by funds from the Inter-American Development Bank, which, unlike the IMF and the IBRD, continued its operations in Bolivia even during the darkest hours of hyperflation.

Since 1985, multilateral organizations have been the mainstay of Bolivian external finance as commercial lenders have continued their boycott on fresh loans. Bolivia received net transfers in the late 1980s from the IMF, the World Bank, the IDB, and the Andean Development Corporation (the last on near-market terms). Bolivia has now reached the end of this approach, having exhausted its loan quotas with these organizations and is now obligated to make net repayments to them. Apart from an initial flight capital reflux, absent participation in an entirely new program like the EAI, there simply is no external source to provide the financing necessary to restart the Bolivian economy.

External Liberalization

As part of the 1985 package, the Paz Estenssoro government eradicated Bolivia's long-standing protectionist trade regime. In place of the traditional fragmented tariff system and its accompanying import licensings and exonerations, Paz instituted a single uniform tariff for all imports, with no exceptions whatsoever. As has been the experience elsewhere, the move actually increased the central government's revenues from trade while lowering the average tariff rate. Widespread loopholes and opportunities for fraud were eliminated, tariff enforcement was simplified, and taxes replaced nontariff barriers.

Adhering to strict free-market principles, Bolivia did not make direct at-

tempts to stimulate foreign direct investment through special incentives, but
it did make a sincere effort to lay a groundwork for it by making commitments for investment insurance with, inter alia, the United States Overseas
Private Investment Corporation. Nor did Bolivia engage in a formal program
of debt-equity swaps, since this would have entailed a sharp increase in the
money supply and thereby undermined crucial domestic stabilization aims.
Paz's team did undertake a wholesale revision of its exchange-rate policy,
shifting from fixed rates to rate determination by daily currency auctions.
That this has yielded a realistic exchange rate is seen in the unity between the
official rate and the black market rate since 1987. By floating its currency
and unifying the rate, Bolivia protected itself from long periods of overvaluation (and subsequent need for maxidevaluations), while avoiding the corruption and political favoritism that occur when foreign exchange is granted
at an official rate below parity.

Domestic Stabilization

The 1985 approach to domestic stabilization was straightforward with reference to fiscal policy: Paz demanded zero tolerance for central-government
and state-enterprise deficits. The turnabout in the central government's
books was immediate. The overall balance of the nonfinancial public sector
moved from a deficit equivalent to more than 25 percent of GDP in 1984 to
10 percent by 1985 and 3.2 percent in 1986. Fiscal discipline, however, was
undercut in 1987 as a consequence of externalities, notably the sharp drop
in tin prices and Argentina's nonpayment for gas exports. Nevertheless, the
extent of fiscal closure that Bolivia has attained is remarkable.

Near balance of the central government's internal accounts came about
through radical expenditure cuts and the revamping of Bolivia's tax structure.
All consumption subsidies, including those on staples, were eliminated in a
stroke. Prices on public-sector goods and services were brought into line
with real factor costs. For example, the price of a liter of gasoline increased
some thirtyfold in the days following the start of the adjustment program.
Simultaneously, the salaries of all public-sector employees were frozen,
and, more important, illegal cash bonuses paid to workers at state enterprises,
which often amounted to twice the value of above-board annual wages,
were abolished, as was the absurdly subsidized commissariat system.

On the revenue side of the ledgers, after the imposition of an indirect tax
of fuel, comprehensive tax reform was undertaken. The tax reform bill dismantled an outmoded system of some 450 separate levies directed primarily
at income and replaced it with a regime based on nine new taxes targeted at
consumption and wealth. Tax revenues rose from slightly more than 1 percent
of GDP to approximately 9 percent by 1987. By bringing Bolivia's 24,000
percent annual rate of inflation to a halt, the Paz Estenssoro government
signaled its departure from the long-standing practice of monetizing domestic
debt. Bolivian government revenues, however, were arguably held down by the

Tanzi-Olivera effect, since rapid price inflation decimated the real value of taxes paid with a time lag. Thus, while the central government's domestic debt burden was no longer amortized through monetary policy, by shifting to taxes on value added and quelling hyperflation public-sector tax revenues increased commensurately.

Domestic Liberalization

Domestic structural adjustment included the liberation of interest rates from administrative control. The 1985 program provided for interest rates to be set freely in the financial markets for both Bolivian pesos and foreign currency. This bold step amounted to a tacit acknowledgment that foreign currency was an acceptable medium of exchange. This move had favorable consequences for the repatriation of flight capital and helped to cushion external shocks upon Bolivia's export earnings. In the area of privatization, the Bolivian program did *not* parallel the orthodox line. A higher priority was accorded to making state-owned enterprises self-financing rather than on divestiture. Paz's team was understandably concerned about the inflationary undertow of privatization, the depressed value of real assets in the public sector, and the public perception of the adjustment package as a giveaway to national and foreign elites. Deregulation featured the removal of all price controls, which had been hallmarks of Bolivian economic policy for more than half a century. Deregulation was clearly welcomed by small farmers, who had borne the brunt of a hidden tax that favored urban areas, while exchange-rate reform acted as a spur to the production of tradables.

ECONOMIC PERFORMANCE

Bolivia's economic performance has improved dramatically since the institution of the Paz package. In the late 1980s, GDP growth ranged between 2 percent and 3 percent a year. This growth, however, has not kept pace with population growth, so that in per-capita terms Bolivian GDP rates remain negative. Today, with hyperflation vanquished, Bolivia's chief problem as a small, open economy is the narrow, underdeveloped nature of its export basket, with tin comprising more than half its outward trade flows by value. Plainly, Bolivia needs liberalized access to export markets for its traditional commodities; but in the long run, it must also develop nontraditional exports. Precisely where the capital required for export diversification will be found is a mystery. Clearly, Bolivia's membership in an economic alliance led by the United States would help on both these fronts.

POLITICAL FACTORS

On the other hand, there is no country in Latin America where a popular consensus for the continuation of a market approach to development is more firmly grounded than Bolivia. Despite a resumption of real per-capita growth, in 1989, after four years of orthodox adjustment, nearly two-thirds of the electorate endorsed the austerity approach to adjustment by voting for the incumbent regime. Somehow, President Paz Estenssoro in his now-famous "Bolivia is dying" speech rekindled hope for progress among his people.

Two factors account for popular support of the adjustment program in the ensuing years. First, although Paz's economic team received technical assistance from the IMF and the World Bank, they designed the adjustment program themselves and used it as an internal blueprint rather than the basis for a letter of intent to the IMF. In each dimension of the program, the Bolivians proved that its was not intended to enrich foreign creditors but to place the economy on a sound footing for the benefit of all. In particular, the cessation of commercial debt payments allowed the results of the sacrifices incurred by adjustment to be legitimately portrayed as going to the Bolivians themselves. Second, Paz drew upon his own authoritarian reputation, taking a no-nonsense position toward the most powerful workers group in his country, the tin miners' union. When the adjustment package was announced, the union struck, and Paz immediately declared a state of siege. With the collapse of tin prices in 1987, some financial assistance was furnished to the miners, but Paz responded to the adverse price movement by shuttering capacity and laying off mineworkers. Seeing the decisiveness of their government and convinced that reform was for their ultimate benefit, Bolivian taxpayers demonstrated that they would pull their weight and subsequently endorsed the Paz Estenssoro adjustment program in the 1989 elections.

COLOMBIA

After experiencing an unprecedented foreign-exchange boom and high growth rates during the last four years of the previous decade, the Colombian economy began to show signs of trouble in the early 1980s, partly because the government allowed the currency to become overvalued and lost fiscal discipline. Colombia chose early to pursue a comprehensive adjustment package, and it now faces comparatively modest further policy adjustments. Largely because it avoided the drastic policy lurches that the rest of Latin America has suffered, Colombia finished the 1980s with the region's best growth record.

ADJUSTMENT

The General Course of Adjustment

Adjustment was first undertaken in 1984, as the government instituted a stabilization drive aimed at reducing the public-sector and current-account deficits, promoting exports and export-led growth and restoring access of the country to international capital markets. The program was accompanied by a gradual devaluation of the currency, and Colombia was able to achieve this very large adjustment of the exchange rate without devaluing abruptly. Moreover, the devaluation did not stimulate inflation beyond traditional levels, and the gradual adjustment of the mid-1980s did not prompt significant net capital flight because the speculative outflows were compensated by the return of illegal capital from North American banks.

Although stabilization was pursued through orthodox means, no wholesale liberalization of the domestic or external sectors of the economy was undertaken. Advocates of free-market adjustment tend to shun reference to Colombia's positive performance, fearing that critics might use Colombia's example to claim "that the preservation of positive growth in Colombia is due to its retention of the statist model."[23]

External Stabilization

Because foreign debt was not a major problem for Colombia, its external stabilization has been fairly constant. Although Colombian debt paper trades at a discount between 30 and 35 percent on the secondary market, this ratio to par has remained stable throughout the Latin American debt crisis. Colombia has managed this without renegotiation of its foreign commercial liabilities. Indeed, although Colombia has refinanced its commercial debt with voluntary new loans, it is the only major borrower in Latin America to have avoided rescheduling of its bank debt. The Colombians have never received balance-of-payments assistance from the IMF, and they have no intention of blotting this record by engaging in a Brady Plan debt reduction. Extensive capital flight has been prevented, in part by Colombia's use of exchange controls. Its disciplined macroeconomic policies are probably more important in this regard than legal prohibitions against the export of capital.[24] In particular, by pursuing a policy of flexible exchange-rate management, Colombia avoided substantial overvaluation and allowed interest rates to remain close to equilibrium, limiting the influence of pull and push incentives toward flight capital movements.

External Liberalization

Structural adjustment of its foreign sector, other than the maintenance of a competitive exchange rate, has been virtually absent from Colombia's stabilization-oriented adjustment efforts. Colombia has retained a protectionist trade regime, replete with administrative import controls and indiscriminate export subsidies and incentives. In fact, under emergency balance-of-payments conditions, the Colombia government tends to intensify its protectionist trade regime through the mechanism of import licensing. Since 1984 a timid trade liberalization has been at work, featuring modest tariff reductions and the elimination of some formal red-tape nontariff barriers; and Colombia's current president, César Gaviria, is committed to gradual trade liberalization. But the economy is inwardly oriented and based on an import-substitution industrialization strategy which, when coupled with macroeconomic discipline, has served the economy remarkably well. Consistent with that approach, Columbia has a restrictive foreign direct investment regime grounded in the theoretical tenets of the Andean Pact. Some liberalization of foreign investment rules is expected under the Gaviria administration.[25] The government of Colombia has not adopted any debt-reducing program that would also promote foreign investment. Gaviria's policy advisors, who feel that foreign direct investment is insensitive to artificial inducements, do not foresee that additional investment would flow from debt-equity swaps and similar incentives. Moreover, debt conversions are regarded as an obstacle to the present foreign-financing strategy of the government, which is based on maintaining the relative exposure of the different types of lenders, thereby "blocking exit doors for the commercial banks to reduce their exposure."[26] What has allowed this illiberal trade and FDI policy to work is the government's commitment to flexible exchange-rate management.

Domestic Stabilization and Liberalization

Colombia's traditional commitment to fiscal and monetary discipline has kept its domestic economy stable. The Gaviria regime has shifted budget outlays away from expensive capital projects and toward infrastructure and human-capital investment. Similarly, there is no perception on the part of the government that the domestic economy requires structural reform through privatization or deregulation, while administratively determined bank lending rates have been kept close to equilibrium.

ECONOMIC PERFORMANCE

What bothers many orthodox economists is that this fairly heterodox approach has paid off for Colombia during Latin America's lost decade to an extent not seen in economies undertaking far deeper reforms. GDP growth has ranged between 3 percent and 4 percent throughout the 1980s and into the start of the 1990s, making Colombia the only Latin American nation to experience GDP growth in per-capita terms. A heightened energy import bill did contribute to Colombia's less than favorable inflation rate in 1990 (nearly 30 percent), but this is interpreted as a cyclical phenomenon arising outside a noninflationary policy nucleus.

CHAPTER 6

Second-Tier EAI Economies: Brazil, Argentina, and Peru

The chief criteria employed in the classification of Brazil, Argentina, and Peru as second-tier economies are their relative failure to attain stabilization goals and restructure their economies along free-market lines. This aside, both Brazil and, to a lesser extent, Argentina could be highly attractive free-trade partners for the United States. Both feature the natural ingredients needed for dynamic export and investment outlets. In Argentina's case at least, some liberalization of the external sector has taken place. But until these countries can get their fiscal and monetary policies in order and achieve a realistic, stable exchange rate, their capacity to function in a hemispheric free-trade arrangement is questionable. As for Peru, it lacks the inherent growth potential of the larger second-tier countries; and, as a consequence of gross mismanagement by the regime of Alan Garcia, must atone for the sins of the immediate past while undergoing painful adjustment, a tall order that does not augur well for Peru's readiness to participate in a regional trade partnership.

Plainly, these nations would like to benefit from EAI treatment and Presidents Collor and Menem were among the first Latin American heads of state to respond positively to President Bush's EAI proposal. At the same time, of the continent's larger states, they are the furthest from creating the requisite conditions for EAI eligibility. In this context, the EAI could act as a conditional incentive toward further adjustment. It could, however, prompt the formation of a competitive subregional trading bloc led by Brazil and Argentina and a possible return to the inward orientation of past Latin American integration efforts. For the EAI proposal, then, these second-tier nations hold forth the promise of moving Latin America toward a sound basis but also the danger of coopting other economies into a populist confederacy.

BRAZIL

In Brazil, the world's largest Third World debtor, no authentic adjustment took place during the 1980s. Rather than adjust, Brazil attempted to grow its way out of its current-account straits, and this approach has left it in the midst of hyperflation. The same can be said of Argentina; but even under Alfonsin, the Argentine government was at least nominally committed to stabilization and structural reform. This cannot be said of Brazil, which even under President Collor has remained basically indisposed to open its economy. The heart of Brazil's problem remains excessive statism, with generally inefficient, loss-making SOEs accounting for over half of GDP and commensurate fiscal imbalance twice as large as that of the United States. What allowed Brazil to continue along this path since the early 1970s are the enormous resource endowments that distinguished Brazil as the "land of the future" during the era of the "Brazilian Miracle" (1968–1973). These natural advantages have never been fully exploited but have been hamstrung and siphoned to mask fundamental structural disequilibria.

The entire mess is paralleled in Brazil's approach to external-debt repayment. Punctuated with suspensions, featuring fierce wranglings with bank steering committees, Brazil's debt policy has consisted largely of flip-flop vacillation on the issue of whether outstanding loans should be repaid at all. The country has decimated its reserves, eviscerated its external sector, and worst of all, paid off comparatively cheap external debt with high-cost domestic debt. These moves were followed by gross monetary expansion and, most recently, by an absolutely unconscionable liquidity mop up that is little less than bank robbery. Finally, a danger of contamination exists so long as Brazilian statism and its attendant import-substitution path survive. Other developing countries could cite Brazil's example as a reason to turn to the disastrous road it has traveled over that past decade and a half, with few of the factor advantages that have allowed the Brazilians to limp along toward inevitable ruin.

ADJUSTMENT

The General Course of Adjustment

When the debt crisis began in Brazil in 1982, President Figuereido steered his country on a quasi-orthodox recessionary course, without deviating from the customary import-substitution path. Administered import compression was the centerpiece of Brazil's initial response to the debt crisis, and it worked reasonably well given Brazil's extensive import-substitution capacity. This was followed by a strong, export-led recovery in 1984 and 1985, and when a moderate and respected Tancredo Neves became Brazil's first popularly elected president in modern times, optimism for Brazil's future was rekindled.

But Neves died shortly before his inauguration, and his vice presidential running mate, Jose Sarney, was left to implement his stabilization blueprints. In February 1986, with inflation running at 400 percent per year, Brazil embarked on a major heterodox stabilization effort, the notorious Cruzado Plan, pivoting upon a wage-price freeze. One year later, when the price freeze was removed, inflation exploded. The government initiated new attempts to control inflation — in mid-1987 under the Bresser Plan and again in January 1989 under the Summer Plan. Once again, the government froze prices, squeezed credit, and lopped zeros off the face of the value of the currency. Sarney, unfortunately, lacked the political gumption to achieve fiscal closure: each of these stabilization programs was doomed by the continued growth of both the state and the parastatals. When Sarney took office in 1985, government employment (including the SOEs) stood at 560,000; when he left five years later the payroll had increased by 140,000, leaving the public sector with an additional $21 billion a year in salary expenditures.

In March 1990, Fernando Collor de Mello became Brazil's head of state and appointed as his economy minister, the 36-year-old Zelia Cardoso de Mello. Elected on a populist platform, Collor delayed unveiling the details of his plan for restoring order to Brazil's economy until the last minute. The package that Collor and Cardoso prepared and pushed through the Brazilian Congress in April 1990 consisted of seemingly radical and orthodox economic and administrative reforms. The economic package contained fiscal, monetary, and tax overhauls; the introduction of a new currency; foreign exchange market reform; price rollbacks; and a commitment to renegotiating Brazil's foreign debt with commercial creditors.

The administrative plank featured restructuring of government ministries, a stiff reduction of the federal civil service, the divestiture of state-owned enterprises through debt-equity swaps, and the withdrawal of privileges for high-ranking government officials. Through these means, Collor proposed to turn the central government's budget deficit, equivalent to 7 percent of GDP in 1989, into a modest surplus by the end of 1990.

All this sounded constructive, if not entirely plausible. But Collor had already demonstrated his willingness to depart from orthodox adjustment upon his assumption of the Brazilian presidency. Two days before taking office, with the cooperation of the outgoing Sarney administration, Collor declared a three-day bank closing, lest uncertainty about his adjustment approach prompt massive bank runs. Collor then announced that his government would freeze for a period of eighteen months some $80 billion in private assets held in Brazilian overnight bank accounts.

The measure sent the Brazilian economy into a production tailspin and an upward price spiral. By November 1990, a record number of companies had declared bankruptcy, while private bank credit was virtually unavailable. In January 1991, Brazil was given yet another bank holiday, and Finance Minister Cardoso announced an indefinite freeze on all wages and prices, to be enforced by reassembling the price-control office she disbanded less than a year before. Public ire with Collor and Cardoso led to the former's dismissal of the latter, and in May 1991, Marcilio Marques Moreira became the new Brazilian finance minister. With Moreira installed, a revised adjustment program was announced with more realistic goals and a stronger emphasis on long-term structural liberalization.

External Stabilization

Debt overhang is a major variable in Brazil's economic performance, its effect being glossed over by unsustainable monetary expansion. The position of the public sector continues to be badly compromised by the need to extract resources from the private sector for the service of external debt. In the last four years of the 1980s, Brazil paid more than $47 billion in interest and $21.6 billion in principal to its foreign creditors. To achieve the fiscal consolidation it needs without a major recession, Brazil must reduce its transfer of resources abroad through comprehensive debt reduction and even the postponement of debt service. Here, however, Brazil risks a permanent rupture with its external creditors, who are already sorely miffed by Brazil's checkered repayment record.

Falling from compliance with its IMF conditional adjustment program in 1986, the Sarney government announced of a debt moratorium in February 1987.[1] Seeking to iron out its differences with the banks, Brazil took a series of high-handed actions that did not ingratiate it with its creditors. Minister of Finance Dilson Funaro unsuccessfully insisted on dealing directly with bank lenders individually rather than through a steering committee. When this failed, the Brazilians tried to create a wedge between the bankers by placing more lenient European bankers on negotiation committees in place of hardline American bankers. They also insisted on a rescheduling agreement before they would enter into a new adjustment program under IMF supervision. In response, U.S. bankers pressured both the IMF and the U.S. Treasury to steer Brazil toward coming to terms with commercial creditors before the multilateral institutions would grant fresh loans. To break the impasse, Brazilian authorities offered in September 1987 to convert half their $68 billion in bank loans into thirty-five-year bonds yielding 6 percent fixed interest per year. This was tantamount to a discount of almost 50 percent on the nominal value of their debt, and the banks rejected the proposal out of hand.[2]

An agreement was finally reached between the Sarney government and Brazil's foreign creditors in August 1988, ending eighteen months of conflict over the moratorium on interest payments. The accord stipulated that Brazil's incipient debt-equity swap auctions would be expanded so that nearly $2 billion of debt would become available for conversion at face value. Exit bonds also appeared on the menu of financial options; and although they were not enhanced with credit guarantees, Brazil sold more than $1 billion to more than 100 banks, some $4 billion short of its target. Swaps, exit bonds, and other secondary-market conversions enabled Brazil to pare its external debt by more than $8 billion in 1988. In sheer volume, it was the largest exercise in debt-equity conversion Latin America had ever witnessed. The program's cost, however, was a surge in inflation resulting from the expansion of the money supply caused directly by the conversion of debt paper into local currency. The 1988 workout also included a substantial prepayment on principal at face value. Consequently, a large share of Brazil's trade surplus was dedicated to making amortization payments ahead of their originally scheduled maturity. To round up these receipts, the Sarney administration issued internal debt at extremely high interest rates. Sweder van Wijnbergen has captured this anomaly: "This is really like using your credit card to pay off your mortgage."[3] The credit shuffle also sent a clear message to investors that high inflation was bound to persist as the government's fiscal position came under even greater pressure.

Two months later, President Sarney issued a decree closing the door on informal debt conversion for state-owned companies. He later reneged on his promise to continue the debt-equity swap program, citing the need to support the antiinflationary Summer Plan. Disturbed at this unilateral revision of the 1988 agreement, the banks reacted by reducing revolving trade and interbank lines of credit. Sarney retaliated by imposing another suspension of interest payments on Brazilian debt. The banks fired back by blocking Brazil's access to short-term trade credit, paradoxically weakening the economy's debt-service capacity. In the final year of the Sarney regime, Brazil simply built up its reserves rather than paying its debts, while the banks diverted money to increase their reserves to cover future loan losses instead of making fresh loans to Brazil.

Although Brazil remained ineligible for a Brady Plan workout, the announcement of the plan and, more to the point, the resistance to it on the part of the international banks created a new situation immediately before the start of Collor's term. Recognizing the growing displeasure of developed-country governments with their international bankers, Brazil started to make repayments to its official Paris Club creditors in February 1990. The bankers looked askance at this move and insisted that Brazil enter into an IMF adjustment program before it could deal with the banking cartel's steering committee. In fact, Brazil did work with IMF, and both the IMF and the World Bank enthusiastically approved much of the Collor plan.[4] But since these organizations were not happy with the banks either, they did not incorporate a requirement for commercial debt renegotiation or even the resumption of payments to the banks for Brazil to remain eligible for disbursements of IMF and World Bank loans.

At the outset, the banks reacted positively to Collor's election. After all, it was the departed Sarney who had raised their ire. Moreover, Collor had defeated his closest rival, Luis Ignacio Lula de Silva (Lula), a left-wing candidate who had vowed to suspend all payments on the foreign debt, to investigate the legitimacy of loan contracts, and to work toward establishing a Latin American debtors' cartel. Bankers were relieved when Collor said that he would renegotiate Brazil's foreign debt but paid considerably less attention to his correlative statement that he would not make sacrifices that would interfere with economic growth.

Shortly after his election, the new president spelled out exactly what he had in mind with regard to his country's foreign debt. Collor suggested pegging bank interest payments to 1 percent of Brazilian GDP and placing a ceiling for total annual payments of just $5 billion, a small fraction of the annual payments due to the banks.[5] Brazil's U.S. bank lenders were hit with a shock from an unexpected quarter in July 1990 when federal bank regulators ordered them to write off one-fifth of the $11.1 billion Brazil owed them. The banks tried to forestall the action and give their Brazilian paper the semblance of performance. Citicorp chairman John Reed even hinted that Brazil would be lent fresh money if only it made some token payments on overdue interest.[6] This ploy failed, and the ensuing write-down caused real damage to bank profit statements and an immediate decline in their stocks. Attempting to find a compromise, Assistant Treasury Secretary Mulford visited Brazil in August 1990 and stressed the need for Brazil to resume repayments to commercial banks. Mulford's visit did not pay off, and Brazil remained defiant.

A parlay between Brazil and its bank creditors was set for September in New York, with Economy Minister Cardoso leading her country's deputation. The attitude of the Brazilian representatives was painfully evident when Cardoso alarmed bankers with a careless comment that both sides would sit down to talk "with loaded pistols."[7] Aside from these rhetorical fireworks, Cardoso insisted on two points. First, debt repayment would not be initiated at all if it interfered with the accomplishment of the Collor Plan's objectives. Second, Brazil would first make repayments to its official multilateral creditors, then to Paris Club members, and last (and perhaps least) to its bank lenders. Disappointment hardly captures the reaction of the bankers to Mrs. Cardoso's ground rules. At the time, Sir Jeremy Morse, chairman of Lloyds Bank in the United Kingdom, stated flat out that he was "very disappointed" by Brazil's continued refusal to make even token payments on the mounting arrears.[8]

A month later, Brazil's ambassador to the United States, Jorio Dauster, met with bankers in New York in October 1990 to discuss the restructuring of Brazil's $70 billion commercial bank debt, holding forth the prospect that token payments would be made, Brazilian paper put back on a performing basis, and another wave of mandatory write-downs avoided. The terms Dauster offered were not what the bankers wanted. They consisted of three options: (1) conversion of the debt into forty-five-year bonds with fixed interest of 9 percent; (2) conversion to twenty-five-year bonds with an interest rate that would rise to 10 percent in the tenth year and remain at that level until maturity; or (3) conversion to fifteen-year debt paper bearing 3 percent interest beginning in the fourth year. Unlike the Mexican restructuring in 1989, none of the Brazilian bonds would be backed by United States Treasury zero-coupon bonds. Incredibly, the Brazilian government insisted on fresh loans of $8 billion to repay the interest arrears (then about $9 billion), and said that it would not pay interest in excess of $1 billion per year. The bankers were flabbergasted. Having fallen from grace with the IMF, they still turned to the IMF and the Bush administration to perform the same sort of arm-twisting that accompanied the Mexican Brady Plan workout.

Currently there is no Brady Plan treatment on the Brazilian debt horizon, and sporadic talks with demoralized bankers have led nowhere. As of mid-1991, Brazil was some $10 billion in arrears on interest payments alone. In the future, as more write-downs are required by U.S. regulatory authorities, Brazil is likely to see its trade credit lines evaporate altogether, and its record of debt repayment does not bode well for any attempt by the government or its SOEs to tap into international capital markets. Even the potential for a flight capital reflux bringing new money into the country is limited. Through the use of exchange controls, Brazil limited capital flight to an estimated $28 billion.[9] It is hardly likely that any of these funds will return to Brazil except through roundabout purchase of private bond and equity issues. In short, Brazil has not attained external stabilization and is unlikely to do so until well into the 1990s.

External Liberalization

Brazil's record on external liberalization is one of half-measures implemented halfheartedly. The sheer size and diversity of its economy have enabled Brazil to function under a protectionist trade and direct-investment regime and without the benefit of a practical exchange rate mechanism.

Over the entire decade of the 1980s, the Brazilian government did very little to liberalize trade. Even during the comparatively orthodox adjustment of the Figuereido government, import liberalization was neglected. Thus far, Brazil has gotten away with the maintenance of high tariff and nontariff barriers to imports. In the near future, however, as prices on intermediate production inputs and capital goods are artificially propped up, Brazil's extraordinary export campaign is likely to wind down. Import substitution has allowed Brazil to nurture infant industries, including some high-tech sectors, but it will not allow Brazil to compete in these same industries on a global or even a regional scale.

At first glance, the Brazilian tariff rate seems only slightly higher than the international norm, but import restriction in Brazil depends on nontariff barriers for its effectiveness. The average legal tariff rate is 35 percent when nonduitable imports of energy and wheat are factored out, but the average implemented rate is only 10 percent. The reason for this difference is straight-forward: when imports are permitted at all, they are almost always exempt from tariff or receive large reductions. It is the import license, not the tariff level, that acts as the effective constraint.[10]

Certainly the most infamous nontariff barrier erected by the Brazilian government is its market reserve protectionism used to "nurture" its computer industry. Although Brazil permits importation of large computers, for per-sonal computers it has erected legal and administrative barriers against both foreign imports and local manufacture by foreign firms. This ban stems from the 1984 Special Informatics Secretariat (SEI) bill, which received nearly unanimous approval by the Brazilian Congress and has even functioned as a constitutionally inscribed model for Brazilian trade and direct-investment policy as a whole. The so-called informatics law is actually a form of import preemption.

Rather than going through a typical import substitution process—first importing small computers and then trying to convince foreign producers to manufacture them in Brazil and hoping that local firms would eventually become involved in their pro-duction, Brazil decided to rely from the beginning on production by locally owned firms.[11]

Some weakening of this ironclad regime occurred when the United States threatened to institute Super 301 trade sanctions against Brazil for its infor-matic policy. Brazilian consumers are not happy with the measure either; they are forced to pay high prices for inferior locally produced PCs or take their chances on purchasing imported PCs on the black market. William Cline has estimated that Brazil's market reserve on small computers costs it some $500 million annually, "even if one allows some benefit for the saving of scarce foreign exchange."[12]

Very modest tariff reductions were initiated at the end of the Sarney ad-ministration. By the end of 1991, the average tariff on imports was expected to decline to around 25 percent. Under the Collor plan, it is expected to be reduced by an additional 10 percentage points by the end of 1994. Addressing U.S. Super 301 trade-sanction threats, as part of an industrial competitiveness program, Collor recently announced a two-year suspension of the industrial products tax (IPI) on machines and equipment, the establishment of simpli-fied technology transfer arrangements, and the elimination of restrictions on the distribution and sale of foreign software. But there are no plans to dismantle the import licensing system as a whole, and this cannot but create enmity between Brazil and its trading partners. At the same time, Brazil of-fers significant subsidies to exporters and a raft of export incentives. Brazil has pledged to gradually phase out the latter, but the incentives will remain in place. By themselves, these measures are suspect departures from authentic reliance on a free market. When combined with nontariff barriers to imports, they create the impression of a predatory Brazil bent on beggar-thy-neighbor trade policies.

Much the same can be said of Brazil's direct investment regime. More than a quarter-century later, foreign investment in Brazil is still basically governed by legislation passed by the military government in 1964. This allows repatriated profits of up to 12 percent of a company's liquid capital to be subject to normal income tax rates. Above that percentage, repatriated profits pay a progressively higher rate. That this law will not be fundamentally altered can be seen from the Brazilian Constitution, passed in the final years of the Sarney regime. The 1988 Constituent Assembly wrote the constitution in a context of militant nationalism around the question of foreign capital and even drew some of its ideas from the informatics law. The basic law of the land expresses naked hostility to foreign investment and specifies impossibly tight regulation over foreign ownership of production assets in Brazil.

Just as some elements of the 1967 constitution were never implemented, the curbs on direct investment in the new constitution may never be fully enforced. In fact, under a national reconstruction program, President Collor has requested the deletion of constitutional disincentives to foreign investment. Brazil's revised privatization program entitles foreign investors to buy up to 40 percent of the voting capital of privatized companies (although little real privatization has been accomplished to date). Even the SEI is now more receptive to proposals that include foreign participation, conditional upon their establishment of research and development centers in Brazil or contributions to the export sector.

For a brief period, Brazil experimented with debt-equity swaps, not to attract foreign direct investment to Brazil but to reduce foreign debt and to use as a bargaining chip in negotiations with commercial creditors. Shortly after the program began, President Sarney began to place restrictions upon it. Within a year, the program was effectively halted when the government announced it would not honor its commitment to allow conversion at par. Since then, there have been no commercial incentives for bank lenders to engage in swaps. During its brief heyday, some $5 billion in swaps took place, and in its wake, another $7 billion in private-sector debt has been converted into equity. But even under Collor, the Brazilians are not avid about attracting direct investment, particularly when it fuels inflation and amounts to a fire-sale bargain for foreign investors. There were rumors in 1991 that the Collor government was actively considering the resumption of a debt-to-equity conversion scheme, some saying that Brazil was holding back on the renewal so it could be used as leverage in rescheduling exercises with its bank lenders.

Recent reform of Brazil's exchange-rate policy has been far more substantial. In the past, the government permitted the national currency (currently the cruzeiro) to become grossly overvalued under a fixed, multiple-exchange-rate regime (billed as a "trotting peg") and then simply replaced that currency with another (e.g., a cruzado novo). In 1990, the Collor government did take an historic step when it allowed all foreign exchange rates to float, discarding the centrally fixed rates the government had used as an economic and political instrument since 1945. Preferential rates are still in place so that the new system is not unified, and the central bank intervenes regularly in the exchange markets with transactions in dollars and gold. Still, this is the one aspect of external restructuring in which Brazil can claim to have made some real reforms.

Domestic Stabilization

Domestic stabilization is now a distant vision in Brazil. The debt crisis manifests itself not only in rising inflation but also in the rapid growth of domestic debt, which results in part from domestic financing of external debt service and in part from high real interest rates on existing domestic debt. In fact, onerous as the external debt problem has been, it pales by comparison with the government's domestic liabilities. The strongest barriers to fiscal discipline are ominously political, the salaries of central government and state-owned enterprise employees accounting for well over half the annual budget. Brazil's sorry privatization record and the opposition of the legislature to cutting public employment make it exceedingly difficult for any sort of fiscal balance to be achieved. Indeed, with the recent change in political regime, Brazil has adopted a new definition for reporting the government's budget deficit, which it claims to have been around 5 percent of GDP in 1990, while independent analysts reckon it to have been as greater at 16 percent.

At the same time, Brazil has an enormous social debt waiting in the wings. Finance Minister Cardoso, ready to make deep cuts in other areas of the budget, nevertheless urged President Collor to invest an additional $14 billion a year in reform programs to promote greater social equity. According to the World Bank, while Brazil spends a comparatively high percentage of its GDP on social services (compared with other middle-income LDCs), social welfare indicators there are alarmingly low. For example, infant mortality in northeast Brazil is higher than the average for sub-Saharan Africa. The World Bank has concluded that Brazil's welfare resources are poorly managed and inefficiently targeted, noting that the poorest fifth of the population receives less than 6 percent of all social benefits.[13]

Monetary stabilization is even further out of sight than fiscal closure. In the past, Brazil has used two policy measures to deal with inflation, wage-price freezes and the maintenance of administratively set and nominally high interest rates to dampen demand. Eventually, the government has been forced to abandon one or both of these measures, and the result has always been the same—a price upsurge. The Sarney government, in its last policy flurry prior to the national elections, tried to avoid hyperflation by raising interest rates and making miniadjustments to the exchange rate. The move failed badly, building still more costs into the price of goods, because the public had simply lost faith in the administration's willingness to stay the course once the election returns were tallied. As always, Brazil's inflation problem does not issue from an oversupply of liquidity in the hands of the private sector but from the government's printing of new money to accommodate its domestic and (indirectly) foreign debts.

With the inflation rate at 80 percent a month, in the first days in office, Collor and Cardoso came up with a stabilization plan that was described as "daring and sweeping" by some observers,[14] and as likely to devastate the Brazilian economy by others.[15] At the time, Minister Cardoso pointed to the endorsement of her plan by Federal Reserve Chairman Alan Greenspan and Treasury Secretary Nicholas F. Brady, both of whom should have known better.[16] The scheme had two provisions, one worse than the other. The first and less harmful involved a price freeze without a corresponding wage freeze. The government ordered a rollback of prices—accompanied, however, by broad administratively determined wage gains—the result being a real wage increase of around 23 percent. It then boosted public service rates (telephone, electricity, postage, gasoline, and public transportation) between 32 percent and 72 percent. Just what net impact all this was supposed to have on inflation rates remains inexplicable. For private producers the path was simple: hold back on deliveries until the scheme petered out of its own accord and then sell inventories at the vastly higher prices that were bound to follow its demise.

The second and more toxic element was the temporary confiscation of Brazilian bank accounts. This provision was intended to drain liquidity from the economy by preventing withdrawals for eighteen months from savings and checking accounts. Some $80 billion in private accounts were placed under the control of the Central Bank at 6 percent interest. After September 1991, account holders were told they could withdraw funds in small amounts. The impact of this gambit was far clearer than its intent. When it was announced, the Brazilian stock market fell by 50 percent and industrial production fell 15 percent.

The freeze applied to the cash balances of businesses, making it impossible for them to meet payrolls and pay suppliers. By freezing 80 percent of all liquid assets in Brazil, the government compelled absurdly high interest rates on loans of all sorts, "turning once-reliable borrowers into dodgy credit risks."[17] As for the measure's impact on inflation, it was genuinely perverse. Private enterprises, unable and unwilling to operate under these conditions, simply accumulated inventory or cut production while retailers jacked up prices on goods that had fallen into extremely scarce supply. Moreover, the plan set the stage for a prolongation of hyperflation by eroding public confidence in government, the banks, and the domestic currency. After the failure of the confiscation program (inflation resumed at breakneck speed), Economic Minister Cardoso and her entire team, as well as the Brazilian Central Bank Governor, were compelled to resign their posts in May 1991. For all of 1990, the Brazilian inflation rate was around 1,800 percent: by the time of Mrs. Cardoso's departure, inflation had subsided to 20 percent per month.

A small bright spot in the domestic stabilization picture appears under the rubric of tax reform. Central to Brazil's fiscal difficulties, central government tax revenues fell substantially during the 1980s. As times have gotten tougher for private citizens, already rampant tax evasion has grown worse. Today, an estimated 40 percent of Brazilian taxes are evaded, meaning that government revenues are less than they should be, by some $20 to $25 billion, an amount sufficient to eliminate the deficit.[18] The tax base itself is inordinately thin. Only 4.5 million of Brazil's 140 million people pay income taxes. Collor's tax reform package pushes on all fronts: rates have been increased; the tax base has been expanded; a strong crackdown on evasion has been initiated. The expansion of the tax base has been accomplished by extended levies on previously untaxed capital gains from stocks and bonds, interest income from savings, and profits from gold and real estate transactions. In addition, a 30 percent value-added tax has been placed on exports and services. To make all this stick, Collor appointed Romeu Tuma, the former federal police chief, to head the tax collection and enforcement campaign. This is one area, confiscation of private holdings through tax levies, in which the current administration may register gains.

Domestic Liberalization

It is not possible to speak of financial or interest-rate liberalization in Brazil today given the extent of repression applied to the banking system by the Collor government. Evidence that the financial system is troubled beyond the dictates of government can be seen in the inherently high cost of financial intermediation. Traditional wisdom has it that Brazil's high-tech, highly staffed retail banks cannot survive monthly inflation of less than 5 percent without drastic cutbacks. Most of their profits derive from exploiting non-indexed money lying idle in current accounts, which they invest in high-yield treasury bills. Realizing that this was the case, Collor slapped heavy taxes on financial operations and instituted the confiscation program. The question is not whether financial liberalization will occur when the thaw on bank deposits takes place, but rather which banks will survive and what will be left of them.

Privatization is often viewed as a panacea for what ails Brazil, and even the Sarney administration included it in its prescription. The real problem is that no government in recent times has been able to swallow the medicine of divestiture given the political backlash that privatization is bound to arouse. Literally hundreds of public enterprises were created in Brazil in the 1960s, 1970s, and early 1980s. These companies have been universally criticized for losing money because of inadequate managerial skills and excessive labor costs; unclear and contradictory objectives; and privileged access to capital, subsidies, and protection.[19] In 1990, Brazil's state-owned enterprises accounted for almost half the GDP. They also registered a combined deficit of nearly one-fifth of GDP. Simple arithmetic indicates that losses of this magnitude cannot be absorbed indefinitely.

Because of the need to keep the budget deficit down, privatization programs have been initiated in the past, but with little real effect. While methods of divestiture have changed from program to program, the result has been the same. During the first half of the 1980s, Brazilian privatization moved at a snail's pace: total sales between 1980 and 1986 amounted to less than $200 million; in 1987 five firms were sold for another $27 million. By 1989, only seventeen publicly-owned firms had been privatized in nine years.

Collor restarted Brazil's perennially unsuccessful privatization crawl at the beginning of 1991. By the end of 1992, Brazil plans to privatize ninety-two parastatals valued at $17 billion, while the government will retain approximately thirty in the fields of energy, telecommunications, transportation, and mineral resources. Collor has declared that in the future, ports, roads, and large areas of government-owned land will be for sale. Even independent analysts allow that the privatization of Portobras, the port authority, could bring as much as $35 billion.[20]

To oversee the sales, Collor has established the National Commission of Denationalization. Chaired by the president of the National Economic and Social Development Bank (BNDES), the commission is charged with establishing and revising basic rules for privatization and setting the limits on the number of shares individuals and corporations may hold. Under preliminary guidelines set by the commission, individual foreign investors will be limited to owning 35 percent of a privatized enterprise if debt-equity swap money is used and 40 percent if straight direct-investment capital is used. Another 35 percent of the shares have been reserved for individual Brazilian investors; and the last 30 percent must be sold to workers and clerical employees of the firm.

Carrying out the program is another matter, for a catch-22 dilemma faces the government. To reduce the drag on the budget, the government should first privatize the deficit-ridden state companies, thereby ending its responsibility for their losses and halting the printing presses that create the new money to cover the deficit. The question, of course, is who would want to purchase these white elephants? If the government elects to divest itself of its few profitable firms, these might be snapped up; but, sales revenues apart, the government's fiscal situation would deteriorate. This, in turn, would reinforce the depression that makes it hard for even the more efficient SOEs to operate profitably. In the end, privatization is unlikely to work without wholesale restructuring of the economy, a task the government has been unable even to approach. There has been so little dismantling of the apparatus of intervention and so little political will to do so that privatized firms must continue to function in a politicized market economy where their fortunes turn on state action in one guise or another.

The outlook for deregulation of the Brazilian economy is dismal. Consider that the 1988 Brazilian constitution (1) gives civil service employees the security of tenure; and (2) by transferring powers from the central government to the states, complicates the correction of Brazil's fiscal imbalance.[21] In all likelihood, further rigidities will be built into the Brazilian economy, locking it into a downward trajectory and making painful stabilization and liberalization measures all the more difficult to undertake.

ECONOMIC PERFORMANCE

When its natural advantages and occasional overstimulation of the economy are combined with its self-inflicted wounds, Brazilian economic performance must necessarily be erratic, both across and within its several parameters. When Sarney entered office, there was a surge in both investment and consumption, but the year ended in stagnation that lasted until 1988. The prospect of a change in regime and the suspension of transfers to external debtors caused growth to climb again rapidly in the second half of 1989, but the economy contracted by some 4 percent in 1990, and the outlook for 1991 was for another decrease in output. Measured against its potential, Brazil's underperformance becomes evident. A newly industrialized nation that has pursued industrialization by hook and crook, Brazil has neglected its agricultural sector, which nevertheless grew faster than the manufacturing sector. In the second half of the 1980s, agriculture emerged as the most dynamic sector in Brazil, exercising a stabilizing force and limiting the collapse in economic growth and incomes. Apparently the government has found it more difficult to interfere with natural forces than to throw monkey wrenches into the workings of the modern portion of the economy.

Up until 1990, Brazil was exceptional among Latin American countries for having a positive average per-capita growth rate during the 1980s. With the recession of the early 1990s, this is no longer the case. Moreover, during the 1980s, the gap in income between Brazil's richest and poorest strata continued to widen. While average income per capita in Brazil exceeds that of most African or Asian economies, extreme poverty persists as a result of inequitable income distribution.

The Brazilian government's fiscal balance is clearly in deficit, although the size of the deficit is hard to determine since the government routinely cooks its books by excluding interest payments on external and domestic debt from its overall budget figures or by amortizing the latter by adjusting for quadruple-digit inflation. The inflation rate is somewhat plainer. In 1990, Brazil entered the realm of hyperflation; improvement has brought the annualized rate down to 20 to 30 percent a month.

Brazil's dormant power is apparent in the performance of its exports. Although the growth in Brazil's trade surplus during the 1980s (the largest in Latin America in both absolute terms and relative to GDP) can be ascribed in part to its restrictive import regime, Brazil's trade performance was nevertheless nothing short of phenomenal. It has raised trade surpluses through export growth and import substitution every year since 1983, including the 1990s. Even today, Brazil's potential trade surplus remains between $15 billion and $20 billion.

But there are problems here too. For example, along with South Korea and Mexico, Brazil is one of the few nations in the developing world that has managed to export sizable numbers of automobiles ($1.5 billion in 1987), most of them delivered to the United States. The cars differ from those manufactured for the domestic market in that some 90 percent of the latter are equipped to run on ethanol. Since the oil shocks of the 1970s, Brazil has been developing an ethanol-production complex and campaigning for the substitution of this fuel for gasoline. Unfortunately for the Brazilians, although their state-run auto-assembly plants operate at a profit, the ethanol-manufacturing program has generated an unbroken series of multibillion-dollar deficits for the government. Thus, by pursuing an import-substitution industrialization program, Brazil has moved ahead in its product standards at a pace faster than that of the world as a whole, depriving its automotive sector of scale and scope economies that would enable it to compete in a world market. Brazil's recent large trade surpluses tend to obscure the fact that artificially low levels of capital and intermediate imports will, in the long run, stymie exports drives, leaving the country at a technological disadvantage against strengthening competitors from the Pacific Basin. As Brazil shifts into high-tech exports and attempts to compete with them in developed-country markets, the inherent limitations of a closed economy become binding constraints on future export growth.

POLITICAL FACTORS

The Domestic Political Situation

Brazilian adjustment in both its stabilization and liberalization dimensions is heavily constrained by domestic political factors. President Sarney repeatedly tried to put the Brazilian economy on a sounder footing, but he lacked the political will to implement the necessary fiscal consolidation measures. He also lacked credibility, determination, and allies in congress. Whether Tancredo Neves would have been able to make greater progress on the stabilization front is a question that simply cannot be answered. That Collor must look over his shoulder as he and his economic team are at the adjustment drawing board is beyond question.

The Brazilian election campaign of 1989 featured a field of twenty-two declared presidential candidates, including the incumbent Sarney. Collor ran on an anticorruption platform that cast further shadows on the Sarney regime. But Collor's main foe in this contest was Luis Ignacio Lula de Silva, a prominent pro-labor, left-wing leader, known affectionately among Brazil's trade unionists as Lula. It is by contrasting Collor and Lula that the profound polarities of the Brazilian political scene are seen in sharpest relief. During the election Collor called for administrative, fiscal, and monetary reforms that would overhaul the Brazilian economy. Lula vowed to oppose all privatization, expand state intervention in the economy and social entitlement programs, and reform government subsidy programs. Collor said he would renegotiate Brazil's foreign debt; Lula's stance toward Brazil's foreign creditors was one of uncompromising militancy. In the end, Collor won the election with 53 percent of the vote, but Lula placed second. This result is symptomatic of the schizophrenic Brazilian attitudes on the capacity of orthodox adjustment to solve Brazil's economic woes. Collor's election had more to do with popular dissatisfaction with chaos under President Jose Sarney than with conviction about the need for a free-market approach to Brazilian development.

Under Collor, major changes were made in the administrative structure of the Brazilian government, particularly in the area of economic affairs. During Sarney's tenure, the Brazilian cabinet sprawled, having as many as twenty-seven ministers — six of them for the military alone. Collor cut the number down to an even dozen, dropping both the Joint Chiefs and the (infamous) National Intelligence Service. He also merged the Ministry of Finance and the Secretariat of Planning into a Ministry of Economy, Finance, and Planning (headed first by Cardoso and then by Moiera), and created a huge ministry of infrastructure (headed by Ozires Silva, a former director of the state-owned oil company, Petrobras).

Collor's immediate cabinet reshufflings gave him the aura of a man of action. It also contributed to his growing reputation as an authoritarian decisionmaker who charts Brazil's course with little input from outside a small circle of policy advisors. There is in this style an inherent contradiction of free-market reforms being mandated from above. As Pang and Jarnagin have remarked, the Brazilian public "sees Collor as a constitutionally elected imperial President."[22] Under Collor's adjustment program, the public at large seems to have been deprived of a firm anchor. During local elections held in October 1990, no politician of national stature voiced any criticism of the ill-conceived Collor Plan, and the result of the primary campaign implied broad support for the plan. Nevertheless, when runoffs were held the following month, Collor's endorsement was a kiss of death — virtually all the candidates he backed went down to defeat.

It is extremely difficult to gauge the real power that the Brazilian president commands. During his first eighteen months in office, Collor announced sweeping reforms and even instituted some drastic, if heterodox, measures. Yet his political background is extremely thin. He became president after only two relatively undistinguished years as governor of the economically insignificant state of Alagaos. Collor is an outsider atop his nation's power structure, lacking real support from any of Brazil's nationwide parties. This paradox helps to explain both why he has been willing to plan radical change within the Brazilian economy and why he has been unable to accomplish significant reform: he is not beholden to the vested interests and he has little leverage against them.

Brazil's Relations with the United States

In relations with the United States, trade flows have been a salient factor. In 1990, America sold about $5 billion worth of goods and services to Brazil and bought some $8 billion from that economy. The trade deficit was one in an unbroken string, leading to charges of unfair trade practices and, in the case of the informatics law, the threat of Super 301 trade sanctions. Collor has promised to revoke legislation on computer imports, intellectual property rights, and patent protection, which generated a low-level trade war with the United States. Yet the heart of the informatics law remains in place. The modest trade liberalization has had little impact thus far on U.S. exports, which rose only 5 percent in 1990.

Yet, as the provisions of the Industrial Competitiveness and National Reconstruction programs suggest, the Brazilians are interested in importing cutting-edge technology from the United States. In 1990, more than half of U.S. shipments to Brazil consisted of high-tech manufactures such as aircraft, auto parts and engines, chemicals, computers and peripherals, process controls, measuring and testing instruments, telecommunications equipment, and the like.

But Brazil is seen by the United States as a potential security threat, particularly in its willingness to supply military hardware to Third World regimes bent against U.S. interests. For instance, as a major supplier of arms to the Middle East, notably Iraq, Brazil maintained a large technical crew in Iraq until the Persian Gulf conflict was in full swing. Since 1988, Brazil has tried to purchase a supercomputer from IBM. The U.S. government has refused to approve the sale, worried that Brazil will use American technology to further a nuclear weapons development program. In November 1990 (along with Argentina's President Menem), Collor agreed to ratify the Treaty of Tlateleco prohibiting nuclear weapons in his country.

Clearly one of the most prominent issues in which the United States and Brazil have a strong antagonistic stake is the deforestation of the Amazon rain forest. Under Sarney, rapid agrarian development and mineral deposit extraction were allowed, even encouraged, with little thought for the long-term well-being of Brazil's natural landscape and less for the international environmental fall-out of intentionally destroying it. In the final year of his presidency, Sarney responded to criticism of forest burning with a program he called "Our Nature." That some attention was being paid to a potential environmental catastrophe of hemispheric if not global proportions was welcome news in the United States. That little of consequence was accomplished and that the program was cast in nationalistic terms to underscore Brazil's ownership of the Amazon was not.

The Brazilians have sought to create a linkage between their overexploitation of the environment and their debt problems. According to a statement by one senior Brazilian official in 1990, "We can't afford to be the lungs of the world if we are also to pay off our foreign debt and finance our development plans."[23] In October 1990, the U.S. House Foreign Affairs Committee approved official debt forgiveness in exchange for local-currency payments by Latin American governments into environmental protection and clean-up projects. Whether such swaps will ever come about on a large scale is problematical. Approval of debt relief under the EAI requires that recipient nations demonstrate continued commitment to adjustment along several fronts, and thus far Brazil has failed to meet many of these conditions.

To his credit, Collor has tried to attenuate Brazil's image as an environmental spoiler and has stated his willingness to consider debt-for-nature swaps, a debt-relief option that Sarney rejected out of hand. Brazil will host the United Nations Conference on Environment and Development in June 1992, which President Bush said he would attend, where Collor's main proposal was expected to be the imposition of an international tax levy on the emission of polluting gases. This measure would, of course, give new life to Brazil's ethanol technology and automotive industries. However, even within the more environmentally sensitive Collor regime, the crucial tradeoff between environmental safeguards and economic growth has not been resolved. Relations between the Special Secretary for the Environment Jose Lutzenberger and Special Secretary for Science and Technology Jose Goldemberg are stormy, with the development of the Amazon Basin being the chief object of conflict.

ARGENTINA

Argentina is another second-tier major Latin American country that must accomplish considerably more adjustment before it can qualify as a candidate for inclusion in a hemispheric free trade pact. In certain quarters, notably the reform of trade and direct investment laws, Argentina is substantially ahead of Brazil. But in terms of external and, more acutely important, domestic stabilization, Argentina remains on the same low plateau as Brazil and lacks the natural resource endowments of the latter.

To some, the fact that domestic instability has been a source of popular deprivation is an asset in the sense that the political will for radical change is greater in Argentina than in Brazil. On the other hand, the ability of government to carry out such reforms is undermined in the popular view by the adjustment failures of the past. Argentina's current president, Carlos Saul Menem, is committed to a wholesale restructuring of his nation's economy, which his foreign minister, Domingo Cavallo, has characterized as "a mixture of socialism with no central planning and capitalism with no market."[24] The sheer magnitude of the task Menem faces suggests that it will require a decade or so for his reform program to restore financial stability and economic abundance. Unfortunately, Menem's program has not transformed popular expectations for progress, and as time elapses, its credibility may well erode.

The General Course of Adjustment

The adjustment legacy that Menem inherited is a bleak record of radical programs abandoned soon after they were initiated. Under the military juntas of the late 1970s and early 1980s, the Argentine government took on an enormous load of debt; and when the juntas were ousted from power, they left their people with very little to show for this burden. After the disaster of Falklands and the return of civilian government, President Raul Alfonsin's first priority was the restoration of domestic stability. The newly elected leader faced the task of mopping up liquidity resulting from excessive domestic debt issuance.

In June 1985, Alfonsin initiated the Austral plan which hinged upon a fresh start, a new currency, and lip-service to greater fiscal discipline. It was soon followed by the Mini-Austral of March 1987, the Austral II Plan of six months later, the Spring Plan of 1988, and (just two months thereafter) the Primavera Plan. All these schemes collapsed for essentially the same reason: the Alfonsin administration lacked the political gumption to close the government's fiscal gap. By the spring of 1989, Argentina suffered from hyperflation caused by the collapse of the Primavera Plan and the prospect of the Peronist candidate, Menem, assuming power in May's presidential elections.

Menem's populist program proved appealing; and in July 1989, with Argentina experiencing inflation at the rate of 4 percent a day, Menem became president in the first peaceful transition of power in Argentina since 1928. Within days, he introduced an emergency package featuring a major devaluation, a wage-price freeze, a deceleration of monetary expansion, and the promise of further reforms. This promise was kept the next month when Menem asked the Argentine Congress to pass the Economic Emergency Law and the Law on the Reform of the State. Addressed to both stabilization and liberalization objectives, the Menem program pivoted upon strict fiscal austerity, deregulation and privatization, and a negotiated debt-reduction package with external creditors. Toward that end, the Menem approach featured a heterodox emergency stabilization effort but a long-term commitment to orthodox adjustment along free-market lines. Not only did the new president offer the prospect that Argentina might put its house in order, his package went well beyond Alfonsin's stabilization measures toward structural reform.

Initially, at least, Menem and his approach met with high praise from a number of observers, including William Cline who called it "a serious program of adjustment and structural reform."[25] During the three-month honeymoon between July and October, it appeared that there was something to this optimism. The heterodox portion of the plan (a wage-price freeze) worked—the monthly rate of inflation declined from 200 percent in July to 5 percent in October. The effects, however, were short-lived. By November, optimism about Menem's ability to transform Argentina in short order had vanished. Under pressure from organized labor, Menem revised scheduled wage increases upward, permitting a huge increase negotiated between the powerful General Confederation of Labor (CGT) and employers. This, in itself, created expectations of future price increases; it also showed that like Alfonsin Menem would accommodate special political interest groups even if it meant undermining stabilization goals. Moreover, the degree of fiscal and monetary discipline shown by the government fell well short of its own mark.

Sensing an erosion in his credibility, Menem replaced Minister of Economy Nestor Rapanelli with Antonio Erman Gonzalez. The new minister lost no time in initiating a program of a much more orthodox stripe. He lifted all price controls and announced that the Argentine Treasury would no longer finance the government budget deficit by printing money. Of more enduring importance, he liberalized foreign trade, lowering tariff rates and removing NTBs, and he unified the foreign exchange rate, an absolutely stunning austerity measure when combined with strict stabilization.

Thus, the government was expected to withstand extreme stabilization and liberalization at the same time. Two weeks after the Gonzalez decree, Menem approached mopping up liquidity and financing the government budget deficit in a fashion similar to that of Cardoso in Brazil. Two days into 1990, Menem decreed that each bank depositor's savings in Argentine australs must be converted into ten-year government bonds, with interest and principal guaranteed in dollars. Bondholders were allowed to sell their paper, but only at a tiny fraction of their ten-year value. The decree effectively confiscated about 80 percent of the australs in circulation.

As in Brazil, this drastic step did not avert another round of hyperflation, as monthly rates during the winter of 1990 hovered between 60 percent and 100 percent. The government was determined to do even more. In March, the finance minister announced the suspension of payments to thousands of the government's domestic suppliers. In reaction, the economy went into a deep recession, but hyperflation stopped — prices rose only 11 percent in April. In August 1990, Erman Gonzalez tried to rein in Argentina's state-owned enterprises by announcing that no agency or government corporation could set prices for its services or prepare a budget without his approval.[26] Paradoxically, the Menem government was at cross-purposes, trying to redress problems rooted in the extension of the state into productive activities by tightening state control over them.

External Stabilization

The clearest yardstick of Argentina's external instability is seen in the fact that specimens of its $65 billion in debt could be purchased on the secondary market in 1990 at between 11 cents and 14.5 cents on the dollar. Argentina still has one of the highest debt-to-export ratios in Latin America, and while it is possible to quibble over whether foreign debt or domestic instability is the economy's greatest problem, debt overhang is plainly operative.

Under Alfonsin, Argentina tried to reduce its external debt through a last-straw debt-conversion scheme. It attempted to issue exit bonds in 1987, but twenty-five-year paper, offering a 4 percent interest rate without any enhancements, left creditors cold. In April 1988, with substantial interest arrears accumulating, the commercial banks cut Argentina off from any new financing. The action contributed to the advent of hyperflation, which was given a second boost when the IMF and the World Bank also shut down conditional adjustment loan disbursements, triggering an expectational explosion of the exchange rate. With its reserves exhausted, the Alfonsin government simply stopped supporting the austral.

Menem's election afforded Argentina an opportunity to shore up its relations with the IMF and the World Bank; and by December 1989, the IMF released about $250 million to Argentina. Relations between Argentina and the IMF, which had grown acutely confrontational in the final years of the Alfonsin administration, grew more cordial, and IMF director Camdessus even visited Buenos Aires. During 1990, the IMF remained satisfied with Argentina's adjustment effort, and both the World Bank and the IDB made additional policy-based loans to the Menem government in support of trade liberalization.

Having suspended repayments to the banks at the start of 1988, Argentina began making token payments of about $40 million a month in interest to them in June 1990. This was roughly equal to 10 percent of scheduled interest although the banks had called for token remittances in the neighborhood of $100 million a month. They were probably grateful to receive anything at all. Although Argentina has not yet been granted a comprehensive debt rescheduling, the resumption of good-will interest payments prompted the banks to take actions clearing the way for implementation of Menem's structural reforms — for example, allowing for waivers in the privatization of state-owned enterprises like the national telephone company. As of mid-1991, Argentine arrears in interest payments to its commercial creditors were between $6 billion and $7 billion, no formal discussions with the banks about a rescheduling were in place, and Brady Plan treatment was at least a couple of years away. The banks continue to reject any debt conversion without Brady Plan enhancement, since this would involve a substantial writedown in loan assets without a significant reduction in risk. Rather than sell their Argentina paper on the secondary market at a steep discount, major money-center banks have elected to sidestep comprehensive relief and deal with loans case by case. Some of this paper was issued to state-owned enterprises, or even private concerns, that own valuable real assets, and creditors seek either a debt-equity swap or intend to await improvement in the Argentina economy rather than sell for a few pennies on the dollar. Argentina's relations with its bank creditors are somewhat better than Brazil's under Cardoso. The country's chief debt negotiator is now telling them that Argentina has not yet achieved a fiscal condition that would allow it to pay at full schedule. Precisely when that will occur is problematic, to say the least. Nonetheless, under Menem, Argentina has changed its image from that of an unredeemable deadbeat.

With no prospect of fresh bank financing on the horizon and the Argentine economy a shambles, alternative sources of foreign capital are extremely limited and will become more so as Argentina exhausts its quotas with multilateral financial institutions. Some Argentine companies can raise money on the Eurobond market by offering extremely high interest rates, but Mexican, Venezuelan, and Chilean private issues are far more attractive risks.

It has been estimated that Argentine citizens have transferred somewhere around $40 billion in flight capital and that the hemorrhage accelerated in the late 1980s as external financing was cut off and the election of a Peronist candidate loomed large. In light of the economy's disarray, the lack of provisions to tax overseas investments, and the 1990 confiscation of austral deposits, repatriation of these funds in any sizable amount is unlikely. When Argentina began to make token interest payments to the banks, Citicorp Chairman John Reed tried to reciprocate by offering the government a list of Citibank's Argentinean depositors.[27] The real quandary was captured by Argentinean economist and former finance secretary Juan Alemann when he said, "If someone were to bring money back from outside the country and declare it, he'd lose the lot. He'd be forced to pay the highest tax rate, plus fines."[28] Under these circumstances, Argentina's best hopes for stabilizing its external accounts are by running massive trade surpluses, creating incentives for direct investment, expanding its debt-equity swap program, and privatizing some of the more valuable assets that remain in the hands of the government.

External Liberalization

In terms of external structural adjustment, although the decree of December 1990 called for trade liberalization, depressed conditions in Argentina have aborted any major growth in Argentine imports. Although President Menem ended Argentina's trade embargo with Great Britain, currency devaluations, coupled with the scarcity of foreign exchange, have dampened import demand as effectively as the protectionist fences of the past. Trade liberalization measures are in place; how well they will work remains to be seen.

Considerably greater progress has been achieved in rules governing foreign direct investment. Since September 1989, requirements for specific approval of foreign investments have been removed, and there are now no legal distinctions between foreign and domestic investment. Given the depressed state of the Argentine economy, foreign direct investors have limited their interest to natural resources, utilities, and activities with an export dimension. Realizing this, President Menem has eased nationalistic laws on foreign access to petroleum exploration. In 1990, Argentina leased twenty-nine exploratory oil concessions to foreign and domestic oil companies for $250 million plus future royalties.

Since there is a deep discount available for Argentine debt paper on the secondary market, debt-equity swaps are attractive to foreign investors. Argentina launched a debt-equity swap program in January 1988. To compensate for the enormous effective subsidy these swaps entailed, the Alfonsin government insisted that debt-equity conversions be accompanied by additional foreign direct investment inflows. These demands have been dropped by the Menem government, but in the wake of the deposit confiscation measure of 1990, Argentina's ability to convert debt into equity has been constrained by its tiny monetary base. Should trade or nonsubsidized direct investment pick up, it will be supported by an exchange rate that has been unified and allowed to float freely, a marked departure from the traditional overvaluation of Argentine currency that has held back its exports and the flow of investment capital into the economy in the past.

Domestic Stabilization

Domestic stabilization is not yet in sight. This is by no means a novelty. In Argentina the public sector as a whole has very rarely been in equilibrium since World War II. Although Argentina's foreign debt is the most visible outward manifestation of its economic woes, the government's domestic debt is far more debilitating. In fact, the exorbitant interest costs attached to its $15 billion in internal debt (in excess of 10 percent a month) prompted the confiscation program. For decades, public expenditure priorities in Argentina were biased toward consumption subsidies; today, the government has instituted fiscal measures that virtually ban such outlays. As one might expect, in addition to its foreign and domestic debts, neglect of spending on physical and human infrastructure is a liability that must be dealt with if vitality is to be restored to the economy.

The most startling facet of the Argentine economy today is hyperflation. The government's customary approach to this perennial problem was simply to replace one currency with a heavier one, an indirect form of confiscation that prompted short bursts of export growth and extensive capital flight. Between 1969 and 1985, Argentina lopped nine zeros off its currency. The shutdown in foreign bank credit and the later IMF disbursement suspension stimulated quadruple-digit annual inflation rates. Immediately prior to Menem's inauguration, advisor Domingo Cavallo stated bluntly, "As far as our monetary policy goes, we are in a terminal stage."[29]

For a few months, the new regime's commitment to holding down prices appeared credible. Then the wage increase to the General Confederation of Labor was granted, and prices surged. To redress this relapse, Menem instituted the austral deposit holdup of January 1990. The impact was to radically reduce the amount of domestic currency in circulation; but since most Argentine savers hold the bulk of their funds in dollars, having lost confidence in their currency long ago, only a small fraction of total liquidity was affected. Worse, the government started printing more money soon after the savings freeze, and inflation reared again. For 1990 as a whole, the Argentine inflation rate was 1,400 percent. Some progress was made in the first half of 1991, so that inflation ran at only 10 percent a month, but the outlook here is poor. Fiscal closure would help, as would the creation of an independent central bank. But even if these steps are taken in earnest, the government still must reverse popular expectations that they will be rescinded in the future. Heterodox steps to chill inertial inflation such as the initial wage-price freeze of Menem's stabilization program have functioned as an escape hatch; reliance upon orthodox methods of controlling inflation requires time.

If overspending by government is the root cause of hyperflation in Argentina, one means of dealing with price increases is to expand the tax base, institute new levies, and raise the rates on existing taxes. The Argentine tax base is extremely thin, and tax evasion is rampant. In the final year of the Alfonsin government, revenue from taxes on income, profits, and capital gains amounted to less than 3 percent of GNP (as compared to 13 percent in the United States). In terms of the income tax, enforcement is at the heart of the problem. Under Alfonsin, the government simply counted on people dutifully lining up at the tax office to pay their income tax.[30] This honor system simply has not worked. In 1988, out of 32 million Argentineans, only 30,000 paid any income tax. In the original adjustment package the Menem government put together with the assistance of the IMF, the centerpiece was a broad generalization of the value-added tax at 15 percent, a switch away from levies on income and toward taxes on consumption being intended to simplify tax collection. Income taxes were also raised, and a handful of tax cheats were imprisoned; but progress is still slow in this quarter. The Argentine public has found ways to circumvent the value-added tax, and the contraction of the economy has cut into tax revenues.

Domestic Liberalization

The Menem government is committed to deep structural reform of the domestic sector, but it has undermined its program through resort to heterodox stabilization measures. This is most evident in the area of interest rates. Previously suppressed by stop-and-go decrees, bank deposit rates were liberated by Menem, and the initial result was reduced volatility and positive rates. But the interest payments on government debt led to the deposit transmutation scheme so that, for the time being, government control over financial operations has actually been increased. Like Brazil, the government has dealt with the aftereffects of its intervention into the financial sector with still more intervention. Yet another bank holiday was declared at the start of 1991. Again, there is a catch-22 predicament: structural reform requires stabilization, but heterodox methods of achieving stabilization run afoul of liberalization.

Privatization represents a means whereby the government could shed a drain on its fiscal balance, receive a badly needed infusion of capital, and enhance the efficiency of the productive sector. Prior to Erman-Gonzalez's term, Argentina's state-owned enterprises lost some 2 percent to 3 percent of GNP annually, with the central government picking up the tab (although, in fact, the cost was passed down in the form of inflation). Privatization under Alfonsin was used primarily as a rhetorical device for the benefit of external creditors and multilateral institutions. As in Brazil, the few state companies actually sold during Alfonsin's tenure were mostly reprivatizations of firms that had been taken by the state in bankruptcy. Alfonsin remained reluctant to sell off large chunks of the state's real property at a deep implicit discount, even to Argentine nationals, most of whom were equally reluctant to purchase perennial loss-makers. Privatization through debt-equity swaps or even straight purchases by foreign investors came up against a taboo that the Alfonsin government would not violate.

The spirit behind Menem's approach to privatization stands in marked contrast to that of his predecessor. Even profitable SOEs are on the auction block; and while restrictions have been imposed upon the share that can be purchased by non-Argentine investors, they are now welcomed as partners in the current divestiture drive. The most widely publicized privatization to date involved the state-owned telephone company, Entel. The Menem government also sold off the state-owned airline, Aerolineas, to a foreign conglomerate led by Scandinavian Airlines. Privatization of these two entities brought Argentina about $7 billion earmarked for debt reduction. Buoyed by these successes, in October 1990 Menem announced a second phase in the privatization program, aimed at bringing in a like sum through the sale of electric utilities, coal and natural gas firms, shipping lines, railways, and even subways and highways. Political opposition to the privatization program has been strong, but thus far Menem has succeeded in pushing divestiture on the imperative of fiscal closure.

Although deep privatization may round up cash and reduce the drain on the treasury, whether the purported efficiency gains of divestiture will be realized is another matter altogether. There has been little dismantling of the apparatus of intervention, so privatized firms continue to operate in a politicized market economy with all its associated forms of inefficiency. Deregulation campaigns have a long and dank history in Argentina. An attempt at deregulation made during the military junta era of the late 1970s was aborted by the generals who saw it reducing state power. Deregulation during the Alfonsin administration was too tepid to have any real impact. Like Salinas in Mexico, Menem has found that deregulation poses an acute political dilemma for his government: it would reduce the leverage of the government at a time when strong government action is required to carry out deregulation.

ECONOMIC PERFORMANCE

With adjustment falling far short of putting Argentina's economy in order, recent performance has been dismal; and the few bright spots, such as the trade balance, may be temporary. GDP growth rates have been negative for most of the 1980s. In 1989, the economy contracted at a rate of 6 percent of GDP, a rebound to minus 2 percent GDP growth experienced during Menem's first full year in office was expected to continue through 1991.

Following sharp currency devaluations, the trade balance showed a large surplus in 1990, reaching some $6 billion. This is a remarkable accomplishment, despite devaluation and the squeeze on imports stemming from recession, given that Argentina's chief export markets, including the United States and Brazil, were mired in their own recessions. At a realistic currency rate, Argentina can compete in world markets and could become even more competitive should multilateral trade liberalization take place in the GATT or through a regional arrangement such as that proposed under the EAI.

POLITICAL FACTORS

The Domestic Political Situation

In some ways, Menem's position in Argentina is analogous to that of Collor in Brazil. He was elected to the presidency as an outsider on a populist platform primarily out of public frustration with Alfonsin and his Radical party. Paradoxically, the threat of a Peronist taking power actually boosted

Menem's presidential campaign by prompting the inflation that undercut Alfonsin's desperate Primavera Plan and thereby sealed the ouster of the radicals. Menem performed the now standard about-face after his inauguration. He distanced himself from the traditional Peronists and sought alliances with portions of the Argentina's monied establishment. The transformation was facilitated by the weakness of the opposition, both outside and within his own nominal party. The Radical party was so discredited by Alfonsin's presidency that it could hardly voice any objections, and the anachronistic Peronist party was rife with factionalism.

Like Collor, Menem is widely perceived as an elected authoritarian. Upon attaining the presidency, he packed the Argentine Supreme Court, appointed his brother as chairman of the Peronist party, and cut the manpower of the armed forces in half. The strongest organized group in Argentina remains the trade union movement which supported Menem's candidacy in 1989. As Argentina's president, Menem tried to avoid a direct confrontation with the CGT. Nevertheless, in April 1990 he announced that he intended to limit the right to strike for all unions involved in essential public services. When the Argentine Congress, itself beholden to the CGT, refused to pass the measure, Menem took a page from Juan Peron's manual and instituted an injunction against a telephone workers' strike by executive decree. There are rumors that Menem plans to amend the Argentine constitution so that he can run for a second six-year term in 1995. In December 1990, Menem's reduction of the armed forces and their privileges led to military rebellion. Unlike Alfonsin, Menem took immediate and decisive action against the mutiny, declaring a state of siege and sending loyalist troops to put down the ill-conceived insurgency in time for a scheduled visit by President Bush.

Menem's strong tactics have enabled him to persist with orthodox adjustment policies for more than two years in a nation where few policy innovations have been allowed to survive that long. But, as the wage concession of November 1989 shows, he still needs popular support. What Argentina lacks is both faith in its government's capacity to stay the course and a consensus on how the cost of government and national development should be distributed. No segment of Argentine society is willing to shoulder its share of the burden.[31]

Argentina's Relations with the United States

While far less dependent than Mexico on the U.S. export market and direct investment flows, Argentina sells more than 12 percent of its overseas deliveries to the United States. Relations between the Alfonsin government and the Reagan administration were poor to begin with and deteriorated as Argentina made loans to both Nicaragua and Cuba in the mid-1980s, as if to thumb its nose at the U.S. president. After his appointment as foreign minister, Domingo Cavallo urged closer ties with the United States and followed through by settling the issue of the Falkland Islands with U.S. ally Great Britain and signing a nuclear nonproliferation treaty in November 1990.

The Menem government has hinted that further concessions to the United States could come about in the near future, notably over the issue of Argentine arms exports to the Third World. Cavallo has stated that Argentina would cease building the Condor II missile if the United States would reciprocate by lowering some barriers to Argentine imports.[32] Indeed, Menem's administration showed its good will toward the United States by being the only Latin American nation to send a naval contingent to the Persian Gulf in December 1990. Argentina was also the first Latin American nation to respond positively to President Bush's EAI proposal. Of even greater significance, public opinion polls carried out in 1990 indicate, for the first time since the end of World War II, the Argentine people appear to desire closer relations between their country and the United States.

PERU

Among the major debtor nations of Latin America, Peru undoubtedly has the shabbiest adjustment record during the 1980s. By the time of Alberto Keinya Fujimori's election to the presidency in July 1990, the Peruvian economy was shattered, with rampant inflation and rapidly contracting output. Any additional external support was immediately earmarked to pay down arrears on its official foreign debt. Contrary to the wisdom that prevailed in Peru during the 1980s, these conditions were not the side-effects of orthodox adjustment but the direct result of actions taken by the administration of Alan Garcia to forestall and possibly circumvent the tandem imperatives of stabilization and liberalization.

ADJUSTMENT

The General Course of Adjustment

Prior to Garcia's election in 1985, Peru had taken a conventional path to adjustment, following the widespread pattern of formally endorsing orthodox stabilization goals and drawing liberalization plans—then backing away from both when their unpopular impact threatened to evoke a political backlash. Entering to plaudits from media and left-wing intellectuals, Garcia signaled a change from this half-hearted approach to adjustment by immediately adopting a confrontational stance toward its foreign creditors. He would subsequently extend the reach of the government into the economy by nationalizing Peru's private banks and follow a free-spending fiscal policy to counteract the economy's increasing isolation from the outside world. When the inevitable hyperinflationary pressures emerged, the Garcia government tried to curb inflation by maintaining an overvalued currency. This woefully inadequate means of combating rapid price increases merely curtailed exports. Garcia also instituted periodic price freezes (especially on fuels, electricity, and foodstuffs), so that by mid-1988, prices of these goods were only one-third their mid-1985 levels in real terms.

For a brief time, Garcia's strategy yielded startlingly positive results. With the suspension of external debt-service payments, Peru's international reserves mounted, and Garcia applied these funds to a consumption boom. In 1986 and 1987, after spending the first part of the lost decade in a deep recession, Peruvian GNP growth rebounded to between 8 and 9 percent a year, while heterodox stabilization measures reduced annual inflation to double-digits. Eventually, the reserves ran out, however, and inflation intensified because of an increasing fiscal gap as well as domestic-capacity bottlenecks. The consumption orgy had failed to stimulate investment, partly because the private sector was operating in an environment of overregulation and business confidence was extraordinarily low. After Garcia's first year in power, the public-sector deficit amounted to 7 percent of GNP, and rapid inflation eroded the real value of tax revenues.

Determined to grow Peru's way out of contraction, the government imposed higher protectionist fences. In 1989, a dramatic decline in imports, coupled with a continued debt repayment moratorium, allowed the government again to build up international reserves to about $1 billion, which it used to underwrite yet another consumption boom. But these tactics were by now shop-worn. The Peruvian people's enthusiasm for Garcia's blatant refusal to stabilize and liberalize the national economy was tempered by their chaotic experience. It had become evident that adjustment simply could not be avoided and that the government's policy amounted to wishful thinking that would leave Peru in even worse straits.

In this wilderness, voices of sanity were raised as Mario Vargas Llosa, who had opposed Garcia's nationalization and advocated the dismantling of statism, announced his candidacy for the 1990 presidential election. In direct contrast to Garcia, Vargas prescribed severe shock therapy—orthodox austerity and free-market policies—to reduce the inflation rate quickly to 10 percent. He planned to eliminate the budget deficit by ending government subsidies immediately and selling all of Peru's state-owned companies. He promised to resume payment on the foreign debt and work toward genuine stabilization of Peru's external accounts.

Vargas's chief opposition came not from Garcia's party but from a complete outsider, a Peruvian citizen of Japanese descent, Alberto Fujimori. Describing himself as political centrist, Fujimori called for austerity but criticized Vargas's proposed shock treatment as too drastic.[33] Under his program for the economy, Fujimori told the Peruvian voters, he would trim the budget deficit gradually, reducing the rate of inflation to 100 or 200 percent during his first year. While he would end Garcia's confrontational attitude toward the international financial community, he would insist that the nation's creditors provide Peru with substantial debt relief.

Ultimately, this combination of common sense and a promise to soften the inevitable blow of adjustment led to Fujimori's election in July 1990. In the following month, the government announced the first phase of an eighteen-month economic stabilization program that combined the customary heterodox measures with steps toward the permanent reduction of government involvement in production activities. Fujimori ordered all state-owned companies to raise their prices to levels that would make them profitable and to pare back expenses by furloughing employees who had been hired during the final months of the Garcia administration. True to his word, he included some compensatory wage increases in the package and $400 million in relief to cushion the impact on Peru's poorest. Financed by one-time levies on wealth, these were clearly departures from the main road of orthodox reform to which the Fujimori administration was committed. The permanence of the orthodox portion of the program was most apparent in the turnabout of Peru's foreign trade regime. Imports were liberalized as restrictions on most product categories were lifted, the exchange controls eliminated, and tariff rates cut deeply.

After years of repression and mismanagement, even this tempered shift toward reliance upon market forces was bound to have extreme consequences. When the adjustment measures were implemented, what would be termed "Fujishock" resulted in the steepest one-day price increases in modern Peruvian history. The cost of gasoline went from $.07 to $2.25 per gallon; the electricity rate rose 500 percent; the price of most food staples jumped 300 to 400 percent overnight. This was more austerity than the Peruvian people had bargained for, and sporadic looting and rioting in Lima resulted in some 6,000 arrests. Fujimori's popularity plummeted among his poor constituents.

After a year in office, Fujimori has regained some of his popular backing. His commitment to economic reality has earned him the respect of the capitalist opposition, and one supporter of Vargas Llosa allowed that, "Mr. Fujimori has turned out to be much more lucid than we thought."[34] But Peru is by no means out of the woods. Despite a marked improvement in the country's economic performance in 1991, the political cost of cleaning up the excesses of the Garcia years is very high, and whether Fujimori can sustain reform under these conditions is highly problematical. Clearly, Peru needs the sort of multidimensional assistance that participation in an EAI would bring. But just as plainly, it must tough out further adjustment gains before it can become eligible for formal integration into a hemispheric economic alliance.

External Stabilization

This gap between the need for external support and Peru's capacity to use its productivity is apparent in the adjustment dimension of external stabilization. Peru's foreign debt is a textbook case of statism and an import-substituting industrialization strategy being undercut by a secular decline in terms of trade. During the late 1960s, Peru took the role of nationalist leader of the Andean Pact. When payment crises arose in the early 1970s, emergency stabilization measures were introduced by the ruling military junta, without any structural reform. Periodic efforts by the Belaunde government in the early 1980s to liberalize the economy were stymied by the right-wing nationalist military. Then export prices plummeted in the 1983–1984 period, so that when Garcia was inaugurated, external debt stood at $14 billion, with $500 million in accumulated arrears owed to foreign bankers.

Garcia tried to shift the adjustment burden from Peru to the banking community by announcing the limitation of yearly external debt-service payments to 10 percent of annual exports. This unilateral constraint was obviously unacceptable to commercial creditors; rescheduling of bank debt was denied; a complete breakdown in the repayment process led to the accumulation of over $6 billion in open interest arrears. Worse, by the time of Fujimori's inauguration, Peru had amassed some $2 billion in interest arrears on loans from the IMF, the World Bank, and the IDB. By not servicing its obligations to the World Bank and the IMF, Peru cut itself off from these sources of external credit. Confronted with an unprecedented threat of expulsion from the IBRD, Peru earned a reputation as "the world's worst debtor."[35]

Facing this legacy, President Fujimori sought to begin his nation's trek back to international credibility even before he took office. Between the time of his election and his inauguration, Fujimori traveled to Japan and the United States seeking to restore Peru to the good graces of the international financial community. Sympathetic to Peru's plight, the IMF and the Bank were reportedly considering a special exception to their long-standing rule of not rescheduling loans. As it turned out, this departure was not necessary; the Fujimori government was able to borrow funds to repay its arrears on IMF and IBRD debt. In return for a promise of strict austerity and resumption of debt-service payments, Fujimori obtained a commitment for a bridge loan—through an international consortium including Japan, Spain, and the United States—to be transferred to official multilateral lenders. By mid-1991, Peru was sending some $50 million to $60 million a month to the World Bank and the IMF, and Peruvian officials had begun informal talks with other creditors.

However, a workout with the banks will require that arrears be satisfied in preparation for a Brady-style debt-reduction plan. Peru's prospects on this front were boosted by forgiveness on its official debt through the Paris Club, but the commercial debt is a far larger problem in terms of both outstanding sums and the willingness of lenders to undertake rescheduling while huge interest arrears remain. With voluntary fresh loan flows out of the picture, the direct investment outlook adumbrated by the state of the Peruvian economy, and no private firms with the standing to float bond issues on the Eurocredit market, Peru's only remaining sources of credit to cover its con-

tinuing current-account deficits are outright official grants and the repatriation of flight capital which amounted to somewhere between $6 billion and
$7 billion at the end of the 1980s. It is somewhat surprising that Peruvian in-
vestors acknowledged Fujimori's resolve by returning about 10 percent of
flight capital to their homeland in the summer of 1991 after the finalization
of the bridge loan to repay arrears on IMF and World Bank loans.

External Liberalization

In the near term, the liberalization of Peru's external sector is likely to
work against its stabilization efforts. With imports liberalized and exchange
controls rescinded, prices on imports have skyrocketed. Insofar as market
forces compress import volumes, this will help to meet external stabilization
aims; but since even necessary imports like prescription drugs are now more
dear in domestic currency terms, additional inflationary pressures have
accompanied external liberalization. Even if Peru completely erased rules
governing direct investment, few foreign firms would be willing to enter an
economy like that of Peru in the early 1990s. Thus, there is no compensatory
direct-investment capital flow accompanying import liberalization during
its initial stages.

Domestic Stabilization

As for domestic stabilization, adjustment under Fujimori has featured
drastic cuts in government spending and the elimination of indirect consumption subsidies on goods and services supplied by state-owned enterprises.
Fujimori has stopped printing money to bridge the fiscal gap by monetizing
domestic public debt. During his first year as president, tax revenues doubled
from 4 percent of GDP to nearly 8 percent, although the government reckons
that tax receipts must come in at 14 percent for the state to operate.

Domestic Liberalization

With the domestic economy nowhere near stability, Fujimori's liberalization plans cannot unfold smoothly and their near-term costs are considerable.
In 1990, Peru has some 160 state-owned companies, collectively responsible
for losses of more than $2 billion annually. In symbolic terms, no facet of
Fujimori's program is more important than privatization. Yet the government
has been unable to find domestic or foreign investors willing to digest these
white elephants in a single swallow. A few privatization opportunities —
notably those involving oil and gas holdings of the state-owned Petroperu —
may lead somewhere. Thus far, privatization has moved forward through
the sale of real assets and of shares in state-owned companies. Until such

time as buyers can be found, genuine privatization may be advanced by the further deregulation of the economy, an area in which the Fujimori government has made some progress.

ECONOMIC PERFORMANCE

The second year of Fujimori's administration has shown substantial improvement. GDP growth is now positive, and annual inflation has ebbed to double digits. But Peru has a long way to go—personal income was cut in half during Garcia's regime and declined another 25 percent during the initial stages of Fujishock. With 70 percent of the labor force underemployed, half the population suffering from malnutrition, and productivity below the levels of 25 years earlier, the Peruvian economy is in desperate straits. Under Fujimori, it is possible to muster some optimism for the future. The chances for a return to stability and growth, however, hinge upon the continued acceptance of austerity by the Peruvian people. Some of Fujimori's popular support has been restored since the initial shock of August 1990; but organized labor has aligned itself against Fujimori, especially after he dismantled the dockworkers union to facilitate trade liberalization. In 1991 an editorial in a widely circulated union magazine described Fujimori's program as the "harshest and most unimaginative austerity program ever attempted in Latin America."[36] There is further peril from the terrorist political left. Peru's Shining Path (SL) renewed its promise to wage an unrelenting war against the Fujimori government to establish a primitive agrarian communist society. SL not only controls portions of the countryside, it has access to resources through its odd alliances with Peru's drug lords. If the radical left succeeds in undermining order, the credibility of the Fujimori regime could be jeopardized, leaving the door open for a return to statism under the guise of countering the terrorist menace.

Bibliography

Aho, Michael, and Stokes, Bruce. "The Year the World Economy Turned." *Foreign Affairs* vol. 70, no. 1 ("America and the World 1990–1991"), pp. 160–178.

Arnold, Shellye. "The Joint Committee for Investment and Trade." *Business America* vol. 112, no. 7 (8 April 1991), p. 10.

Avery, William P. "The Origins of Debt Accumulation among LDCs in the World Political Economy." *The Journal of Developing Areas* vol. 24 (July 1990), pp. 503–522.

Baker, Stephen, Weiner, Elizabeth, and Borrus, Amy. "Mexico: A New Economic Era." *Businessweek* no. 3187 (12 November 1990), pp. 102–110.

Baker, Stephen, Woodruff, David, and Javetski, Bill. "Along the Border, Free Trade is Becoming a Fact of Life." *Businessweek* no. 3165 (18 June 1990), pp. 41–42.

Baker, Stephen; Weiner, Elizabeth; and Borrus, Amy. "Mexico: A New Economic Era." *Businessweek* no. 3187 (12 November 1990), pp. 102–110.

Baker, Stephen; Woodruff, David; and Javetski, Bill. "Along the Border, Free Trade is Becoming a Fact of Life." *Businessweek* no. 3165 (18 June 1990), pp. 41–42.

Bartholomew, Douglas. "No Time for New Toys." *Euromoney* (September 1988), spec. supp., pp. 19–22.

Benedict, Daniel. "The Lost Decade of Latin America Is Over." *Global Trade* vol. 110, no. 9 (September 1990), pp. 42–43.

Beristain, Javier, and Trigueros, Ignacio. "Mexico." In *Latin American Adjustment: How Much Has Happened?* Edited by John Williamson, pp. 154–168. Washington, D.C.: Institute for International Economics, 1990.

"Best Prospects for U.S. Exports to Mexico." *Business America* vol. 112, no. 7 (8 April 1991), p. 12.

Bienen, Henry, and Waterbury, John. "The Political Economy of Privatization in Developing Countries." *World Development* vol. 17, no. 5 (1989), pp. 617–632.

Bigman, David. "A Plan to End LDC Debt and Save the Environment Too." *Challenge* vol. 33, no. 4 (July-August 1990), pp. 33–37.

Blackwell, Michael, and Nocera, Simon. "The Impact of Debt to Equity Conversion." *Finance & Development* (June 1988), pp. 15–17.

Bock, David R. "The Bank's Role in Resolving the Debt Crisis." *Finance & Development* (June 1988), pp. 6–8.

Borensztein, Eduardo. "Will Debt Reduction Increase Investment?" *Finance & Development* (March 1991), pp. 25–27

"The Bottom Line: Give Brady a Chance." *The Banker* vol. 139, no. 764 (September 1989), p. 120.

Brady, Simon. "Here Comes the Credit Crunch." *Euromoney* (April 1990), pp. 29–37.

Brady, Simon. "Latin America: The Lost Decade." *Euromoney* (August 1990), spec. supp., pp. 26–28.

"Brady's Bazaar." *Economist* vol. 315, no. 7654 (12 May 1990), p. 77.

"Brazil: Out of Style." *Economist* vol. 319, no. 7077 (18 May 1991), pp. 48–50.

"Brazil's Debt: Forgive and Forget." *Economist* vol. 316, no. 7670 (1 September 1990), pp. 70–71.

Bulow, Jeremy, and Rogoff, Kenneth. "Sovereign Debt: Is to Forgive to Forget?" *American Economic Review* vol. 79, no. 1 (March 1989), pp. 43–50.

Bulow, Jeremy, and Rogoff, Kenneth. "Cleaning Up Third World Debt without Getting Taken to the Cleaners." *Journal of Economic Perspectives* vol. 4, no. 1 (Winter 1990), pp. 31–42.

"Bush Urges U.S. Approval of Mexico Trade Pact." *Congressional Quarterly Weekly* (13 April 1991), pp. 937–938.

Cardoso, Eliana A., and Dantas, Daniel. "Brazil." In *Latin American Adjustment: How Much Has Happened?* Edited by John Williamson, pp. 129–153. Washington, D.C.: Institute for International Economics, 1990.

Cariaga, Juan L. "Bolivia." In *Latin American Adjustment: How Much Has Happened?* Edited by John Williamson, pp. 41–53. Washington, D.C.: Institute for International Economics, 1990.

Carvounis, Chris. *The Debt Dilemma of Developing Nations: Issues and Cases.* Westport, Conn.: Greenwood Press, 1984.

Carvounis, Chris. *The Foreign Debt/National Development Conflict: External Adjustment and Internal Disorder in the Developing Nations.* Westport, Conn.: Greenwood Press, 1986.

Chesler-Marsh, Caren. "Carnival Time Again for Latin Borrowers." *Euromoney* (September 1990), pp. 155–161.

"Chile: Building on Success." *Euromoney* (September 1990), spec. supp., pp. 1–3.

Chopra, Karen James. "NAFTA Negotiations Will Be Comprehensive." *Business America* vol. 112, no. 7 (8 April 1991), p. 8.

Cline, William R. "Comment." In *Latin American Adjustment: How Much Has Happened?* Edited by John Williamson, pp. 169–177. Washington, D.C.: Institute for International Economics, 1990.

Cline, William R. "International Debt Progress and Strategy." *Finance & Development* (June 1988), pp. 9–11.

Cloud, David S. "Highlights of the 'Action Plan'." *Congressional Quarterly Weekly* (4 May 1991), p. 1121.

Cloud, David S. "Fast Track: Congress's Own Creation." *Congressional Quarterly Weekly* (18 May 1991), p. 1259.

Cooper, Richard. "Trade and Non-Tariff Barriers after the Uruguay Round." *Harvard International Review* vol. 13, no. 4 (Summer 1991), pp. 7–8, 58.

Corbo, Vittorio. "Reforms and Macroeconomic Adjustments in Chile During 1974–84." *World Development* vol. 13, no. 8 (1985), pp. 893–916.

Corbo, Vittorio, and de Melo, J. "External Shocks and Policy Reforms in the Southern Cone: A Reassessment." In *Debt, Stabilization and Development,* edited by G. Calvo, et al., pp. 235–264. Oxford: Basil Blackwell, 1989.

Cranford, John R. "Bush Urges Trade, Debt Relief in Plan for Latin America." *Congressional Quarterly Weekly* (30 June 1990), p. 2037.

Crosbie, John. "North American Competitiveness and the Canada–U.S. Free Trade Agreement." *Harvard International Review* vol. 13, no. 4 (Summer 1991), pp. 9–11, 59.

Cuddington, John. *Capital Flight: Estimates, Issues and Explanations.* Princeton Studies in International Finance, no. 58. Princeton, N.J.: Princeton University, 1986.

de Pablo, Juan Carlos. "Argentina." In *Latin American Adjustment: How Much Has Happened?* Edited by John Williamson, pp. 111–128. Washington, D.C.: Institute for International Economics, 1990.

"Debt: A Star Performance." *Euromoney* (September 1990), spec. supp., pp. 7–11.

de Larosière, Jacques. "Economic Adjustment and Growth." *Finance & Development* (March 1986), pp. 28–29.

de Larosière, Jacques. "Progress on the International Debt Strategy." *Finance & Development* (March 1987), pp. 10–11.

"Demand for Computers Strong in Latin America." *Business America* (5 November 1990), p. 20.

Devlin, Robert. *Debt and Crisis in Latin America: The Supply Side of the Story.* Princeton, N.J.: Princeton University, 1989.

Diamond, Jack. "Government Expenditure and Growth." *Finance & Development* (December 1990), pp. 34–36.

Dooley, Michael P. *Country-Specific Risk Premiums, Capital Flight and Net Investment Income Payments in Selected Developing Countries.* Washington, D.C.: International Monetary Fund, 1986.

Dooley, Michael P. "Buy-Backs and Market Valuation of External Debt." *IMF Staff Papers* vol. 35, no. 2 (June 1988), pp. 215–229.

Dooley, Michael P., and Watson, C. Maxwell. "Reinvigorating the Debt Strategy." *Finance & Development* (September 1989), pp. 8–11.

Dornbusch, Rudiger. "It's Time to Open Up Trade with Mexico." *Challenge* vol. 33, no. 6 (December 1990), pp. 52–55.

Dornbusch, Rudiger. "Panel Discussion on Latin American Adjustment: The Record and the Next Steps." In *Latin American Adjustment: How Much Has Happened?* Edited by John Williamson, pp. 312–326. Washington, D.C.: Institute for International Economics, 1990.

Edwards, Sebastian. *Real Exchange Rates, Devaluation, and Adjustment: Exchange Rate Policy in Developing Countries.* Cambridge: Massachusetts Institute of Technology Press, 1989.

Edwards, Sebastian. "Comment." In *Latin American Adjustment: How Much Has Happened?* Edited by John Williamson, pp. 177–181. Washington, D.C.: Institute for International Economics, 1990.

Edwards, Sebastian, and Cox-Edwards, Alejandra. *Monetarism and Liberalization: The Chilean Experiment.* Cambridge, Mass.: Ballinger, 1987.

Edwards, Sebastian, and Larrain, Felipe. "Debt, Adjustment and Recovery in Latin America: An Introduction." In *Debt, Adjustment and Recovery: Latin America's Prospect for Growth and Development,* edited by Sebastian Edwards and Felipe Larrain, pp. 1–27. Oxford: Basil Blackwell, 1989.

Elving, Ronald. "Looking South for Agreement Suddenly Gains Currency." *Congressional Quarterly Weekly* (16 June 1990), pp. 1864–1865.

"Enormously Consequential." *Forbes* vol. 145, no. 9 (30 April 1990), p. 20.

Fauriol, Georges A. "The Shadow of Latin American Affairs." *Foreign Affairs* vol. 69, no. 1 ("America and the World, 1989–1990"), pp. 116–134.

Feinberg, Richard. "Comment." In *Latin American Adjustment: How Much Has Happened?* Edited by John Williamson, pp. 21–24. Washington, D.C.: Institute for International Economics, 1990.

Felix, David, and Caskey, John P. "The Road to Default: An Assessment of Debt Crisis Management in Latin America." In *Debt and Transfiguration: Prospects for Latin America's Economic Revival,* edited by David Felix, pp. 3–35. Armonk, N.Y.: M. E. Sharpe, 1990.

"A Firm Hand on the Tiller." *Euromoney* (December 1989), spec. supp., pp. 3–12.

Fischer, Stanley. "Comment." In *Latin American Adjustment: How Much Has Happened?* Edited by John Williamson, pp. 25–28. Washington, D.C.: Institute for International Economics, 1990.

Fischer, Stanley, and Husain, Ishart. "Managing the Debt Crisis in the 1990s." *Finance & Development* (June 1990), pp. 24–27.

Fishlow, Albert. "The Latin American State." *Journal of Economic Perspectives* vol. 4, no. 3 (Summer 1990), pp. 61–74.

"Fortress North America." *Economist* vol. 314, no. 7648 (31 March 1990), p. 67.

Foxley, Alejandro (interview). "A Calm Hand on the Tiller." *Euromoney* (September 1990), spec. supp., p. 6.

"Free Trade Moves South." *Economist* vol. 316, no. 7663 (14 July 1990), p. 40.

"Free Trade With Mexico Means Oil, Too." *Businessweek* no. 3181 (8 October 1990), p. 162.

"From the Yukon to the Yucatan." *Economist* vol. 315, no. 7659 (16 June 1990), pp. 21–22.

Froot, Kenneth A., Scharfstein, David S., and Stein, Jeremy C. "LDC Debt: Forgiveness, Indexation and Investment Incentives." *Journal of Finance* vol. 44, no. 5 (December 1989), pp. 1335–1350.

Garcia, Alvaro, Infante, Ricardo, and Tokman, Victor E. "Paying Off the Social Debt in Latin America." *International Labour Review* vol. 128, no. 4 (1989), pp. 467–483.

Giraldo, German, and Mann, Arthur J. "Latin American External Debt Growth: A Current Account Explanatory Model, 1973–1984." *The Journal of Developing Areas* vol. 24 (October 1989), pp. 47–58.

Glade, William. "Privatization in Rent-Seeking Societies." *World Development* vol. 17, no. 5 (1989), pp. 673–682.

Gordon, Bernard K. "The Asian-Pacific Rim: Success at a Price." *Foreign Affairs* vol. 70, no. 1 ("America and the World, 1990–1991"), pp. 142–159.

Grayson, George W. "Mexico Moves toward Modernization." *Current History* vol. 90, no. 554 (March 1991), pp. 109–112, 135–136.

Griffin, Keith. "Toward a Cooperative Settlement of the Debt Problem." *Finance & Development* (June 1988), pp. 12–14.

Hausman, Ricardo. "Venezuela." In *Latin American Adjustment: How Much Has Happened?* Edited by John Williamson, pp. 224–244. Washington, D.C.: Institute for International Economics, 1990.

Helpman, Elahan. "Voluntary Debt Reduction." *IMF Staff Papers* vol. 36, no. 3 (September 1989), pp. 580–611.

Hieronymus, Bill. "Debt Swaps — Yes, But Who Pays?" *Euromoney* (September 1988), spec. supp., pp. 24–36.

Hoffmann, Stanley. "A New World and Its Troubles." *Foreign Affairs* vol. 69, no. 4 (Fall 1990), pp. 115–122.

Holstein, William J., Borrus, Amy, Baker, Steven, and Drohan, Madelaine. "Inching toward a North American Market." *Businessweek* no. 3166 (25 June 1990), pp. 40–41.

Holstein, William J., Woodruff, David, and Borrus, Amy. "Is Free Trade with Mexico Good or Bad for the U.S.?" *Businessweek* no. 3187 (12 November 1990), pp. 112–113.

Hommes, Rudolf. "Columbia." In *Latin American Adjustment: How Much Has Happened?* Edited by John Williamson, pp. 199–223. Washington, D.C.: Institute for International Economics, 1990.

Howard, Richard. "U.S.-Mexico Cooperation Goes Far Beyond Trade." *Business America* vol. 112, no. 7 (8 April 1991), pp. 9–10.

Husain, Ishart. "Recent Experience with the Debt Strategy." *Finance & Development* (September 1989), pp. 12–15.

Husain, S. Shahid. "Reviving Growth in Latin America." *Finance & Development* (June 1989), pp. 2–4.

"IDB: Renewed Growth in Latin America in 1990s." *Business America* (5 November 1990), p. 20.

Iglesias, Enrique. "From Policy Consensus to Renewed Economic Growth." In *Latin American Adjustment: How Much Has Happened?* Edited by John Williamson, pp. 345–350. Washington, D.C.: Institute for International Economics, 1990.

International Monetary Fund, World Bank, Organization for Economic Cooperation and Development, and European Bank for Reconstruction and Development. *The Economy of the USSR.* Washington, D.C.: World Bank, 1990.

Islam, Shafiqul. "Going Beyond the Brady Plan." *Challenge* vol. 32, no. 4 (July-August 1989), pp. 39–46.

Johnson, Christopher. "Left Hand, Right Hand." *The Banker* vol. 139, no. 765 (November 1989), p. 144.

Kenen, Peter B. "Organizing Debt Relief: The Need for a New Institution." *Journal of Economic Perspectives* vol. 4, no. 1 (Winter 1990), pp. 7–18.

King, Elliot. "The Impact of the Free Trade Act." *Global Trade* vol. 111, no. 3 (March 1991), pp. 16–18.

Krause, Lawrence B. "Regionalism in World Trade: The Limits of Economic Independence." *Harvard International Review* vol. 13, no. 4 (Summer 1991), pp. 4–6.

Kuczynski, Pedro-Pablo. "Peru." In *Latin American Adjustment: How Much Has Happened?* Edited by John Williamson, pp. 86–94. Washington, D.C.: Institute for International Economics, 1990.

"Labor Groups Pan Mexico Pact." *Congressional Quarterly Weekly* (30 June 1990), p. 2039.

Larrain, Felipe. "Comment." In *Latin American Adjustment: How Much Has Hap-

pened? Edited by John Williamson, pp. 247–253. Washington, D.C.: Institute for International Economics, 1990.

"The Latin Market Comes to Life." *Economist* vol. 319, no. 7710 (8 June 1991), pp. 77–80.

Lessard, Donald R., and Williamson, John, eds. *Capital Flight and Third World Debt.* Washington, D.C.: Institute for International Economics, 1987.

Lindow, Herbert A. "Venezuela: Imports Expected to Rise as Economy Recovers." *Business America* vol. 112, no. 8 (22 April 1991), p. 14.

"Living with the Giant Next Door." *Euromoney* (December 1989), spec. supp., pp. 23–36.

Looney, Robert E. "The Influence of Arms Imports on Third World Debt." *Journal of Developing Countries* vol. 23, no. 1 (January 1989), pp. 221–232.

Lowenthal, Abraham F. "Rediscovering Latin America." *Foreign Affairs* vol. 69, no. 4 (Fall 1990), pp. 27–41.

Lowry, Andrew. "Mexico: Market Is Large, Especially for U.S. Goods." *Business America* vol. 112, no. 8 (22 April 1991), p. 10.

Magnusson, Paul, Baker, Stephen, Beach, David, DeGeorge, Gail, and Symonds, William C. "The Mexico Pact: Worth the Price?" *Businessweek* no. 3215 (27 May 1991), pp. 32–35.

Main, Jeremy. "How Latin America Is Opening Up." *Fortune* vol. 123, no. 7 (8 April 1991), pp. 84–88.

Mandelbaum, Michael. "The Bush Foreign Policy." *Foreign Affairs* vol. 70, no. 1 ("America and the World, 1990–1991"), pp. 5–23.

McNeill, William H. "Winds of Change." *Foreign Affairs* (1990–1991), pp. 153–175.

Meller, Patricio. "Chile." In *Latin American Adjustment: How Much Has Happened?* Edited by John Williamson, pp. 54–85. Washington, D.C.: Institute for International Economics, 1990.

Meller, Patricio. "Comment." In *Latin American Adjustment: How Much Has Happened?* Edited by John Williamson, pp. 32–35. Washington, D.C.: Institute for International Economics, 1990.

Melton, Sara K. "U.S.–Mexico Business Experience." *Business America* vol. 112, no. 7 (8 April 1991), p. 11.

"Mexico Beckons, Protectionists Quaver." *Economist* vol. 319, no. 7703 (20 April 1991), pp. 23–24.

Meyer, Arno, and Bastos, M. Silva. *The Flight of Capital from Brazil.* Rio de Janeiro: Getulio Vargas Foundation, 1989.

Mohammed, Azizali F. "The Case by Case Approach to Debt Problems." *Finance & Development* (March 1985), pp. 11–14.

Morgan Guaranty. "LDC Capital Flight." *World Financial Markets* (March 1986), pp. 46–57.

Musumeci, James J., and Sinkey, Joseph F. "The International Debt Crisis, Investor Contagion, and Bank Security Returns in 1987: The Brazilian Experience." *Journal of Money, Credit, and Banking* vol. 22, no. 2 (May 1990), pp. 209–220.

Musumeci, James J., and Sinkey, Joseph F. "The International Debt Crisis and Bank Loan-Loss Reserve Decisions: The Signaling Content of Partially Anticipated Events." *Journal of Money, Credit, and Banking* vol. 22, no. 3 (August 1990), pp. 370–387.

Nagourney, Steve (interview). "Latin America, Si!: Go South, an Analyst Urges U.S. Investors." *Barron's* vol. 70, no. 50 (10 December 1990), pp. 18–19.

Novak, Michael. "A Malthusian Vision." *Forbes* vol. 145, no. 10 (14 May 1990), p. 80.

Nowzad, Bahram. "Lessons of the Debt Decade." *Finance & Development* (March 1990), pp. 9–13.

Pang, Eul-Soo, and Jarnagin, Laura. "Brazil's Catatonic Lambada." *Current History* vol. 90, no. 553 (February 1991), pp. 73–75, 85–87.

Peagam, Norman. "Returning to the Fold." *Euromoney* (1990) spec. supp., pp. 15–17.

Perera, Tino. "Despite Debt Troubles, Latin America Is Still a Key U.S. Trading Partner." *Business America* vol. 111, no. 12 (22 October 1990), pp. 20–21.

Perry, William. "In Search of a Latin American Policy: The Elusive Quest." *The Washington Quarterly* (Spring 1990), pp. 125–134.

Piorkowski, Anne. "Brazilian Computer Import Restrictions: Technological Independence and Commercial Reality." *Law and Policy in International Business* vol. 17, no. 3 (1985), pp. 619–645.

Poole, Claire. "Cement Wars." *Forbes* vol. 146, no. 7 (1 October 1990), pp. 99–102.

Psacharopoulos, George. "Poverty Alleviation in Latin America." *Finance & Development* (March 1990), pp. 17–19.

Reier, Sharon. "The Last Tango." *Financial World* vol. 158, no. 11 (30 May 1989), pp. 14–17.

Reier, Sharon. "Lessons of a Samba Dancer." *Financial World* vol. 159, no. 5 (6 March 1990), pp. 66–67.

Remmer, Karen L. "Debt or Democracy: The Political Impact of the Debt Crisis in Latin America." In *Debt and Transfiguration: Prospects for Latin America's Economic Revival,* edited by David Felix, pp. 63–78. Armonk, N.Y.: M. E. Sharpe, 1990.

"Respectability Brings Investment." *Euromoney* (September 1990), spec. supp., p. 20.

Roberts, Paul Craig. "Brazil's One-Way Ticket to Disasterville." *Businessweek* no. 3158 (7 May 1990), p. 20.

Roett, Riordan. "Peru: The Message From Garcia." *Foreign Affairs* vol. 64, no. 2 (Winter 1985–1986), pp. 274–286.

Rogoff, Kenneth. "Symposium on New Institutions for Developing Country Debt." *Journal of Economic Perspectives* vol. 4, no. 1 (Winter 1990), pp. 3–6.

Rustow, Dankwart A. "Democracy: A Global Revolution." *Foreign Affairs* vol. 70, no. 2 (Winter 1990), pp. 75–91.

Ryser, Jeffrey. "Brazil Finally Catches Free-Market Fever." *Businessweek* no. 3128 (16 October 1989), p. 51.

Ryser, Jeffrey. "Collor Really Knows How to Make an Entrance." *Businessweek* no. 3151 (26 March 1990), p. 54.

Sachs, Jeffrey D. "Strengthening IMF Programs in Highly Indebted Countries." In *The International Monetary Fund in a Multipolar World: Pulling Together,* edited by C. Gwin and Richard E. Feinberg, pp. 275–285. Washington, D.C.: Overseas Development Council, 1989.

Sachs, Jeffrey D. "A Strategy for Efficient Debt Reduction." *Journal of Economic Perspectives* vol. 4, no. 1 (Winter 1990), pp. 19–29.

Scott, Charles. "Menem Scores a Home Goal." *Euromoney* (1990), spec. supp., pp. 25–28.

Selowsky, Marcelo. "Adjustment in the 1980s: An Overview of the Issues." *Finance & Development* (June 1987), pp. 11–14.

Selowsky, Marcelo. "Stages in the Recovery of Latin America's Growth." *Finance & Development* (June 1990), pp. 28–31.

Smith, Wayne. "The United States and South America: Beyond the Monroe Doctrine." *Current History* vol. 90, no. 553 (February 1991), pp. 49–52, 88.

Stallings, Barbara, and Kaufman, Robert. "Debt and Democracy in the 1980s: The Latin American Experience." In *Debt and Democracy in Latin America,* edited by Barbara Stallings and Robert Kaufman, pp. 156–194. Boulder, Colo.: Westview Press, 1989.

Steel, David. "Breaking Through the Bureaucracy." *Euromoney* (September 1990), pp. 177–179.

"Suddenly the Money Goes Home to Peru." *Economist* vol. 319, no. 7712 (22 June 1991), p. 43.

Sunkel, Osvaldo. "Structuralism, Dependency and Institutionalism: An Exploration of Common Ground and Disparities." *Journal of Economic Issues* vol. 23, no. 2 (June 1989), pp. 519–533.

Teske, Gary. "U.S. Trade with Mexico in Perspective." *Business America* vol. 111, no. 12 (18 June 1990), pp. 20–22.

Tharp, Paul. "Dancing the Samba of Debt." *Euromoney* (March 1990), pp. 97–102.

Tharp, Paul. "There's Life after Hyperinflation." *Euromoney* (September 1990), pp. 169–174.

Thuermer, Karen E. "Will a North American FTA Become a Reality?" *Global Trade* vol. 111, no. 3 (March 1991), pp. 10–14.

"Trade Block Folly." *Economist* vol. 319, no. 7703 (20 April 1991), pp. 11–12.

Truman, Edwin M. "U.S. Policy in the Problems of International Debt." *Federal Reserve Bulletin* vol. 75, no. 11 (November 1989), pp. 727–735.

Turner, Roger. "Brazil: U.S. Outlook is Promising, Despite Some Uncertainties." *Business America* vol. 112, no. 8 (22 April 1991), p. 11.

"Twins That Won't Tango." *Economist* vol. 310, no. 5793 (11 March 1989), pp. 17–18.

Uhlig, Mark A. "Latin America: The Frustrations of Success." *Foreign Affairs* vol. 70, no. 1 ("America and the World, 1990–1991"), pp. 103–119.

Urquidi, Victor L. "Panel Discussion on Latin American Adjustment: The Record and the Next Steps." In *Latin American Adjustment: How Much Has Happened?* Edited by John Williamson, pp. 333–337. Washington, D.C.: Institute for International Economics, 1990.

Valenzuela, Arturo, and Constable, Pamela. "Democracy in Chile." *Current History* vol. 90, no. 553 (February 1991), pp. 53–56, 84–85.

van de Walle, Nicolas. "Privatization in Developing Countries: A Review of the Issues." *World Development* vol. 17, no. 5 (1989), pp. 601–615.

Van Wijnbergen, Sweder. "Comment." In *Latin American Adjustment: How Much Has Happened?* Edited by John Williamson, pp. 181–187. Washington, D.C.: Institute for International Economics, 1990.

"Venezuela: Tomorrow They Will Agree." *Economist* vol. 315, no. 7660 (23 June 1990), pp. 38–39.

Vernon-Wortzel, Heidi, and Wortzel, Lawrence H. "Privatization: Not the Only Answer." *World Development* vol. 17, no. 5 (1989), pp. 633–641.

"Virtues Reward." *Economist* vol. 317, no. 7685 (15 December 1990), p. 79.

Wallace, Roger W. "North American Free Trade Agreement: Generating Jobs for Americans." *Business America* vol. 112, no. 7 (8 April 1991), pp. 3–5.

Wanamaker, Melissa. "No Easy Path for Debt/Equity Swaps." *Euromoney* (September 1989), spec. supp., pp. 2–18.

Weintraub, Sidney. "The New U.S. Economic Initiative toward Latin America." *Journal of InterAmerican Studies and World Affairs* vol. 21, no. 2 (Summer 1991), pp. 1–17.

Werlich, David P. "Fujimori and the 'Disaster' in Peru." *Current History* (February 1991), pp. 61–64, 81–83.

Williamson, John. "Introduction." In *Latin American Adjustment: How Much Has Happened?* Edited by John Williamson, pp. 1–3. Washington, D.C.: Institute for International Economics, 1990.

Williamson, John. "What Washington Means by Policy Reform." In *Latin American Adjustment: How Much Has Happened?* Edited by John Williamson, pp. 7–20. Washington, D.C.: Institute for International Economics, 1990.

Williamson, John. "The Progress of Policy Reform in Latin America." In *Latin American Adjustment: How Much Has Happened?* Edited by John Williamson, pp. 353–420. Washington, D.C.: Institute for International Economics, 1990.

Wilson, Neil. "Light at the End of the Tunnel." *The Banker* vol. 139, no. 765 (November 1989), pp. 134–135.

Wynia, Gary W. "Argentina's Economic Reform." *Current History* vol. 90, no. 553 (February 1991), pp. 57–60, 83–84.

Yotopoulos, Pan A. "The (Rip) Tide of Privatization: Lessons from Chile." *World Development* vol. 17, no. 5 (1989), pp. 683–702.

Notes

CHAPTER 1

1. International Monetary Fund, World Bank, Organization for Economic Cooperation and Development, and European Bank for Reconstruction and Development, *The Economy of the USSR* (Washington, D.C.: World Bank, 1990), p. 1.

2. Robin Leigh-Pemberton, cited in Simon Brady, "Here Comes the Credit Crunch," *Euromoney,* April 1990, p. 29.

3. Enrique Iglesias, "From Policy Consensus to Renewed Economic Growth," in *Latin American Adjustment: How Much Has Happened?* ed. John Williamson (Washington, D.C.: Institute for International Economics, 1990), p. 346.

4. Caren Chesler-Marsh, "Carnival Time Again for Latin Borrowers," *Euromoney,* September 1990, p. 155.

CHAPTER 2

1. John Williamson, "The Progress of Policy Reform in Latin America," in *Latin American Adjustment: How Much Has Happened?* ed. John Williamson (Washington, D.C.: Institute for International Economics, 1990), p. 353.

2. Victor L. Urquidi, "Panel Discussion on Latin American Adjustment: The Record and the Next Steps," in *Latin American Adjustment,* p. 336.

3. Enrique Iglesias, "From Policy Consensus to Renewed Economic Growth," in *Latin American Adjustment,* p. 345.

4. William R. Cline, "International Debt Progress and Strategy," *Finance & Development,* June 1988, p. 9.

5. Chris Carvounis, *The Debt Dilemma of Developing Nations: Issues and Cases* (Westport, Conn.: Greenwood Press, 1984); idem., *The Foreign Debt/National Development Conflict: External Adjustment and Internal Disorder in the Developing Nations* (Westport, Conn.: Greenwood Press, 1986).

6. Steven Kamin, Robert Kahn, and Ross Levine, "External Debt and Developing Country Growth," *International Finance Discussion Paper 352* (Washington, D.C.: Board of Governors of the Federal Reserve System, May 1989), p. 52.

7. Edwin M. Truman, "U.S. Policy in the Problems of International Debt," *Federal Reserve Bulletin,* vol. 75, no. 11 (November 1989), pp. 728–729.

8. S. Shahid Husain, "Reviving Growth in Latin America," *Finance & Development,* June 1989, p. 2.

9. Robert E. Looney, "The Influence of Arms Imports on Third World Debt," *Journal of Developing Countries,* vol. 23, no. 1 (January 1989), p. 230.

10. Bahram Nowzad, "Lessons of the Debt Decade," *Finance & Development,* March 1990, p. 11.

11. Sebastian Edwards and Felipe Larrain, "Debt, Adjustment and Recovery in Latin America: An Introduction," in *Debt, Adjustment and Recovery: Latin America's Prospect for Growth and Development,* eds. Sebastian Edwards and Felipe Larrain (Oxford: Basil Blackwell, 1989), p. 4.

12. David Felix and John P. Caskey, "The Road to Default: An Assessment of Debt Crisis Management in Latin America," in *Debt and Transfiguration: Prospects for Latin America's Economic Revival,* ed. David Felix (Armonk, N.Y.: M. E. Sharpe, 1990), p. 12.

13. Bianchi et al., cited in *Debt, Adjustment and Recovery: Latin America's Prospect for Growth and Development,* eds. Edwards and Larrain, p. 4.

14. Keith Griffin, "Toward a Cooperative Settlement of the Debt Problem," *Finance & Development,* June 1988, pp. 12–14.

15. Nowzad, "Lessons," p. 10.

16. Kenneth Rogoff, "Symposium on New Institutions for Developing Country Debt," *Journal of Economic Perspectives,* vol. 4, no. 1 (Winter 1990), p. 5.

17. Jeffrey D. Sachs, "A Strategy for Efficient Debt Reduction," *Journal of Economic Perspectives,* vol. 4, no. 1 (Winter 1990), p. 24.

18. Eduardo Borensztein, "Will Debt Reduction Increase Investment?" *Finance & Development,* March 1991, p. 27.

19. Ibid.

20. Jeremy Bulow and Kenneth Rogoff, "Cleaning Up Third World Debt without Getting Taken to the Cleaners," *Journal of Economic Perspectives,* vol. 4, no. 1 (Winter 1990), p. 32.

21. Ibid., p. 35.

22. Ibid., p. 36.

23. Michael Novak, "A Malthusian Vision," *Forbes,* vol. 145, no. 10 (14 May 1990), p. 80.

24. Donald R. Lessard and John Williamson, eds., *Capital Flight and Third World Debt* (Washington, D.C.: Institute for International Economics, 1987), pp. 14–15.

25. John Cuddington, *Capital Flight: Estimates, Issues and Explanations,* Princeton Studies in International Finance, no. 58 (Princeton: Princeton University, 1986), p. 105.

26. Ibid., p. 20.

27. Michael P. Dooley, *Country-Specific Risk Premiums, Capital Flight and Net Investment Income Payments in Selected Developing Countries* (Washington, D.C.: International Monetary Fund, 1986), p. 77.

28. Felix and Caskey, "Road to Default," p. 14.

29. Morgan Guaranty, "LDC Capital Flight," *World Financial Markets,* March 1986, p. 49.

30. Lessard and Williamson, eds., *Capital Flight,* p. 34.

31. Ibid., p. 23.

32. L. William Seidman, cited in Sachs, "A Strategy for Efficient," p. 19.

33. Jacques de Larosière, cited in Truman, "U.S. Policy," p. 729.

34. Husain, "Reviving Growth," p. 3.

35. Jacques de Larosière, "Progress on the International Debt Strategy," *Finance & Development,* March 1987, p. 11.

36. Truman, "U.S. Policy," p. 731.

37. James J. Musumeci and Joseph F. Sinkey, "The International Debt Crisis and Bank Loan-Loss Reserve Decisions: The Signaling Content of Partially Anticipated Events," *Journal of Money, Credit, and Banking,* vol. 22, no. 3 (August 1990), p. 371.

38. Kenneth A. Froot, David S. Scharfstein, and Jeremy C. Stein, "LDC Debt: Forgiveness, Indexation and Investment Incentives," *Journal of Finance,* vol. 44, no. 5 (December 1989), p. 1335.

39. Nicholas F. Brady, cited in Shafiqul Islam, "Going Beyond the Brady Plan," *Challenge,* vol. 32, no. 4 (July-August 1989), p. 39.

40. Ibid.

41. Keith Griffin, "Toward a Cooperative Settlement of the Debt Problem," *Finance & Development,* June 1988, pp. 12–14; Robert Devlin, *Debt and Crisis in Latin America: The Supply Side of the Story* (Princeton: Princeton University, 1989).

42. Rudiger Dornbusch, "Panel Discussion on Latin American Adjustment: The Record and the Next Steps," in *Latin American Adjustment: How Much Has Happened?* ed. John Williamson (Washington, D.C.: Institute for International Economics, 1990), p. 321.

43. "Brady's Bazaar," *Economist,* vol. 315, no. 7654 (12 May 1990), p. 77.

44. Wayne Smith, "The United States and South America: Beyond the Monroe Doctrine," *Current History,* vol. 90, no. 553 (February 1991), p. 89.

45. Shafiqul Islam, "Going Beyond the Brady Plan," *Challenge,* vol. 32, no. 4 (July-August 1989), p. 41.

46. Bulow and Rogoff, "Cleaning Up Third World Debt," p. 41.

47. "The Bottom Line: Give Brady a Chance," *The Banker,* vol. 139, no. 764 (September 1989), p. 120.

48. Stanley Fischer and Ishart Husain, "Managing the Debt Crisis in the 1990s," *Finance & Development,* June 1990, p. 27.

49. Williamson, "Progress," p. 402.

50. William Glade, "Privatization in Rent-Seeking Societies," *World Development,* vol. 17, no. 5 (1989), p. 675.

51. Marcelo Selowsky, "Adjustment in the 1980s: An Overview of the Issues," *Finance & Development,* June 1987, p. 14.

52. Jacques de Larosière, "Economic Adjustment and Growth," *Finance & Development,* March 1986, p. 28.

53. David R. Bock, "The Bank's Role in Resolving the Debt Crisis," *Finance & Development,* June 1988, p. 7.

CHAPTER 3

1. Jeffrey D. Sachs, "A Strategy for Efficient Debt Reduction," *Journal of Economic Perspectives,* vol. 4, no. 1 (Winter 1990), p. 19.

2. John Williamson, "What Washington Means by Policy Reform," in *Latin American Adjustment: How Much Has Happened?* ed. John Williamson (Washington, D.C.: Institute for International Economics, 1990), p. 8.

3. See for example, Georges A. Fauriol, "The Shadow of Latin American Affairs," *Foreign Affairs,* vol. 69, no. 1 ("America and the World, 1989–1990") pp. 116–134; William Perry, "In Search of a Latin American Policy: The Elusive Quest," *The Washington Quarterly,* Spring 1990, pp. 155–178.

4. Abraham F. Lowenthal, "Rediscovering Latin America," *Foreign Affairs,* vol. 69, no. 4 (Fall 1990), p. 27.

5. *The Wall Street Journal,* 13 September 1990.

6. John R. Cranford, "Panel Approves Debt Relief, Development Bank Funds," *Congressional Quarterly Weekly* (30 June 1990), p. 2038.

7. Cited in John R. Cranford, "Bush Urges Trade, Debt Relief in Plan for Latin America," *Congressional Quarterly Weekly* (30 June 1990), p. 2037.

8. Daniel Benedict, "The Lost Decade of Latin America Is Over," *Global Trade,* vol. 110, no. 9 (September 1990), p. 42.

9. Ibid.

10. "Demand for Computers Strong in Latin America," *Business America,* 5 November 1990, p. 20.

11. Steve Nagourney, quoted in "Latin America, Si!: Go South, an Analyst Urges U.S. Investors," *Barron's,* vol. 70, no. 50 (10 December 1990), p. 19.

12. Cited in Benedict, "Lost Decade," p. 43.

13. Osvaldo Sunkel, "Structuralism, Dependency and Institutionalism: An Exploration of Common Ground and Disparities," *Journal of Economic Issues,* vol. 23, no. 2 (June 1989), p. 521.

14. Enrique Iglesias, "From Policy Consensus to Renewed Economic Growth," in *Latin American Adjustment,* p. 348.

15. Lowenthal, "Rediscovering Latin America," p. 38.

16. Donald R. Lessard and John Williamson, eds., *Capital Flight and Third World Debt* (Washington, D.C.: Institute for International Economics, 1987), p. 42.

17. Cited in Neil Wilson, "Light at the End of the Tunnel," *The Banker,* vol. 139, no. 765 (November 1989), p. 134.

18. Michael Mandelbaum, "The Bush Foreign Policy," *Foreign Affairs,* vol. 70, no. 1 ("America and the World, 1990–1991"), p. 20.

CHAPTER 4

1. Cited in "From the Yukon to the Yucatan," *Economist,* vol. 315, no. 7659 (16 June 1990), p. 21.

2. Cited in "Mexico: The New Model Debtor," *Economist,* vol. 317, no. 7675 (6 October 1990), p. 86.

3. Cited in "Bush Urges U.S. Approval of Mexico Trade Pact," *Congressional Quarterly Weekly* (13 April 1991), p. 937.

4. Ibid.

5. Paul Magnusson, Stephen Baker, David Beach, Gail DeGeorge, and William C. Symonds, "The Mexico Pact: Worth the Price?" *Businessweek,* no. 3215 (27 May 1991), p. 34.

6. Ronald Elving, "Looking South for Agreement Suddenly Gains Currency," *Congressional Quarterly Weekly* (16 June 1990), p. 1864.

7. Cited in ibid., p. 1865.

8. "Mexico Beckons, Protectionists Quaver," *Economist,* vol. 319, no. 7703 (20 April 1991), p. 24.

9. "Best Prospects for U.S. Exports to Mexico," *Business America,* vol. 112, no. 7 (8 April 1991), p. 12.

10. Roger W. Wallace, "North American Free Trade Agreement: Generating Jobs for Americans," *Business America,* vol. 112, no. 7 (8 April 1991), p. 4.

11. Cited in "Living with the Giant Next Door," *Euromoney* (December 1989), spec. supp. (Mexico), p. 36.

12. Ibid., p. 33.

13. Ibid., p. 36.

14. "Europe and Japan Close the Gap," *Euromoney* (September 1989), spec. supp. (Mexico), p. 14.

15. George W. Grayson, "Mexico Moves toward Modernization," *Current History,* vol. 90, no. 554 (March 1991), p. 110-111.

16. Stephen Baker, Elizabeth Weiner, and Amy Borrus, "Mexico: A New Economic Era," *Businessweek,* no. 3187 (12 November 1990), p. 108.

17. "Free Trade with Mexico Means Oil, Too," *Businessweek,* no. 3181 (8 October 1990), p. 162.

18. "Labor Groups Pan Mexico Pact," *Congressional Quarterly Weekly,* 30 June 1990, p. 2039.

19. Rudiger Dornbusch, "It's Time to Open Up Trade with Mexico," *Challenge,* vol. 33, no. 6 (December 1990), p. 54.

20. Karen E. Thuermer, "Will a North American FTA Become a Reality?" *Global Trade,* vol. 111, no. 3 (March 1991), p. 10.

21. William J. Holstein, Amy Borrus, Steven Baker, and Madelaine Drohan, "Inching toward a North American Market," *Businessweek,* no. 3166 (25 June 1990), p. 40.

22. Cited in Elving, "Looking South," p. 1865.

23. Cited in "Bush Urges U.S. Approval," p. 938.

24. "Enormously Consequential," *Forbes,* vol. 145, no. 9 (30 April 1990), p. 20.

25. William R. Cline, "Comment," in *Latin American Adjustment: How Much Has Happened?* ed. John Williamson (Washington, D.C.: Institute for International Economics, 1990), p. 175.

26. Cited in Bahram Nowzad, "Lessons of the Debt Decade," *Finance & Development,* March 1990, p. 11.

27. "The Bottom Line: Give Brady a Chance," *The Banker,* vol. 139, no. 764 (September 1989), p. 120.

28. "Mexican Debt: To Him That Hath Not," *Economist,* vol. 319, no. 7704 (27 April 1991), p. 82.

29. Cline, "Comment," p. 175.

30. Victor L. Urquidi, "Panel Discussion on Latin American Adjustment: The Record and the Next Steps," in *Latin American Adjustment,* p. 336.

31. Douglas Bartholomew, "No Time for New Toys," *Euromoney* (September 1988), spec. supp., p. 20.

32. Sebastian Edwards, "Comment," in *Latin American Adjustment,* p. 180.

33. Javier Beristain and Ignacio Trigueros, "Mexico," in *Latin American Adjustment,* p. 161.

34. William Glade, "Privatization in Rent-Seeking Societies," *World Development,* vol. 17, no. 5 (1989), pp. 673–674.

35. Cited in "A Firm Hand on the Tiller," *Euromoney* (December 1989) spec. supp. (Mexico), p. 7.

36. Cited in Magnusson et al., "Mexico Pact," p. 33.

37. Abraham F. Lowenthal, "Rediscovering Latin America," *Foreign Affairs,* vol. 69, no. 4 (Fall 1990), p. 35.

38. Philip A. Davis, "Environmental Opposition Fading," *Congressional Quarterly Weekly* (18 May 1991), p. 1258.

39. Cited in Elving, "Looking South," p. 1864.

40. "From the Yukon to the Yucatan," p. 21.

41. Wallace, "North American Free Trade Agreement," p. 5.

42. Holstein, Borrus, Baker, and Drohan, "Inching toward a North American Market," p. 41.

43. Wallace, "North American Free Trade Agreement," p. 5.

44. Sara K. Melton, "U.S.–Mexico Business Experience," *Business America,* vol. 112, no. 7 (8 April 1991), p. 11.

45. Cited in "Bush Urges U.S. Approval," p. 938.

46. William J. Holstein, David Woodruff, and Amy Borrus, "Is Free Trade with Mexico Good or Bad for the U.S.?" *Businessweek,* no. 3187 (12 November 1990), p. 113.

47. Elving, "Looking South," p. 1865.

48. Cited in "Labor Groups," p. 2039.

49. Ibid.

50. Mark A. Uhlig, "Latin America: The Frustrations of Success," *Foreign Affairs,* vol. 70, no. 1 ("America and the World, 1990–1991"), p. 118.

51. Stephen Baker, "Salinas's Plan: First Feed the People, Then Talk Reform," *Businessweek,* no. 3215 (27 May 1991), p. 35

52. "Fortress North America," *Economist,* vol. 314, no. 7648 (31 March 1990), p. 67.

53. "Trade Block Folly," *Economist,* vol. 319, no. 7703 (20 April 1991), pp. 11–12.

54. John Crosbie, "North American Competitiveness and the Canada–U.S. Free Trade Agreement," *Harvard International Review,* vol. 13, no. 4 (Summer 1991), p. 11.

55. Thuermer, "North American FTA," p. 10.

56. Cited in Baker, Weiner, and Borrus, "Mexico," p. 108.

CHAPTER 5

1. Patricio Meller, "Comment," in *Latin American Adjustment: How Much Has Happened?* ed. John Williamson (Washington, D.C.: Institute for International Economics, 1990), p. 106.

2. "Debt: A Star Performance," *Euromoney,* spec. supp. (September 1990), p. 10.

3. Melissa Wanamaker, "No Easy Path for Debt/Equity Swaps," *Euromoney,* spec. supp. (September 1989), p. 2.

4. Interview with Alejandro Foxley, "A Calm Hand on the Tiller," *Euromoney,* spec. supp. (September 1990), p. 6.

5. Pan A. Yotopoulos, "The (Rip) Tide of Privatization: Lessons from Chile," *World Development,* vol. 17, no. 5 (1989), p. 687.

6. Patricio Meller, "Chile," in *Latin American Adjustment,* p. 83.

7. Ibid., pp. 83–84.

8. Ibid., p. 54.

9. "Respectability Brings Investment," *Euromoney,* spec. supp. (September 1990), p. 20.

10. Arturo Valenzuela and Pamela Constable, "Democracy in Chile," *Current History,* vol. 90, no. 553 (February 1991), p. 54.

11. Ibid., p. 56.

12. Felipe Larrain, "Comment," in *Latin American Adjustment,* p. 247.

13. Stanley Fischer and Ishart Husain, "Managing the Debt Crisis in the 1990s," *Finance & Development,* June 1990, p. 25.

14. David Felix and John P. Caskey, "The Road to Default: An Assessment of Debt Crisis Management in Latin America," in *Debt and Transfiguration: Prospects for Latin America's Economic Revival,* ed. David Felix (Armonk, N.Y.: M. E. Sharpe, 1990), pp. 3–35.

15. Ricardo Hausman, "Venezuela," in *Latin American Adjustment,* p. 241.

16. Cited in David Steel, "Breaking through the Bureaucracy," *Euromoney* (September 1990), p. 178.

17. Ibid.

18. "Venezuela: Tomorrow They Will Agree," *Economist,* vol. 315, no. 7660 (23 June 1990), p. 39.

19. John Williamson, "The Progress of Policy Reform in Latin America," in *Latin American Adjustment: How Much Has Happened?* ed. John Williamson (Washington, D.C.: Institute for International Economics, 1990), p. 355.

20. Ibid., p. 356.

21. Juan L. Cariaga, "Bolivia," in *Latin American Adjustment,* p. 50.

22. Williamson, "Progress," p. 341.

23. Ibid., p. 391.

24. Donald R. Lessard and John Williamson, eds., *Capital Flight and Third World Debt* (Washington, D.C.: Institute for International Economics, 1987), p. 25.

25. Larrain, "Comments," p. 252.

26. Rudolf Hommes, "Columbia," in *Latin American Adjustment,* p. 216.

CHAPTER 6

1. James J. Musumeci and Joseph F. Sinkey, "The International Debt Crisis, Investor Contagion, and Bank Security Returns in 1987: The Brazilian Experience," *Journal of Money, Credit, and Banking,* vol. 22, no. 2 (May 1990), p. 219. Sarney would later call the 1986–1987 moratorium the "biggest error" his government had made.

2. Sebastian Edwards and Felipe Larrain, "Debt, Adjustment and Recovery in Latin America: An Introduction," in *Debt, Adjustment and Recovery: Latin America's Prospect for Growth and Development,* eds. Sebastian Edwards and Felipe Larrain (Oxford: Basil Blackwell, 1989), p. 19.

3. Sweder van Wijnbergen, "Comment," in *Latin American Adjustment: How Much Has Happened?* ed. John Williamson (Washington, D.C.: Institute for International Economics, 1990), p. 181.

4. Eul-Soo Pang and Laura Jarnagin, "Brazil's Catatonic Lambada," *Current History,* vol. 90, no. 553 (February 1991), p. 86.

5. Paul Tharp, "Dancing the Samba of Debt," *Euromoney* (March 1990), p. 100.

6. "Brazil's Debt: Forgive and Forget," *Economist,* vol. 316, no. 7670 (1 September 1990), p. 70.

7. Paul Tharp, "There's Life after Hyperinflation," *Euromoney* (September 1990), pp. 169–174.

8. Ibid., pp. 170, 173.

9. Arno Meyer and M. Silva Bastos, *The Flight of Capital from Brazil* (Rio de Janeiro: Getulio Vargas Foundation, 1989), p. 17.

10. Eliana A. Cardoso and Daniel Dantas, "Brazil," in *Latin American Adjustment,* p. 133.

11. Ibid., p. 135.

12. William R. Cline, "Comment," in *Latin American Adjustment,* p. 171.

13. Cited in Cardoso and Dantas, "Brazil," p. 150.

14. Pang and Jarnagin, "Brazil's Catatonic Lambada," p. 74.

15. Paul Craig Roberts, "Brazil's One-Way Ticket to Disasterville," *Businessweek,* no. 3158 (7 May 1990), p. 20.

16. Ibid.

17. "The Collor of Money," *The Banker,* vol. 140, no. 771 (May 1990), p. 3.

18. Sharon Reier, "Lessons of a Samba Dancer," *Financial World,* vol. 159, no. 5 (6 March 1990), p. 67.

19. Cardoso and Dantas, "Brazil," p. 143.

20. Pang and Jarnagin, "Brazil's Catatonic Lambada," p. 75.

21. "Brazil: Out of Style," *Economist,* vol. 319, no. 7077 (18 May 1991), p. 50.

22. Pang and Jarnagin, "Brazil's Catatonic Lambada," p. 73.

23. Wayne Smith, "The United States and South America: Beyond the Monroe Doctrine," *Current History,* vol. 90, no. 553 (February 1991), p. 88.

24. Cited in Charles Scott, "Menem Scores a Home Goal," *Euromoney,* spec. supp. (1990), p. 25.

25. William R. Cline, "Comment," p. 170.

26. Gary W. Wynia, "Argentina's Economic Reform," *Current History,* vol. 90, no. 553 (February 1991), p. 58.

27. Norman Peagam, "Returning to the Fold," *Euromoney,* spec. supp. (1990), p. 17.

28. Cited in Scott, "Menem Scores," p. 28.

29. Cited in Sharon Reier, "The Last Tango," *Financial World,* vol. 158, no. 11 (30 May 1989), p. 14.

30. Ibid., p. 16.

31. Sebastian Edwards, "Comment," in *Latin American Adjustment,* p. 179.

32. Wynia, "Argentina's Economic Reform," p. 83.

33. David P. Werlich, "Fujimori and the 'Disaster' in Peru," *Current History* (February 1991), p. 64.

34. "Suddenly the Money Goes Home to Peru," *The Economist,* vol. 319, no. 7712 (22 June 1991), p. 43.

35. Pedro Pablo-Kuczynski, "Peru," in *Latin American Adjustment,* p. 89.

36. "Suddenly the Money Goes Home," p. 43.

Index

Adjustment, 41–46; critique of, 45–46; external liberalization measures and, 41; external stabilization measures and, 42–43; internal liberalization measures and, 43; internal stabilization measures and, 44; International Monetary Fund and, 41; Latin progress in 20, 32, 46, 55–57; nature of, 41–42; United States progress in, 65–68. *See also* specific countries

Africa, 3–4

Alemann, Juan, 164

Alfonsin, Raul, 144, 161, 162, 163, 165, 167, 168–69

Alvarez, Luis, 109

Andean Development Corporation, 137

Andean Trade Association 64, 142, 173

Anderson, Mark, 107

Argentina, 160–70; adjustment approach of 143, 160–63; adjustment, external in, 163–65; adjustment, internal in, 165–68; capital flight from, 164; deregulation of business in, 168; debt (external) of, 163–64, 167; debt (public/internal) of, 165–66, 167, 168; debt-equity swaps used by, 165; direct investment in, 165, 169; Enterprise for the Americas Initiative and, 143, 160–70; exchange rate policy of, 165; exports of, 168; financial sector in, 162–63, 166, 167; fiscal policy of, 165–66, 167; growth rate of, 168;

Argentina *(continued)* imports of, 168; inflation in, 162–63, 166; International Monetary Fund and, 163, 166; political situation in, 168–69; privatization in, 164, 167–68; tax policy in 166–67; trade balance of, 168; trade liberalization in, 165; trade pattern of, 64–65, 169–70; United States relations with, 168, 169–70; weapons exports of, 60, 170; World Bank and, 163

Asian-Pacific Economic Cooperation (APEC), 6

Association of South East Asian Nations (ASEAN), 6

Aylwin, Patricio, 115–16, 123–25

Baker, James, 9, 31, 32

Baker Plan, 29–34, 48

Banzer, Hugo, 135

Bensten, Lloyd, 74

Bolivia, 133–40; adjustment, approach of, 113, 134–36; adjustment, external of, 136–38; adjustment, internal of, 138–39; capital needs of, 139; capital flows to, 137; capital flight of, 135; current account balance of, 135; deregulation of business in, 139; debt buybacks of, 137; debt (external) of, 134–35, 136–37; debt (public/internal) of, 134, 138; debt-equity swaps and, 138; direct investment in, 137–38;

Bolivia *(continued)*
  Enterprise for the Americas Initiative
    and, 133-40; exchange rate policy of,
    138, 139; exports of, 136; financial
    sector in, 139; fiscal policy of, 134-38;
    growth rate of, 136-37, 139; inflation
    in, 134-35, 140; International Mone-
    tary Fund and, 135, 136, 137, 140;
    political situation in, 139-40; privati-
    zation in, 139; tax policies in, 138-39;
    trade liberalization in, 137; World
    Bank and, 135, 136, 137, 140
Borzenzstein, Eduardo, 25
Brady, Nicholas, 34, 35, 36, 51, 69-70,
  92, 153
Brady Plan, 1, 9, 12, 29, 34-37, 50, 62,
  92-94, 117. *See also* specific countries
Brazil, 144-60; adjustment, approach
  of, 143, 144-46; adjustment, external
  of 146-52; adjustment, internal of,
  152-57; Brady Plan and, 147, 149;
  capital flight from, 149; de-regulation
  of business in, 156; debt (external)
  of, 33, 144-49, 158; debt (public/
  internal), of 144, 145, 152; debt-equity
  swaps used by, 147-47, 151; direct
  investment in, 151; Enterprise for the
  Americas Initiative and, 143, 144-60;
  environmental policy of, 60, 159-60;
  exchange rate policy of, 151-52;
  financial sector in, 144, 145, 153-54;
  fiscal policy of 144, 145, 152, 156-57;
  growth rate of, 144, 156; inflation
  in, 145, 147, 152-54, 156-57; International Monetary Fund and, 146-47,
  149; per capita GDP of, 18, 152, 156;
  political situation in, 157-59; privatization in, 151, 152, 155-57, 158; tax
  policies of, 154; trade balance of,
  144, 147, 149, 157; trade liberalization
  in, 149-51; trade pattern of, 64-65,
  150-51, 159; United States relations
  with, 150-51, 159-60; weapons exports
  of, 60, 159; World Bank and, 147
Bulow, Jeremy, 25, 26, 37
Bush, George: Action Plan of, 74,
  102-104; EAI and, 1-2, 51-52; Fast-

Bush, George *(continued)*
  Track authority and, 71-75; Latin
  policy of, 48, 127, 169; NAFTA, and
  69-72, 76, 83, 100-101, 107, 110-11.
  See also Enterprise Initiative for the
  America and North American Free
  Trade Area.
Business Roundtable (U.S. business
  association), 105

Capital Flight, 25-28; causes of, 20,
  26; magnitude of, 26; effects of, 27;
  policies toward, 27-28, 60-61; repatriation of, 27, 28. *See also* specific
  countries
Camdessus, Michel, 62, 163
Canada, 71-72, 80
Cardenas, Cuauhotemoc, 101, 108-109
Cardoso, Zelia, 145-46, 148, 152, 153,
  154, 158
Cavallo, Domingo, 161, 166, 169-70
CEMEX, 76, 80-81, 95
Central American Common Market, 64
Chile, 113-125; adjustment, approach
  of, 113, 114-16; adjustment, external
  of, 116-19; adjustment, internal of
  119-21; current account balance of,
  122; debt (external) of, 31, 114, 116,
  117; debt (public/internal) of, 115,
  119; debt-equity swaps used by, 116,
  118-19, 120-21, 122; direct investment in, 118, 121-22; Enterprise for
  the Americas Initiative and, 113-25;
  exchange rate policy of, 115, 119;
  exports of, 122; financial sector, in
  115, 119-20; fiscal policy of, 114-15,
  119; growth rate of, 115, 121; human
  rights in, 123, 124, 125; imports of,
  117; inflation in, 115, 119; International Monetary Fund and, 117;
  political situation in, 59, 123-25;
  privatization in, 120-21, 122; trade
  balance of, 114, 115, 122; trade liberalization in, 118; United States
  relations with, 124-25; World Bank
  and, 117
Chrysler Motor Corporation, 84

Citibank, 33, 93
Cline, William, 19, 86, 94, 162
Collor, Fernando 143, 144, 145–46, 147–48, 151, 153, 154, 157–59, 160, 168, 169
Colombia, 140–42; adjustment, approach of, 113–14, 140–41; adjustment, external of, 141–42; adjustment, internal of, 142; capital flight from, 141; debt (external) of, 141; Enterprise for the Americas Initiative and, 113, 140–42; exchange rate policy of, 141; exports of, 18; fiscal policy of, 141, 142; growth rate of, 142; imports of 19; inflation in, 142; International Monetary Fund and, 141; per capita GDP of, 18; trade liberalization in, 141–42; trade of, 18–19
Confederation of Mexican Workers, 108
Costa Rica 1, 33, 35, 62
Council for Mutual Economic Assistance (CMEA), 3
Crafton, Richard, 54
Crosbie, John, 109–110

Dauster, Jorio, 148–49
Debt Buybacks, 33, 39, 137
Debt Conversion Bonds, 34–37, 40
Debt-Equity Swaps, 39–41
Debt Overhang, 23–25
Dorgan, Byron, 74
Dornbusch, Rudiger, 35

Entel (Argentine Telephone), 164, 167
Enterprise for the Americas Initiative (EAI), 12–15, 48–68; adjustment, gains from, 13–15, 55–57; barriers to, 64–65; commercial gains from, 13, 52–55; conditionality of, 14, 50, 67–68; debt relief under, 49–50; direct investment incentives under, 49; GATT and, 13; historical background to 1, 50–52; Latin American reception of, 1–2, 113–14, 143, 170; political gains from, 13, 57–61; trade liberalization under, 49. *See also* specific countries

Eastern Europe, 2, 3, 5, 51, 70
Economic Dislocation and Work Adjustment Act, 74
Ecuador, 33
European Community, 2, 5–6, 71; EC-92 program of, 2, 5–6, 71, 85–86

Fast-Track Authorization, 71, 72–75
Federation for Industrial Retention & Renewal, 107
Figuereido, Joao, 144
Foley, Thomas, 74
Ford Motor Corporation, 84, 111
Foreign Debt: causes of, 19–23, 58; capital flight and 20, 25–28; effect on debtor economy of, 23–25; growth of 18–19; international strategy for, 29–37; secondary market for, 37–41
Foxley, Alejandro, 117, 118, 119
Fujimori, Alberto, 28, 170, 171–75
Funaro, Dilson, 146

Galbraith, James, 100
Garcia, Alain, 90, 142, 170–71, 173
Gaviria, Cesar, 113, 142
General Agreement of Tariffs and Trade (GATT), 5, 23, 56, 66, 73, 76, 95, 109–110, 128
General Confederation of Labor (CGT, Argentina), 162, 166, 169
General Electric, 111
General Motors Corporation, 81
Gephart, Richard, 74
Germany, 5, 9
Globalization (economic), 2, 4–5
Goldemberg, Jose, 160
Gonzalez, Antonio, 162, 163
Greenspan, Alan, 153
Guarini, Frank, 107
Gurria, Angel, 93

Hills, Carla, 70, 72, 76, 79–80, 103
Hollings, Ernest, 74
Honduras, 33
Hong Kong, 6

Iglesias, Enrique, 18, 63

Inter-American Development Bank
(IDB), 1, 8–9, 18, 49, 54, 62–63,
117, 137, 163, 173
International Monetary Fund: adjustment, approach of, 41–45; loans
from, 9–10, 30–31, 63; role in developing country debt crisis of, 12,
30–37, 61–62; studies by, 3. *See also*
specific countries

Japan: Latin American debt policy of,
9, 54–55, 173; Latin America, direct
investment in, 55; Mexico, direct
investment in, 55, 84–85

Kaifu, Toshiki, 9,
Korea, South, 6, 157
KPGM Peat Marwick, 80

de Larosiere, Jacques, 30, 32
Latin America: adjustment, progress
of, 45–46, 55–57; capital needs of,
9–11; capital flight from, 25–28; debt
(external) of, 18–23; debt (public/
internal) of, 20; democratization in,
2, 59–60; development strategies in,
20, 57–59; direct investment in, 54–56;
Enterprise for the Americas Initiative
and, 1–2, 11–15, 57–58; environmental
policies of, 60; foreign investment
flows to, 8–11; growth rates in, 17;
immigration to U.S. from, 60; inflation in, 17; investment rate in, 17–18,
25; lack of economic integration within, 63–65; lost decade in, 17, 33;
narcotics flows from 60; per capita
GDP of, 18; regionalism impact
upon, 8–11; tax treaties of, 60–61;
trade balance of 21–23; trade patterns of, 63–65; United States trade
exchanges with 52–55. *See also* specific
countries
Latin American Free Trade Association
(LAFTA), 64
Leach, James, 51
Leigh-Pemberton, Robin, 7
Llosa, Mario Vargas, 171, 172
Lopez-Portillo, Jose, 87, 88, 91

Lula (Luis Igancio Lula de Silva), 148,
158
Luschini, Jaime, 126
Lutzenberger, Jose, 160

Macomber, John, 54
de la Madrid, Miguel, 88–90
Maquiladoras, 81–82, 84, 103
Meller, Patricio, 116
Menem, Carlos, 142, 161–63, 164, 165,
166, 167–70
Mexican Foreign Investment Commission, 82
Mexico, 68–111; adjustment, approach
of 87–90; adjustment, external of,
90–97; adjustment, internal of, 97–
100; Brady plan and, 1, 28, 62, 92–94,
95–96, 99, 101–102, 128; capital needs
of, 94–95; capital flight from, 28,
95, 104–105; current account balance
of, 86; debt (external) of 88, 89, 90–
95; debt (public/internal) of, 88, 98;
debt-equity swaps used by, 95–96;
de-regulation of business in, 82, 99,
100; development strategy of, 87–90;
direct investment in, 70, 81–86, 96–97,
101, 106–107, 108–109; direct investment from the United States in,
81–86; environmental policy of, 70,
74–75, 102, 103, 107; exchange rate
policy of, 88–89, 97; exports of,
53–54, 77–81, 86–87; financial sector
in, 99; fiscal balance of, 88, 97–98;
fiscal policy of, 87–88, 97–98; growth
rate of, 86, 88, 102; human rights
issue in, 104; immigration to U.S.
from, 102–103; imports of, 53–54,
77–81, 86–87; inflation in, 86, 89, 98;
infrastructure in, 98; International
Monetary Fund and, 62, 91; investment rate in, 86; North American
Free Trade Area and, 68–87, 101–111;
per capita GDP of 81, 110; petroleum
resources of, 77, 78, 82–83, 87–88,
89; political situation in, 59, 99,
101–102, 105, 107–108; privatization
in, 83, 88, 99–100; trade balance of,
70, 77–81, 88, 89; trade liberalization

Mexico *(continued)*
  in 71, 75-77, 78, 95-96; U.S. direct
  investment in, 81-84; U.S. trade
  exchanges with, 53-54, 74-75, 77-81,
  86-87, 89
Middle East, 3, 4
Morgan Guaranty, 27, 91
Moreira, Marcillo, 146, 158
Morse, Jeremy, 148
Mosbacher, Robert, 69, 70
Mulford, David, 35, 148
Multi-Fibre Agreement (MFA), 23, 75

National Association of Manufacturers,
  105
National Foreign Investment Commission (Mexico), 96
Neves, Tancredo, 144-45, 157
New World Order, 2
Nicaragua, 33, 47, 52, 169
North American Free Trade Agreement
  (NAFTA), 69-111; Action Plan and,
  74, 102-104; advocates of, 105-106,
  107-108, 110-11; Canadian role in,
  71-72, 80; commercial gains from,
  77-78; contents of 75-77; direct investment under, 77; environmental
  issues and, 70, 74-75, 102, 103, 107;
  Fast-Track authorization and, 72-75;
  GATT and, 109-110; historical evolution of, 1, 51, 69-72; human rights
  and, 104; immigration policy and,
  102-103; narcotics traffic and, 70,
  102, 103-104; opponents of, 73-74,
  101-102, 105, 106-107, 108-109, 110;
  outlook for, 110-11; political gains
  from, 100-105; rules of origin in, 76;
  size of resultant market from, 72,
  85, 110; snap-back clause in, 75;
  trade liberalization under, 77-81
Nowzad, Bahram, 21, 23

Organization of American States (OAS)
  48
Organization for Economic Cooperation
  and Development (OECD), 3
Organization of Petroleum Exporting
  Countries (OPEC), 3, 87, 126

Pacific Basin, 2, 6, 85-86
Paraguay, 59
Paris Club, 12, 36, 37, 51, 173
Paz Estenssoro, Victor, 114, 135, 140
Perez, Carlos, 124, 125, 126, 128,
  133-34
Peru, 170-75; adjustment, approach of
  28, 143, 170-72; adjustment, external
  of, 172-74; adjustment, internal of,
  174-75; Brady Plan and, 173; capital
  flight from, 28, 174; debt (external)
  of, 170-71, 172-74; debt (public/
  internal) of, 174; direct investment
  in, 173; Enterprise for the Americas
  Initiative and, 143, 170-75; fiscal
  policy of, 172, 174; growth rate of
  171, 175; imports of, 171; inflation in,
  170-71, 172; International Monetary
  Fund and, 171, 173, 174; narcotics
  issue and, 175; political situation in,
  171, 175; privatization in, 174; tax
  policies in, 172, 174; trade liberalization in, 174; United States relations
  with, 175; World Bank and, 174
Petroleos Mexicanos (PEMEX), 77,
  82-83, 95, 100, 103
Petroleos Venezolanos (PDVASA),
  126, 130
Pinochet, Augusto, 59, 113, 114, 115,
  116, 121, 123-25
Privatization, 44. *See also* specific
  countries
Prebisch, Raul, 57
Puche, Jaime Serra, 70

Rangel, Charles, 104
Rapanelli, Nestor, 162
Reagan, Ronald, 47, 51
Reed, John, 148, 162
Regionalism, 4-11
Religion & Labor Council, 107
Richardson, William, 69
Rio Group, 123
Roett, Riordan, 100
Rogoff, Kenneth, 25, 26, 37
Rostenkowski, Daniel, 74

Sachs, Jeffrey, 25, 47, 136-37

Salinas, Carlos, 51, 69–72, 83, 85, 86,
96, 101–102, 105, 107–108, 110–11
Sarney, José, 47, 90, 145, 147, 151,
156, 157, 158, 160
Scheele, Nicholas, 111
Secondary Debt Market, 37–41; dis-
counts on, 33, 38; growth of, 33,
37–38; size of, 37; transactions forms
in, 37–38, 39–40. *See also* debt buy-
backs, debt conversion bonds, and
debt-equity swaps
Seidman, L. William, 29
Selowsky, Marcelo, 45, 57
Sendero Luminoso (Shining Path), 175
Silva, Ozires, 158
Singapore, 6
Stroessner, Alfredo, 59
Sunkel, Osvaldo, 58

Taiwan, 6
TELMEX (Mexican Telephone Com-
pany), 99–100
Thatcher, Margaret, 71
Trade Adjustment Assistance Program,
74
Tuma, Romeu, 154

Union of Soviet Socialist Republics
(USSR/CIS), 3
United States: adjustment in 65–68;
current account deficit of, 65; debt,
external of, 65; Latin America policy
of 11–12, 47–48; monetary policy in,
21, 67; protectionism in, 12, 53,
66–67; regionalism impact on, 6–8;
trade balance of, 53–54. *See also*
direct investment; Enterprise for the
Americas Initiative; general foreign
relations; North American Free Trade
Agreement; specific countries; trade

U.S.–Canadian Free Trade Agreement,
70–71, 80
U.S. International Trade Commission,
80, 81, 105–106
U.S.–Mexico Joint Commission for
Trade and Investment, 70, 83

Venezuela, 125–33; adjustment, approach
of, 113, 128–29; adjustment, external
of, 127–31; adjustment, internal of,
131–33; Brady Plan and, 1, 28, 62,
128–29; capital flight from, 28, 127,
129; capital flows to, 128–29; current
account balance of, 126, 133; debt
(external) of, 125, 127–31; debt
(public/internal) of, 126; debt-equity
swaps used by, 131; direct investment
in, 130; Enterprise for the Americas
Initiative and, 125–33; exchange rate
policy of, 126, 131; financial sector
in, 127, 132; fiscal policy of, 126,
127, 131–32; growth rate of, 125,
133; imports of, 133; inflation in,
125, 132, 133; International Monetary
Fund and, 62, 128, 129; petroleum
resources in, 125–27, 130–31; political
situation in, 133–34; privatization in,
132–33; tax policies of, 132; trade
balance of, 133; trade liberalization
in, 129–30; World Bank and, 128

Williamson, John, 17, 135
van Wijnbergen, Sweder, 147
World Bank (IBRD): loans from, 9–10,
63; roles in debt crisis of, 12, 31, 34,
62; studies by, 3

Yerxa, Rufus, 72

Zenith Corporation, 106

About the Authors

CHRIS C. CARVOUNIS is a Professor of Economics and Finance at St. John's University. He is co-author of *U.S. Commercial Opportunities in the Soviet Union: Marketing Production, and Strategic Planning Perspectives* (Quorum, 1989), and author of *The U.S. Trade Deficit of the 1980s: Origins, Consequences, and Responses* (Quorum, 1987), *The Foreign Debt/National Development Conflict: External Adjustment and Internal Disorder in the Developing Nations* (Quorum, 1986), and *The Debt Dilemma of Developing Nations: Issues and Cases* (Quorum, 1984).

BRINDA Z. CARVOUNIS is an instructor at Rutgers University's New Brunswick campus. She is co-author of *U.S. Commercial Opportunities in the Soviet Union: Marketing, Production, and Strategic Planning Perspectives* (Quorum, 1989).

DATE DUE

MAY 16 1994